Polish Catholicism between Tradition and Migration

From a critical realist perspective, this book examines the manner and the extent to which religion is shaped by modernity. With a focus on Poland, one of the most monolithic and religiously active Catholic societies in the world – but which has undergone periods of intense transformation in its recent history – the author explores the transformations that have affected Catholicism from a position of reflexivity. Viewing Catholicism as a system of ideas elaborated by tradition, the author considers the relationship between human subjectivity and social structure by examining the shift from traditional religious practice to modern religious observance, particularly in an era of migration in which many Polish Catholics have relocated to western European countries, with profound changes in their religious outlook. Presenting a new approach to understanding religious change from the perspective of religious reflexivity, *Polish Catholicism between Tradition and Migration* will appeal to scholars across the social sciences with interests in religion, research methods, social change and critical realist thought.

Wojciech Sadlon is Director of the Institute for Catholic Church Statistics, Poland, and Assistant Professor in the Faculty of Humanities, Cardinal Stefan Wyszynski University in Warsaw.

Routledge Studies in the Sociology of Religion

A platform for the latest scholarly research in the sociology of religion, this series welcomes both theoretical and empirical studies that pay close attention to religion in social context. It publishes work that explores the ways in which religions adapt or react to social change and how spirituality lends meaning to people's lives and shapes individual, collective and national identities.

Sacred Marriages
A Discourse Analysis
David Mullins

A Visual Approach to the Study of Religious Orders
Zooming in on Monasteries
Edited by Marcin Jewdokimow and Thomas Quartier

Bisexuality, Religion and Spirituality
Critical Perspectives
Edited by Andrew Kam-Tuck Yip and Alex Toft

The Transformation of Religious Orders in Central and Eastern Europe
Sociological Insights
Edited by Stefania Palmisano, Isabelle Jonveaux and Marcin Jewdokimow

Society and the Death of God
Sal Restivo

Polish Catholicism between Tradition and Migration
Agency, Reflexivity and Transcendence
Wojciech Sadlon

For more information about this series, please visit: https://www.routledge.com/Routledge-Studies-in-the-Sociology-of-Religion/book-series/RRSR

Polish Catholicism between Tradition and Migration

Agency, Reflexivity and Transcendence

Wojciech Sadlon

Routledge
Taylor & Francis Group

LONDON AND NEW YORK

First published 2021
by Routledge
2 Park Square, Milton Park, Abingdon, Oxon OX14 4RN

and by Routledge
605 Third Avenue, New York, NY 10158

Routledge is an imprint of the Taylor & Francis Group, an informa business

British Library Cataloguing-in-Publication Data
A catalogue record for this book is available from the British Library

Library of Congress Cataloguing-in-Publication Data
Names: Sadlon, Wojciech, 1983- author.
Title: Polish Catholicism between tradition and migration : agency, reflexivity and transendence / Wojciech Sadlon.
Description: Abingdon, Oxon ; New York, NY : Routledge, 2021. | Series: Routledge studies in the sociology of religion | Includes bibliographical references and index.
Identifiers: LCCN 2021001116 (print) | LCCN 2021001117 (ebook) | ISBN 9780367551872 (hbk) | ISBN 9781003092339 (ebk)
Subjects: LCSH: Catholic Church—Poland. | Change—Religious aspects—Catholic Church.
Classification: LCC BX1566.2 .S155 2021 (print) | LCC BX1566.2 (ebook) | DDC 282/.438—dc23
LC record available at https://lccn.loc.gov/2021001116
LC ebook record available at https://lccn.loc.gov/2021001117

ISBN: 9780367551872 (hbk)
ISBN: 9780367551889 (pbk)
ISBN: 9781003092339 (ebk)

Typeset in Times New Roman
by KnowledgeWorks Global Ltd.

To my mother, Wanda (1949-2019), who wanted to read this book.

Contents

List of tables, photos and figures   viii
Acknowledgements   x
Foreword by Margaret Scotford Archer   xii

Introduction   1

PART 1
Theoretical   17

  1 **Religion – between subjectivity and structure**   19

  2 **Religious identity from the perspective of critical realism**   42

PART 2
Empirical   67

  3 **Traditional Polish religiosity**   69

  4 **Modern Polish society and religious identity**   106

  5 **Migration and the shaping of religious identity**   143

Epilogue   178

  Index   188

Tables, photos and figures

Table

3.1 Religious affiliation in some Eastern Polish Voivodeships in 1931
(census data in units of 1000)   72

Photos

1   Procession in Lichwin (South Poland) in the 1930s.   69
2   Priests during Youth Mass in Lednica in 2018   106
3   Polish Catholics during a Sunday Mass in Dublin   143

Figures

4.1 Number of Catholic parishes and priests from 1974 to 2017.   113
4.2 Percentage of Catholics participating in parish-based
     organizations (*participantes*) between 1993 and 2018.   119
4.3 Changes in moral attitudes in Polish society from
     2005 to 2016.   122
4.4 Basis of moral attitudes in Polish society from
     2005 to 2016.   122
4.5 Declared frequency of religious practice in Poland
     (1990-2017).   125
4.6 The proportion of *communicantes to dominicantes* in
     Roman catholic dioceses in Poland in 2017.   127
4.7 Attitudes towards easter in Poland from 1994 to 2018
     (in percent).   128
4.8 Declared importance of 'God in one's life' in Poland
     (1990-2017).   129
4.9 Declared frequency of religious practice of high school
     students (in percent).   130
4.10 Declared religiosity of high school students (in percent).   130
4.11 Declared relationship to the Church in Poland (1990-2017)
     (in percent).   131

4.12 Faith in various beliefs (1997 and 2011) (in percent).   132
4.13 Declared belief in god, life after death, heaven and hell,
     in Poland (1990–2017) (in percent).   133
5.1 The attitude towards abortion in Ireland and in Poland
     in 2008.   149
5.2 Religious beliefs and religious concerns of Polish migrants
     to Ireland in 2018.   150
5.3 'If you had problems in finding a proper job, after finishing
     your studies would you go abroad?' Percent of respondents
     at high school (mostly 18–19 years of age).   152
5.4 Declared religious attitudes before and after migration to
     Ireland in 2018.   155
5.5 Reasons for leaving Poland according to Polish migrants in
     Ireland in 2018 (in percent).   156
5.6 Reasons for remaining in Ireland according to Polish migrants
     in 2018 (in percent).   157
5.7 The practice of Polish traditions in Ireland by Polish migrants
     in 2018 (in percent).   165

Acknowledgements

The project of writing of this book commenced many years ago and numerous people and institutions have made its publication possible. In completing this work, I would like to commemorate the lives of my mentors, Witold Zdaniewicz (1928–2017), my first teacher and subsequently my colleague in sociological research, and Lucjan Adamczuk (1938–2019) who showed me the way to approach the study of religion statistically.

Special thanks are due to Margaret Archer whose encouragement and generous intellectual support accompanied me in conceptualizing, writing and revising the manuscript. I really appreciate her friendship throughout the years and the insightful foreword she has written for the book. I would also like to express thanks to all my colleagues at the Institute for Catholic Church Statistics, and especially Krzysztof Kosela, Jaroslaw Horowski and Slawomir Nowotny with whom I have been enjoying friendly and committed discussions on critical realism for the past two years.

I had the opportunity to study the transformation of Polish Catholicism in the context of migration thanks to Marcin Lisak and his research project 'Religion versus Migration: the Determinants of Religiosity of Polish Immigrants in Ireland' (National Science Centre, Grant no. 2017/25/B/HS1/02985). Wendy Smith made an enormous effort to edit the manuscript of the book as a native speaker.

I was very inspired by discussions on earlier drafts of this book with my colleagues Marcin Jewdokimow, Slawek Mandes, Dorota Hall and Marta Kolodziejska. Moreover I am very grateful to Slawek Nowotny who has kindly agreed to translate the book into Polish. I would also like to thank my family especially my brother Narcyz Sadlon, his wife Gosia and their daughters, my sister Kinga Papiez and her husband Bartek, my father and my other two sisters, Ania and Gosia, who have given me excellent support during my work over the past three years. I would also like to thank my Pallottine community in Poland, Germany, France, Rome and the United States and many friends especially Michalina Jankowska, Aneta Kowalewska, Aneta Kobylinska, Jerzy Dmochowski and Rafal Lange. I'd also like to extend my gratitudeto Marek and Katarzyna Rymsza, Asia and Bartek Salamon, Teresa and Darek Kowalscy, Maryla and Slawek Legat and to the many friends in the Rodzina Rodzin [Catholic Community founded by the Blessed Cardinal Stefan Wyszynski] who cordially live out their personalist faith.

Foreword

Margaret Scotford Archer

It is an honour to be invited to provide this brief introduction to *Polish Catholicism between Tradition and Migration*. However, its title already poses a question; why should its subject matter be of interest in the English-speaking world – particularly in the UK and USA? After all the historical trajectories of their religious institutions could hardly be more different; with Poland being a case of considerable institutional continuity, England one of discontinuity from the 16th century break from Rome and persistent denominational fissiparousness thereafter, and the USA stirring its melting pot, adding ingredients beyond the range of Protestant, Catholic and Jew. Nevertheless, the temptation should be resisted of remaining within the confines of the old 'sociology of religion' and reading this book as either a deliberate accentuation of national contrasts requiring explanation, or another attempt to revive the theme of 'secularization' with the explanandum reducing to an account of international variations in its speed.

Instead, Wojciech Sadlon has confronted and now confronts his readers with a much greater challenge. Effectively he asks, 'Has Social Theory provided a better toolkit than the functionalism and empiricism that were the main resources available to researchers in the second half of the Twentieth century'? As the Head of Poland's Institute for Catholic Church Statistics, this is a bold starting point and bolder still in his adoption of Critical Realism with which to explore Polish religiosity in a full-length book. It is even more courageous than when Roy Bhaskar engaged with 'Meta-reality', as the last Phase he demarcated in his own theorizing, because he already had a group of well-known social theorists dedicated to the philosophical under-labouring he had already done for the ontology of social science. Some of these stuck to the earlier 'Phases' of his work as the initial reception of what was often called Bhaskar's 'spiritual turn' was distinctly chilly, including from certain of my own post-doctoral students.

Probably the critical realist closest to Sadlon's starting point would have been Douglas Porpora, not simply because he spurned a closet for his Catholicism but also because he refused to anathematise empirical studies; electrifying the 1998 annual Realist conference with his unlikely title 'Do

Realists run Regressions?', reproduced in his 2015 book on *Restructuring Sociology*. He was orthodox in dismissing Humean 'constant conjunctions' as causal explanations, but resolute in maintaining that significant correlations (in all their various forms) set explanatory problems for the Realist that deserved better than dismissal.

Allowance for contingency has always been a crucial part of the Critical Realist charter, which is why our accounts are in terms of tendencies and never a search for laws in open systems – and all societies are such, since they can never be closed against influences from their external environment, unlike the artificial laboratory closure possible in much natural science. Openness and its unpredictable consequences seem undeniable during the current pandemic. (Further reasons for contingency are the coincidence of two or more generative mechanisms, pulling in different directions, and the intrinsic creativity, originality or ingenuity of social agents.)

One contingent circumstance that is relevant to Sadlon's current volume is that it happened to be me who was giving the regular Masterclasses at University of Cardinal Stefan Wyszynski in Warsaw when we first met 4 or so years ago. I suppose that Poland being faithful to the memories of the deceased, I came with a character reference since Pope Saint John Paul II had appointed me to the governing body of his new Pontifical Academy of Social Science in 1994. What sustained our conversation was that I had written a lengthy (815 page) book on the *Social Origins of Educational Systems* (1979 [2013]), which was the origin of my Morphogenetic/Morphostatic Approach (M/M) to explaining institutional change over long temporal stretches. In the beginning I had no idea that Wojciech Sadlon was contemplating a similar study about the historical trajectory of Polish Catholicism, or that this was to ripen into presenting it "from the inside, for an English-speaking audience" (p. 14).

This notion of Catholicism "from the inside" is key to the present book and to Sadlon's theoretical creativity and sure-footedness because he integrated two parts of my theorizing that needed the substantive exemplification that he has provided and I had never undertaken in detail. These were my M/M approach and the later trilogy I wrote on Reflexivity. It is the religious reflexivity that makes his approach to 'Traditionalism', a 'lived tradition' in his own words (p. 7), a real insider's account and not the repetitive assumption that by virtue of its being inherited, it acts upon agents – regardless of time, place or circumstances – like a slab that crushes active agents into passive recipients through the unerring process of its internalization. That image recalls to me the fate of the English Saint Margaret Clitheroe, crushed to death in 1586 for harbouring Catholic priests; a witness undoubtedly, but through her reflexive acceptance of her fate, which she could possibly have evaded. As the author himself puts it, 're-reading traditional religiosity from a realist perspective reveals the reflexive dimension of folk religiosity' (p. 16).

Sadlon is consistent in using the insider's religious reflexivity 'to avoid the vicious circle of trapping our understanding of religion within the concepts of culture and social structure'. Both the latter are conflationary moves that deprive agency (individual or collective) of making their own contribution(s) since they become puppets of their social circumstances, be these materially or ideationally based. Rather, as Norbert Wiley put it, 'we are little gods in the world of inner speech' (Conference of American Sociological Association, 2004), free to share it and free to withhold it, but always free to engage or indulge in it – for good or ill.

One very interesting and largely unexplored theme in sociology is how personal reflexivity can percolate upwards through the practical action that ensues from it, networking its way through the meso-level and finally penetrating the macro-institutional level and issuing in social transformation or reproduction. Importantly, it can spatially shift the social institutions responsible for commemorating religious *anamnesis* from the public to the private sphere. I venture that we are more accustomed to matters working the other way around, for example the many hermits etc. whose personal reflexivity was central to them adopting an isolated *modus vivendi* but who magnetically drew a 'following' to them –St Bernard being the most obvious exemplar. Conversely, it is when social and most usually socio-political structures are hostile to the hierarchy, to Church observances, and the catechesis of the young that gradually a transposition takes place in which the domestic role of the family changes places with that of the Church – special meals for significant dates, fabrication of objects for religious occasions (baking breads, weaving crosses for funerals etc). 'Domestic' is a term to be treated cautiously, partly because it may involve a whole apartment building, partly because it can later be interpreted as a communal act (which it is), but without the reflexive religious initiative of those starting such practices it would not have become common practice as it remains in Poland and is also in Romania (a different Church and different structural constraints). Exactly the same points can be made about culture.

Potentially, the above considerations could be facilitating factors towards migration in the sense that the migrant family 'carries the Church with it'. However, what of those without a family with them (young, old, bereaved etc.)? Are these the 'sojourners', there for the better pay and conditions but not committed to remaining? We don't know, but what Sadlon's stress upon reflexive religiosity does is to open up a new area of research that does not succumb to materialism or to a willingness to adopt local cultural conventions, wherever migrants find themselves, in a process of quasi-automatic hybridization.

What shines through this, which is not intended as a deviation, is that Wojciech Sadlon's approach is firmly anchored in explanations that endorse the acronym I coined, namely SAC, meaning that Structure, Agency and Culture are all indispensable to any adequate sociological explanation, even when the distinctions have to be analytical ones. Explanations are always structurally-dependent, because there is no such thing as contextless-action; culturally-dependent, because agents and actors have to have some idea of what they are doing and pursuing; and agentially-dependent since ultimately it is only agency that makes anything social happen.

Acknowledgement and application of SAC will take different forms, accentuating differing features depending on the level, in Realist terminology, the stratum at which it is pitched. Strata are differentiated on the causal criterion of the properties and causal powers they exercise. Conventionally, those distinguished are the macro-, meso- and micro-levels, although another stratum or strata can be added, provided they are demonstrated to exert causal import. As ever, it is the nature of the research question that is crucial in determining whether or not this transpires. In Sadlon's case, his principal aim is to account for the historical trajectory of Polish Catholicism. Obviously, this is a macro-level question and this means that the Morphogenetic Approach can be adopted in its original form.

Just for clarification, a micro-level study of how particular Catholic girls and boys come to marry one other would usually involve an application of the M/M sequence and its three phases over a relative short period of time. T^1 would account for the structural and cultural factors that accounted for the two attending the same course at University or being members of the same Youth Club, but these organizations could involve hundreds if not thousands of young people. T^2 ------ T^3 (interaction) would account for how these specific two people came to know one other and could be as simple as regularly sharing the same bus. If both liked the look of the other, they might come to sitting at the same table in the cafeteria. That could segue into T^4 (elaboration) when they start dating, with all its possible outcomes and vicissitudes; from its cessation (supposing their respective parents disapprove) to marriage if matters run smoothly. The only point I am making is that the timespan of such a study would be relatively short, perhaps only months long. It would likely take several years if the research addressed the meso-level, with institutional issues of representation, collaboration, and both vertical and horizontal stratification. At the national level and above, such as the as emergence and maintenance of the nation's Church or State educational system, centuries if not millennia are usually involved and frequently the examination of multiple M/M cycles in succession.

Moreover, if the phenomenon proves durable then morphostasis will require closer attention than morphogenesis and involves just as much analysis of the interplay between the SAC components, which generate this relative stability. Wojciech Sadlon's impressive study takes all these points on board and works on them to advance a convincing panorama of the resilience of Polish Catholicism inside and outside of Poland. He honestly explores the slow millennial spread of 'religious indifference' among some

Polish migrants to the Republic of Ireland but resolutely teases out some of its varied main causes, rather than concealing these beneath that blanket descriptive term 'secularization'. Just as importantly, this book refuses to condone one tendency within Critical Realism, namely the attempt by some to normalize an 'indifference towards Transcendence'.

Margaret S. Archer, September 2020

Introduction

> Religion will become a more important source of meaning and continuity because of increasing information connectedness, the extent of state weakness in much of the developing world, and the rise of alienation due to the dislocation from traditional work in the developed world. Rapid change and conditions of political and economic uncertainty, if not insecurity, will encourage many people to embrace ideologies and identities for meaning and continuity.
>
> (National Intelligence Council, 2017, p. 42)

This opinion formulated recently by the United States National Intelligence Council describes the growing potential of religion in the global world. Despite supposed trends towards secularization in Western Europe, Australia or Israel, nowadays over 80 percent of the world's population is religiously affiliated and that figure is increasing. Religions embody ideas that go beyond traditional social borders, which is especially important in this era of massive migration. Religions not only play key roles in social conflicts or situations of polarization but, at the same time, they represent universal values which contribute to global homogenization. Currently religious institutions and actors are more powerful because of their enhanced relational, informational and communicative capabilities.

The growing importance of religion in global perspective reveals the complex nature of acts of faith. Moreover, emerging new social forms and the shifting nature of social bonds are transforming religion. The very dynamism of religion in the modern world is a challenge for the sociologists who set out to study it. The sociology of religion is attempting to catch up theoretically with the deluge of religious transformations on the world stage, as traditional categories and research methods fail to capture the fluctuations which have been affecting religious experience and religious organizations. Elements of religion cultivated in traditional, stable communities contrast strikingly with the core beliefs of transnational nomads of the modern era and the way they worship their Gods.

Poland from such a perspective is one of the most monolithic and religiously active Catholic societies in the world. The country has the eleventh largest Catholic population globally and plays an important role in the universal Catholic Church. The significance of Poland in the history of Europe became apparent in the personage of the Polish Pope, John Paul II, whose figure and life still resonates within global Catholicism. Personalism, an intellectual stance which he vigorously advanced during his tenure at the Catholic University in Lublin, has affected not only philosophical schools of thought but also public life and popular ways of thinking, and is often cited by such well-known American thinkers as George Weigel and Richard Neuhaus, or the Italian politician Rocco Buttiglione. As I will show in this book, personalism corresponds with the sociological approach of critical realism and the work of one of its major exponents, Margaret Archer.

The story of 'Polish Catholicism' includes such glorious chapters as the Solidarity Movement (Solidarnosc) which initiated the long path towards the fall of Communism. Polish Catholicism went on to play an important role in opposing the official Communist state in Poland and later, in the general collapse of Communism in the late 1980s. Recently traces of Polish Catholicism are to be found all over the world thanks to the devotional movement of Divine Mercy, initiated by the Polish nun, Saint Faustina.

But Polish Catholicism expands not only through ideas. For centuries Poles have migrated and settled in different regions throughout the world. Millions of Polish Catholics currently live abroad; they have made important contributions to global society for hundreds of years, in the US, France, Germany, Italy, Argentina, Australia and more recently in the UK, Ireland, Norway and Iceland. Polish language parishes for decades have been enriching the landscape of the Catholic Church, from Rome, through Western Europe, to North and South America.

The unique situation of Polish Catholicism results from the complex history of Poland. Polish society, being located in the middle of Europe, sandwiched between various political and military regimes, underwent both magnificent and dramatic periods of flowering and oppression in turn. After the 'Baptism of Poland' in 966, which corresponded with the personal baptism of Mieszko I, the first ruler of the future Polish state, the process of Christianization of Poland was achieved. After several decades the country was recognized by the papacy and the Holy Roman Empire, and joined the ranks of the established European states. Poland has been developing culturally, especially since the 14th century and gave birth to such personalities as Nicolaus Copernicus and Pawel Wlodkowic. After its territorial expansion during the era of the so-called Polish-Lithuanian Commonwealth, the country was subsequently partitioned between neighbouring countries. By the late 18th century, Poland had disappeared from the political map of Europe. The outbreak of the First World War gave Poles unexpected hope for achieving independence and in 1918 a free Polish nation with an outlet to the sea was established. This so-called 'Second Republic of Poland' ceased to exist in 1939 when Poland was invaded as a nation by Germany and two weeks later by the Soviet Union. After the Second World War Soviet

domination in Poland was apparent from the beginning. The Polish gov-
ernment-in-exile, lacking international recognition, continued to exist until
1990. It is also worth mentioning that Catholicism played an important role
in several Polish national uprisings and that the Polish national assembly
signed, in 1573, one of the first European Acts granting religious freedom
(the so-called Warsaw Confederation).

I stand at the end of this long and compelling historical path of Polish
Catholicism and wish to study the dynamics of religion as an important
aspect of Polish history. The key question which has motivated my research
is why, after the repressive Communist era and more than 30 years of
political and economic transformation, Polish Catholicism is still vibrant
especially in comparison to other Western European countries, so much
so that we can speak of a distinct form of Polish religious history. Polish
society represents an exception on the world map in terms of religious attitudes. Rates of attendance at Mass in some regions in Poland exceed those
of most other strongly Catholic parts of the world, for instance in South
America, Africa or the Philippines. Religious statistics from Polish society
still surprise or even astonish some sociologists, journalists, politicians and
others. Yet the Polish religious landscape is rich in new religious movements and social mobilization. While highlighting the dynamism of Polish
religious life, I do not wish to overestimate its religious vitality and, in
doing so, truncate aspects of the erosion of religious faith. Indeed, Polish
Catholicism has experienced turbulent change; in recent years the religiosity of Polish youth has shown the most rapid decline internationally. But
my focus is not on the question of one-dimensional growth or decline but
rather on the reconfiguration of religious identity. I have been stimulated
to begin writing this book with the simple observation that, in the case of
Poland, traditional and folk religiosity should not be regarded as a phenomenon from the past.

The book is an attempt to present knowledge about Polish Catholicism
using the most recent theoretical perspectives in the field of sociology. My
intention is to present Polish Catholicism in terms of the most essential
aspects of social order in Polish society and history, and incorporate into
this study the relationship between social structure, agency and culture. The
project is built upon the epistemology of critical realism initiated by Roy
Bhaskar[1] and the social ontology formulated by Margaret Archer, a leading
contemporary scholar within the critical realist tradition. Because critical
realism as a philosophical approach is very extensive, I have pitched the
focus of the book on the implementation of Margaret Archer's morphogenetic approach, one of her pathbreaking theoretical achievements and the
methodological complement to critical realism.

In a critical realist approach religious identity is not a given or even an
intrinsic characteristic of an individual. It is a relational manifestation
of human reflexivity in relation to transcendence and with reference to
other orders of reality. Religious identity encompasses power in both the

subjective and social structural realms and refers not only to institutions and social bonds but also to the experience and ultimate concerns of individuals. Religious change refers to the reconfiguration of the relationship between the individual and the social structure. In this study religious identity emerges within the configuration of social, practical, natural and transcendental concern, which represent the corresponding orders of reality, as delineated by Margaret Archer (2000; and 2006). The realist paradigm which I apply in this book is based on the assumption that a human being's relationship to the transcendental order reflects a configuration of human concerns. What is more, religious identity from the point of view of reflexivity is not limited to a distinct reference to the transcendental or social orders but can include also reference to the relationship between transcendence and other orders of reality.

In a realist perspective, human reason should not be detached from human emotions. Emotions play an important role as outcomes of our relationship with reality, including experiences of transcendence, and thus represent an 'output' of religious experience or what has been behaviorally understood; a motivation for action. The nature of religious experience is composed of emotions, which emerge from the relationship between human beings and transcendence. Religious identity represents the emotional commitment of human beings to a 'discipleship of lived practice' (Archer, 2000, p. 186) and the reflexive configuration of natural, social and transcendental concerns, activated especially in the performance of rituals (representing the practical order).

That is why the dynamics of religious identity include rich systems of symbols and rituals which play a very important part in shaping religious experience. Religious experience represents much more than transcendent forms of illumination. In a critical realist perspective, religion is far more than a system of logical and propositional or discursive knowledge accumulated within the cultural system of a society. Rather, religiosity is the 'feeling' of the sacred, a matter of doing, or, as Margaret Archer outlines, a spiritual 'know how' (Archer, 2000, p. 184). Religion represents a 'codification of practice' (Archer, 2000, p. 184) and is essentially liturgical precisely because of this. The socio-cultural system of Catholicism, that is, the way religion is embedded in the social life of its adherents, is rooted in 'symbolic remembering' [*anamnesis*]. Religion lives and is expressed within and through material artefacts, such as paintings, sculptures, shrines, liturgical vestments or even books and performative elements, such as gestures, cultic celebrations and rituals. Performative and material symbols represent 'embodied spirituality'. Religions persist within socio-cultural systems thanks to performative order, in other words, lived tradition. Ritual practices within a community, symbols inherited from generation to generation, form a social environment for religious experience. Religious experience is embodied in cultural practices and encompasses all dimensions of reality. For the stability or even the setting up of religious identity, the integration of transcendence within the wider social order of the individual is necessary. Critical realist social ontology corresponds well with some new concepts of religion, especially the category of 'lived religion'. But my main intention is to stay at the sociological level of analysis and not descend to the anthropological level of detail for its own sake.

The book is strongly grounded in the sociology of religion; from the beginning it discusses sociological theories and diverse concepts of religious experience, religiosity and religiousness and it features an approach based on an empirical, statistical research methodology. Besides the direct inspiration of Margaret Archer's work in the theoretical inquiry, it includes broad theoretical views on religion provided by various contemporary social scientists. It should be noted that the original sociological studies on religiosity have been reframed by rational choice theorists and implemented within empirical research, especially by the famous French researcher Gabriel Le Bras (1955; and 1956) and American sociologists, particularly Charles Glock and Rodney Stark (Stark and Glock, 1970), who attempted to reconcile a pragmatic approach to religion with a more sophisticated conception of religiosity. Gabriel Le Bras in his studies on rural Catholicism in France used indicators of religious practice in order to characterize the degree of 'religious vitality' in France, an approach I also use in my research. In this quest, he investigated the relationship between the individual and the group and pointed out that 'Christianism is the life of the soul: sentiments which are awakened by religion and directed towards God and one's neighbours' (Le Bras, 1956, p. 561) I should also mention here the scholars of our Polish Lublin-Warsaw School of the Sociology of Religion who made great efforts to conceptualize religiosity in terms of social attitudes (for example, Piwowarski, 1986). Being educated within this theoretical framework I try to show that critical realism in the sociological context opens up new horizons for religious studies.

The theoretical framework of this book may seem to share many similarities with the phenomenological understanding of religious experience introduced into the sociology of religion by Peter Berger especially. I follow his way of understanding religious experience when he recommends returning to a perspective of the phenomenon 'from within', and grasping religion in terms of the meanings intended by the religious consciousness (Berger, 1974, p. 129). Berger studies the relationship between 'transcendental' experience and everyday life from the perspective of constructed meaning, using the categories of 'legitimization', 'relativization' and 'alienation'. Ontologically, religious experience and everyday life are – in Berger's viewpoint – 'coming from' the same order of the social world and they represent knowledge which is socially constructed. The role of 'human biological nature' is reduced to the world of constructed meaning. In this domain my perspective is evidently more 'realist'. I try to avoid this position – what Margaret Archer calls a 'central conflation' (Archer, 1995, p. 93–134). That is why I focus instead, not on the socially constructed 'cognitive dynamics' of Berger (1967), but on the dynamics of the realistically understood, individual and social identity of a human person. What is more, my approach to religious experience is more analytical. My intention is to distinguish and examine mechanisms which underpin the process of the shaping of personal and social identity by religious experience. This means that, to some extent, I try to include both a phenomenological approach to religious experience and to acknowledge the claim that social structures are realistically 'objective'. In this way I hope to respect Berger's belief that 'whatever religious apparitions the future may bring forth, it would be regrettable if the scientific study of religion were systematically blinded to them by its conceptual machinery' (Berger, 1974, p. 133). It is also worth noting, that – in my opinion – the concept of agency which is a focus of this book has already been explored in Berger's sociology when he outlined the 'deductive', 'reductive' and 'inductive' relationships between religious experience and religious tradition (Berger, 1979, p. 66–156).

The morphogenetic approach to religious identity delivers new theoretical tools for studying the relationship between religious experience and social structure and moreover provides a systematic and comprehensive background for the conceptualization of 'religious identity'. Following this direction, the book applies the concept of 'reflexivity' as a pathway to studying the processes of cultural change, which shape religious identity and the concept of 'transcendence' which emerged in Archer's later publications on social ontology (Archer, 2006; Archer, S. Collier and Porpora, 2004). The implementation of the concept of transcendence is some kind of 'hat trick' for sociology of religion scholar and my focus on it here is an attempt to avoid the vicious circle of trapping our understanding of religion within the concepts of culture and social structure.

Another issue is the problem of 'theodicy' in relation to the scientific study of religion. The reference to transcendence included in the book follows the 'scientific' approach to religion as it puts to one side the question of ultimate truth. As Berger put it so well, 'the gods are not empirically available, and neither their nature nor their existence can be verified through the very limited procedures given to the scientist' (Berger, 1974, p. 125). Following Berger's epistemology, the approach presented in the book assumes that transcendence appears as immanence, and transcendence is '*only* available *qua* contents of human consciousness' and within human experience, to use Berger's explanation (Berger, 1974, p. 126). In this context critical realism does not add anything new to the phenomenological approach apart from strongly opposing the reductionist tradition which understands religious experience as 'false consciousness'. Following Peter Berger and Margaret Archer, I affirm that 'The scientific study of religion cannot base itself on any affirmation of the ultimate truth claims of religion. But it must no more constitute itself on the basis of atheism (that is, atheism *tout court* as against the aforementioned "methodological atheism")' (Berger, 1974, p. 133). It is important to note that the introduction of the concept of 'transcendence' into the study of religion, as proposed by Margaret Archer in her critical realist approach, is not the same as 'theologizing' the sociology of religion (Doak, 2018).

The guidelines inherent in the morphogenetic methodology deliver a conceptual framework for investigating Polish society. The pivotal perspective of this book is the incorporation of the morphogenetic approach in the study on Polish Catholicism. That is why I have sought to use analytical mechanisms at the macro level, rather than delivering a causal explanation of religious identity in Polish society. My aim in this book is to make a significant contribution as one of the first attempts to implement critical realism in the analysis of empirical data on religion.

Polish Catholicism is an especially convenient area for implementing Archer's morphogenetic approach and studying the cultural dynamism of religion. Religious identity has played, and there is no doubt that it still plays, an important role in shaping the form of Polish society. The long and dynamic history of Polish Catholicism overlaps with social agency in the transformation of the interrelationship between culture and social structure and the elaboration of new social forms and configurations. Especially unique is the dominant role of Catholicism in Polish society after the Second World War.

In a morphogenetic approach, Catholicism is a cultural system. Basing on critical realism's distinction between cultural and socio-cultural systems, I describe Catholicism in Poland as a system of theological ideas referring to transcendence and formulated in theoretical categories and concepts elaborated within Roman Catholic tradition. Catholicism represents all theological *intelligibilia* which have a dispositional capacity for being understood and which are governed by logical rules. My focus however is on socio-cultural aspects of Catholicism, distinguished in an analytical way, which encompass social interactions and spheres of mutual influence. Especially significant in my study is the place of transcendence, how it is understood, how it is transformed and evolves, or even how it plays a role in Polish culture, but taking a much wider perspective than a merely functionalist one. I describe the general characteristics of Polish religious history and the relationship between religious experience and the socio-cultural system of the Polish society. In this context, critical realism delivers new theoretical and analytical tools for characterizing religion, not only in its functional aspect, but also much more significantly, in its personal and individual experiential aspect, without neglecting to examine its degree of dissemination within society.

The study of religious identity attempts to describe how and to what extent different cultural configurations shape a person's relationship to transcendence is in Polish society and how the relationship with transcendental concerns impinges upon other human concerns. In this way, the book examines the relationship between human subjectivity, social structure and religion, taking Poland as a case study to investigate these issues in Poland. Following critical realist ontology my study of Catholicism includes also perspectives on the transformation of Polish social structure and social interactions. Margaret Archer claims that: 'every theory about the social order necessarily has to incorporate SAC: Structure, Agency and Culture' (Archer, 2013). Change in the religious life in Poland 'comes in' terms of (Archer, 2013, p. 5) structure, agency and culture. My intention is to present Polish Catholicism as a complex reality of interrelationships between structure, agency and culture. Beginning with a social morphogenetic approach, within a critical realist approach, the study delivers a new theoretical framework for studying religious identity in its social context. In my understanding, being a religious person means integrating religious experience within the wide range of relationships that shape the identity of that individual in society.

My attention is more focused on the practical aspects of social life. By 'practical' I do not mean that my study of Polish Catholicism is empiricist. The purpose of this book is not to deliver merely statistical data on Polish Catholicism in its different historical phases. The analysis is a search for explanatory mechanisms which operate within Polish Catholicism and an attempt to explain patterns of religious change in Poland. I study how religious institutions in traditional society profited from the synergy between structure and culture and how the strong link between political and religious life in Poland contributed to the social morphogenesis of Polish Catholicism, and to what extent the new configuration of religious institutions in the context of emigration has shaped the religious identity of Polish migrants. The study also includes a discussion of agency (individual or collective) and of the actors who confront changing structural and cultural contexts in daily life. In this domain, my focus is both on the structural and cultural motivations derived especially from the relationship of persons to the transcendental order and on how these are represented by their ultimate concerns.

The analysis of the changes in Polish Catholicism within the context of a morphogenic cycle, from the traditional era to the modern era of globalization, includes three phases. The traditional configuration of structure, agency and culture represents the first phase of the morphogenetic cycle. Socio-cultural conditioning characterizes traditional Polish society because, in traditional societies, religious institutions retain the unification of culture and structure, and individuals are grounded in a stable cultural context. In Poland itself, ignoring the Polish diaspora, before and after the Second World War traditional Polish Catholicism was located mainly in local rural communities. Despite the industrialization and urbanization programmes by the Communist state, and strong patterns of social change after 1945, a form of traditional peasant religiosity survived in Poland until the 1990s, when strong social transformation was initiated. My focus on the dynamics of modern Polish religion starts in the 1980s when resilient elements of Catholicism in the society played an important role in initiating social transformation. The period after 1989 represents the strong transition phase which was made up of individual and group interactions. Structural and cultural elaboration takes place in this phase and I highlight its manifestation in the form of vigorous social interactions at the individual and institutional level. Here, the changes inherent in Polish Catholicism include striking turbulence and social tension. The resultant elaboration of social transformation is represented by an empirical case study of Polish Catholicism in the context of migration. The book presents how structural, cultural and agential influences operate within Polish Catholicism in 'late modernity'. Tracing the changes within Polish society I highlight how 'late modernity' and especially the 'situational logic of opportunity' (Archer, 2013, p. 11) affects Polish Catholicism.

A description of traditional Polish Catholicism (in Chapter 3) establishes a claim that structural and cultural features from past actions now condition and contextualize contemporary Polish Catholicism. However, the generative mechanisms of Polish Catholicism at the macroscopic level, (the Archerian third-order level) (Archer, 1995) are different in the traditional system and the global social system in 'late modernity'. In traditional Polish Catholicism, both structure and culture were mutually reinforcing and as a consequence traditional society was static and 'cold', as will be outlined in Chapter 3. The traditional religious structures and cultural characteristic of Polish Catholicism have shaped the religious identity of individuals within modern Polish society and also that of Polish migrants. 'Late modernity' as Archer claims is characterized by new configuration of structure and culture.

In the last twenty-five years [...] structure and culture have come into synergy with one another with far reaching morphogenetic consequences [...] cultural and structural morphogenesis are becoming increasingly symbiotic through the perceived benefits of pursuing their positive feedbacks simultaneously and synthesising them.

(Archer, 2013, p. 13)

Three chapters of my book, (Chapters 3, 4 and 5), adopt Archer's morphogenetic approach and its dynamic interplay between structure and culture, useful for observing the different temporal phases of Polish Catholicism. Traditional Catholicism represents structural and cultural antecedent circumstances. Embroiled in the process of structural and cultural elaboration, actors within Polish Catholicism act within their structural circumstances and cultural conditions and, over time, they both alter and sustain them.

This study of Polish Catholicism underlines the fact that the results of past actions which dominated traditional religiosity are deposited in the form of current situations. Religious identity is a matter of the interplay between structural aspects, represented especially by religious institutions, and social interactions which are a matter of human agency. Any study of agency must include reflexivity and, in the case of religious studies, religious experience. Modern religious forms within Polish Catholicism are not just based on the eradication or modification of previous structural and cultural properties and powers. Instead, the nature of the Polish religious configuration results from a process of constant elaboration, consisting of changing organizational relations and new social opportunities.

Following Margaret Archer, I assume that Polish Catholicism is strongly shaped by the mutually modifying interrelationship between social structure, culture and agency. In other words the purpose of this book is threefold: (1) to present how the changing relationship between structure, culture and social agency shapes in a nonlinear fashion, the process of morphogenesis in Polish Catholicism; (2) to explain how Polish Catholicism still strongly affects social life in Poland through collective interactions and why migration represents a discontinuity within Polish Catholicism; (3) to describe how different cultural contexts affect and shape religious identity in Poland.

In the empirical sections, it presents a broad spectrum of sociological research conducted by Polish sociologists, who are often not known to the English-speaking academic audience. The book stands in a long line of publications, the majority in the Polish language, which focus on Polish Catholicism and more generally, religiosity in Polish society. Some of these belong to a most important genre: historical sociological studies of Polish society. This is because, since its inception, Polish social science included a focus on religious institutions as an important facet of the research. The famous study of Polish peasants in America by Florian Znaniecki and William Thomas (1920 and 1927) is also widely cited in this book and finds common ground with the issues of modern Polish migration which I have researched. What is not seen, even in mainstream Polish sociology of religion publications, and what has inspired my study, is the approach of my family ancestor, Franciszek Bujak (1903 and 1908), the pioneer in the use of statistical methods and the presentation of these data in a monograph format, for the study of Polish social and economic history. In the study of traditional Catholicism, I am also inspired by recent authors who have examined 'folk religiosity' in Poland. Many of them take a rather ethnographic approach, especially Stefan Czarnowski (1956), Jozef Chalasinski (2013[1934]) and Jan Bystron (1936). The book follows especially many sociologists of religion who have explored Polish religious attitudes in the different phases of development of Polish Catholicism. To mention the most distinguished: Jozef Majka, Wladyslaw Piwowarski, Edward Ciupak, Janusz Marianski, Witold Zdaniewicz, and more recently, Krzysztof Kosela, Irena Borowik, Miroslawa Grabowska and also those more familiar with the Central European religious situation, such as Miklos Tomka.

My aim is to overcome a degree of reductionism, Archer's 'conflations', in understanding the religious configuration of Polish society and to present Polish Catholicism from the inside, for an English-speaking audience. Most importantly, I endeavour to avoid the simplistic, one dimensional and linear 'secularization' perspective on religious change in Poland, and to grasp both elements, religious change and also religious continuity, in the dynamics of Polish religion. In my study of 'religious history' in this book, I try to avoid explaining 'religious facts' with reference to no more than the structural configuration of the culture. By introducing the concept of agency as a central category in the book, I try to integrate a sociological perspective of religion with the ontological category of 'time' and to 'dynamize' a quantitative approach to the study of religion. I want to avoid the dualistic approach to religion. Instead I propose a new direction in the study of religion which would overcome – on the one side – reducing religion to subjective experience and – on the other – to the structural aspect of social life. In my opinion the perspective presented in this book could be labelled as 'personalistic' in the tradition of Jacques Maritain (1930), Karol Wojtyla (1979[1969]) or Hans Joas (2011). My intention is to show that at the heart of the sociology of religion is a human person which integrates subjective and objective aspects of social life, and that religion is a relational phenomenon. To some extent I try to follow some postulates of relational sociology formulated by Pierpaolo Donati (2010). I want to show that if scholars of the sociology of religion wish to avoid the 'shallows' of reductionism, they need to take a relational approach. Indeed, the relational approach to my central concept of transcendence opens up new perspectives for the sociological study on religious life because it overcomes the dualistic approach inherent in many studies which distinguish between 'sacred' and 'profane' and between the individual and the collective.

My book not only adds to the studies that strive to avoid reductionist accounts of Polish religiosity but also brings together theoretical understanding of religion and modernity and the existing theoretical studies of Polish religion. In avoiding a reductionist account of Polish religiosity, it delivers a more complex and nuanced interpretation of 'folk' or 'traditional' religiosity in general. With these new insights into traditional folk religiosity, I also shed new light on the phenomenon of religious pluralism in the modern world by highlighting that religious pluralism should not be approached within a dualistic paradigm, either as a structural process or as a matter of one sided individualization. In fact, the book could be classified as a study on 'religious individualization' only if individualization is understood as a relational process. By introducing such concepts as reflexivity and agency I reveal new aspects of a complex social process of individualization in the field of religion. I highlight the fact that religious pluralization in 'late modernity' is a matter of a dynamic relational process of the interplay between religious experience and social structure, in other words, that pluralisation is a matter of agency. I try to demonstrate how religion plays an important role in the social dynamics of some of the most crucial processes of contemporary times, migration and globalization. Hence, the contemporary Polish diaspora in Ireland has been studied as a context for exploring these ideas. In this way I aim to make a contribution to aspects of religiosity in the sociology of migration.

The perspective of this book is to some extent 'post-secular'. As the work of Hans Joas demonstrates, secularization in Western Europe does not necessarily lead to moral decline (2014). In other words, it has become evident that Christianity or Catholicism represents much more than a normative system. Some similarities could also be found between my search for the significance of transcendence in the religious life of contemporary Polish Catholics and the perspective presented by Charles Taylor in his monumental historical book *A Secular Age*. Here he carefully tracks the emergence of the 'immanent frame' which he sees as a process of detachment from the transcendent (Taylor, 2007). Following the intuitive insights found in such classical works, a motivational perspective for me has been to relocate the question of religion within a central sociological issue concerning the relationship between the individual and social structure and to respond to critical remarks formulated by Thomas Luckmann when he claimed in the 1960s that the sociology of religion has become 'divorced from the main issues of social theory' (Luckmann, 1963, p. 148).

This book summarizes important research on Polish Catholicism and use many data from both past and present sources. Empirical data were mostly collected from studies which adopted a different theoretical perspective from mine. Some of them were historical studies, some represent the most recent knowledge on Polish Catholicism and were published by such institutions as the Polish Public Opinion Research Center, the Polish Central Statistical Office or even the American Pew Research Center. A huge range of data comes from Poland's Institute for Catholic Church Statistics, of which I am currently the Director. This study includes my original research, in the context of Poland, concerning traditional Catholic religiosity, Catholic organizations, religious social capital, civil society, youth religiosity, general trends within religiosity in recent decades, as well as significant research on World Youth Day, held in Poland in 2016. This has provided me with firsthand knowledge of the most general trends in Polish religiosity. Original data on modern Polish migration, derived from the quantitative and qualitative research I conducted in Ireland in 2018 and 2019, with a collaborative research team of scholars from the Institute for Catholic Church Statistics, are presented in the last chapter of the book.[2] The initial proposal for this research project was based on critical realism and included the concept of reflexivity.

The book is organized as follows. Chapter 1 deconstructs the current sociological understanding of the complex nature of religious phenomenon and focuses on the relationship between religious experience and religious structures. From the perspective of agency, I review different theories and numerous concepts involving various configurations of religious forms and demonstrate how the sociology of religion distinguishes between subjective and structural aspects of religion. I carefully deconstruct the concept of 'folk religiosity', highlighting some reductionist elements of our understanding of this form of religious life. In doing so I assess the work of classical and modern scholars that highlights reflexive aspects of traditional religiosity. I examine in detail our sociological understanding of traditional religiosity and how religious identity was shaped in the past. As the relationship between religious experience and social structures is crucial, especially in the study of the dynamism of religious life, I give special attention to religious transformation and examine religious change from the perspective of the complex relationship between the individual and social structure, reflexivity and culture. The central question of this part of the book is how social change affects the shaping of religious identity and how sociological theories of religion address the question of social agency in the context of religion. I carefully deconstruct the sociological category of individualization and demonstrate the complexity of this process. The general conclusion from the first chapter is a firm statement that the systematic study of religion requires a very solid and well-founded ontological framework. Especially the study of religious change requires a clear, methodical conceptualization of the process of constructing religious identity.

Chapter 2 is a response to the need for an ontological understanding of the complex nature of religious phenomena. Therefore, this chapter outlines the critical realist understanding of religious identity as primarily proposed by Margaret Archer. It explains how critical realism may contribute to the sociology of religion and it conceptualizes religious identity in terms of reflexivity, transcendence and agency, demonstrating that such an ontological approach corresponds well with the work of some classical authors and well-known concepts in the sociology of religion. Moreover, a discussion of the structural aspects of religiosity, and the processual approach to cultural change proposed by Margaret Archer, are included. These concepts represent my theoretical framework for studying Polish Catholicism and religiosity within Polish society.

Chapter 3 considers in some detail crucial aspects of religious identity in traditional Polish communities and, in this way, analyzes reflexivity in relation to the transcendental order in pre-modern Polish society. It answers the question: to what extent was traditional religiosity reflexive? Some critical descriptions of theoretical concepts concerning the relationship between religion, culture and identity are presented, and classical conceptions of Polish 'folk' and 'popular' religiosity are examined. Traditional religiosity has often been understood as unreflexive and habitual or even akin to magic. A critical realist focus facilitates a review of the prevailing understanding of traditional Polish Catholicism. The chapter demonstrates that rereading the literature on traditional religiosity from a realist perspective reveals the reflexive dimension of folk religiosity. My discussion here shows that traditional religiosity was both reflexive and deliberative, despite the fact that it was strongly influenced by social structures. Some crucial aspects of Polish Catholicism are described which show the degree to which Polish religious faith mobilized social change in Poland and shaped human agency. I also discuss how religion played an important role when members of traditional society migrated in the past.

In Chapter 4 the focus is on changes in Polish Catholicism in the modern era: how cultural dynamism has shaped religion in Polish society in recent decades; and how institutional aspects of Catholicism have provided a context for religiosity in contemporary Polish society. Then the discussion moves to tracing how transcendence is integrated with social concerns and to what extent religious concerns shape Polish identity. A focus on the shift in social concerns after 1989, when Poland embarked upon a path of political and economic transition, elucidates the direct relationship of Poles to transcendence. A central question in the chapter is: what relationships represent the transcendental order in Polish society? Later I describe in detail how religious rituals in modern Polish Catholicism may be seen as the performative dimension of religious identity, and in this context, I mention some continuities with traditional religiosity. An important part of this section is the characterization of modern Polish Catholicism from the perspective of agency. For instance, attention is devoted to new religious movements and associated phenomena. This section is another context for highlighting aspects of agency in Polish Catholicism and their impact on religious identity. Other key questions in this chapter are: what does it mean that the Catholic faith has become a matter of choice; what changes can be observed in the religious values of believers and clergy; and how has it happened that, at the beginning of the 21st century, Catholicism still strongly influences Polish society?

Polish migrants who were socialized in traditional Catholic social environments have been leaving their country for centuries. Chapter 5, the final chapter, surveys how recent migration shapes Polish Catholicism. It examines the dominant concerns which form their decision to migrate and the relationship of their experience of migration to their experience of transcendence, within the context of their religious beliefs. The chapter provides some basic social facts on the new wave of Polish migration and presents modern academic literature and research which concerns Polish migrants to Great Britain especially, but also to other European countries. I review the literature on Polish migration from the point of view of the theoretical concept of reflexivity. Then I develop the analysis based on empirical research conducted among Polish migrants in Ireland. Based on the results of this study I argue that the natural concerns of the migrants, labeled as 'well-being', shape their biographies and also their relationship to the transcendental order. The next part of this chapter concerns the link between transcendental and social concerns. Here I focus on how Polish identity is related to Catholicism in a migratory context. Pertinent questions here are: to what extent are religious rituals shaped by migration; and how does Polish Catholicism lose its agency outside Poland? A key issue is explaining the link between the decline in religiosity, observed among recent Polish migrants, and the process which is often labeled as 'individualization'. I make the case that this needs to be studied as a relational process. The empirical data contained in this chapter demonstrate that the new social context which Polish migrants encounter in Ireland, affects their religious identity indirectly. The overall conclusion of my analysis is that religious change is, to a degree, the result of social adaptation in a diaspora, but the factor of reflexivity, and migrants' concerns shaped before leaving their home country, must also be considered.

Notes

1. At the end of his life, Roy Bhaskar revealed his own approach to the topic of religion, which he called 'Meta-Reality', and tried to present religiosity in some kind of 'neutral' terminology.
2. National Science Centre, grant no. 2017/25/B/HS1/02985: 'Religion versus Migration: the Determinants of Religiosity of Polish Immigrants in Ireland (2018-2020)'

References

Archer, M. S. (1995). *Realist Social Theory: the Morphogenetic Approach*. Cambridge: Cambridge University Press. DOI: 10.1017/CBO9780511557675.

Archer, M. S. (2000). *Being Human. The Problem of Agency*. Cambridge, UK: Cambridge University Press. DOI: 10.1017/CBO9780511488733.

Archer, M. S. (2006). Persons and Ultimate Concerns: Who We Are Is What We Care About, Conceptualization of the Person in Social Sciences. *Pontifical Academy of Social Sciences*, 11, pp. 261–283.

Archer, M. S. (2013). Social Morphogenesis and the Prospects of Morphogenetic Society. In: M. Archer ed., *Social Morphogenesis*. Dordrecht: Springer, pp. 1–24. DOI: 10.1007/978-94-007-6128-5.

Archer, M., S. Collier, A., Porpora, D. (2004). *Transcendence. Critical Realism and God*, London: Routledge. DOI: 10.4324/9780203420683.

Berger, P. (1967). *The Sacred Canopy*. Gadern City, NY: Doubleday.

Berger, P. (1974). Some Second Thoughts on Substantive Versus Functional Definitions of Religion. *Journal for the Scientific Study of Religion*, 13(2), pp. 125–133.

Berger, P. (1979). *The Heretical Imperative. Contemporary Possibilities of Religious Affirmation*. Garden City, NY: Doubleday.

Bujak, F. (1903). *Zmiaca. Wies powiatu limanowskiego. Stosunki gospodarcze i spoleczne* [Zmiaca; A Village in the Limanowski District]. Krakow: G. Gebethner i Spolka.

Bujak, F. (1908). *Galicya. Tom I. Kraj. Ludnosc. Spoleczenstwo. Rolnictwo* [Galicyja: Volume I. Country, Population, Society, Agriculture]. Lwow-Warszawa: Ksiegarnia H. Altenberga, E. Wende i Spolka.

Bystron, J. (1936). *Kultura Ludowa* [Folk Culture]. Warszawa: Nasza Ksiegarnia.

Chalasinski, J. (2013[1934]). Wsrod robotnikow polskich w Ameryce [Among Polish Workers in America]. In: G. Firlit-Fesnak, J. Godlewska-Szyrkowa, C. Zoledowski eds., *Migracje i migranci w pismach Ludwika Krzywickiego, Floriana*

Znanieckiego, Jozefa Chalasinskiego. Wybor tekstow [Migration and Migrants in the Writings of Ludwik Krzywicki, Florian Znaniecka, Jozef Chalasinski. Selected Texts]. Warszawa: Instytut Polityki Spolecznej Uniwersytetu Warszawskiego, pp. 203–220.

Czarnowski, S. (1956). Kultura Religijna Wiejskiego Ludu Polskiego [The Religious Culture of Rural Polish Folk]. In: S. Czarnowski. *Studia Z Historii Kultury* [Studies in the History of Culture]. Vol. 1. Warszawa: Panstwowe Wydawnictwo Naukowe, pp. 88–121.

Doak, P. (2018). Deconstructing Archer's (Un)Critical Realism. In: V. Altglas, M. Wood eds., *Bringing Back the Social into the Sociology of Religion. Critical Approaches, Studies in Critical Research on Religion.* Leiden: Brill, pp. 59–78. DOI: 10.1163/9789004368798_004.

Joas, H. (2011). *Die Sakralitaet Der Person. Eine Neue Genealogie Der Menschenrechte.* Frankfurt am Main: Suhrkamp.

Joas, H. (2014). *Faith as an Option. Possible Futures for Christianity.* Stanford: Stanford University Press.

Le Bras, G. (1955). *Etudes De Sociologie Religieuse,* vol. 1. *Sociologie de la pratique religieuse dans les campagnes francaises.* Paris: Press Universitaires de France

Le Bras, G. (1956). Gabriel Le Bras. *Etudes De Sociologie Religieuse,* vol. 2. *De la morphologie à la typologie,* Paris: Presses Universitaires de France.

Luckmann, T. (1963). On Religion in Modern Society: Individual Consciousness, World View, Institution. *Journal for the Scientific Study of Religion,* 2, pp. 147–162.

Maritain, J. (1930). *Religion Et Culture.* Paris: Desclee.

National Intelligence Council. (2017). Global Trends. Paradox of Progress [online] Available at: www.dni.gov/nic/globaltrends [Accessed 07/11/2019].

Donati, P. (2010). *Relational Sociology. A New Paradigm for the Social Science.* Abingdon: Routledge.

Piwowarski, W. (1986). Teoretyczne I Metodologiczne Zalozenia Badan Nad Religijnoscia [A Theoretical and Methodological Background to Research on Religiosity]. In: W. Piwowarski, W. Zdaniewicz eds., *Z badan nad religijnoscia polska. Studia i materialy.* [From Research on Polish Religiosity. Study and Materials], Warszawa-Poznan: Zaklad Socjologii Religii, Pallottinum, pp. 57–72.

Stark, R., Glock, C. (1970). *American Piety: The Nature of Religious Commitment.* Berkeley: University of California Press.

Taylor, C. (2007). *A Secular Age.* Cambridge: The Belknap Press of Harvard University Press.

Thomas, W., Znaniecki, F. (1920). *The Polish Peasant in Europe and America: A Classic Work in Immigration History. Volume 5: Organization and Disorganization in America.* Boston: The Gorham Press.

Thomas, W., Znaniecki, F. (1927). *The Polish Peasant in Europe and America. Volume I: Primary-Group Organization.* New York: Alfred A. Knopf.

Wojtyla, K. (1979[1969]). *The Acting Person.* Dordrecht: D. Reidel.

Part 1
Theoretical

1 Religion – between subjectivity and structure

When we conduct sociological research on religion we need to specify, for practical purposes, the social theory that will be used and the research questions. Hence, in this chapter I present the theoretical background to my study of Polish Catholicism and I outline the concepts and theories which orient the research. This chapter includes detailed studies of concepts, well-known in the sociology of religion, from the perspective of agency. My intention is not only to give a brief theoretical review of these, as would be found in a dictionary of sociology, but to consider to what extent classical and modern sociological concepts of religion are relevant in my study of Polish Catholicism from the perspective of agency. This section of the book is a quest for theoretical conceptualizations which will cope adequately with the relational dynamism of Polish religious experience and the Polish cultural system. It tracks how different explanatory paradigms and social theories, applied in the field of the sociology of religion, formulate and manage the key social interrelationships between structure, agency and culture within the phenomenon generally labelled as 'religion'.

The following study is focused not only on modern forms of religious dynamism but also on traditional Polish religiosity, because being able to understand traditional religiosity from the perspective of agency is especially important to me. When searching for a better approach to understanding religious change in Poland and incorporating my explanatory approach to Polish Catholicism within sociological theory, I have also carefully considered, to what extent the interrelationship between culture and religious experience plays a role in explaining religious change within sociological theories of religion. I start my study by highlighting the fact that dualism in both a theoretical and a practical approach to religion results from the very fundamental concept, for the sociology of religion, of 'sacred' and the very fundamental distinction, for sociology in general, between the individual and the collectivity. Reviewing classical authors, I show that theoretical or – more specifically – ontological assumptions have far reaching consequences in the understanding of religion. Despite theoretical postulates that religion relates to something transcendental, in academic discourse it can be easily reduced to an aspect of social life, either subjective or structural. These tendencies are especially evident in the study of traditional religious forms which I present below.

In the final part of this chapter I propose a deconstruction of the socio-logical study of religious dynamism which reveals the development of the approach from a dualistic to a more relational perspective. This allows me to focus on the sociological category of individualization and to underline how complex and relational is the process.

Dualism in the study of religion

From the outset, the definition of religious phenomena in sociology has sought to encompass opposite realities. One of the most common elements of the anthropological understanding of religion is the distinction between 'sacred' and 'profane'. According to this paradigm, in the domain of the sacred, acts are carried out with reverence and awe. In the case of magic, priests and sorcerers conduct rites to attain the outcome which they believe is mechanically associated with the magic itself. Human beings when reli-gious, lives in relation to a divided world, one division 'containing all that is sacred and the other all that is profane' (Durkheim, 1995[1912], p. 22). Of course, theoretically Emile Durkheim is fully aware that, 'religion' refers not only to the realm of the supernatural world and 'being religious' implies a relationship between the sacred and everyday life. He admits that humans, when religious, implement transcendence within the profane realm and this process of 'implementation' depends on reflexivity. However, he studies reli-gion as 'objective' knowledge, as 'categories of thought' and cultural ideas such as 'soul', 'spirits and gods'. This results in the clear distinction between religious beliefs and rites; in other words, Durkheim claims that religious phenomena fall into two basic categories: beliefs and rites. Beliefs represent 'states of opinion' and 'consist of representations'. 'Between these two cate-gories of phenomena lies all that separates thinking from doing' (Durkheim, 1995[1912], p. 34). His ontological dualism in the study on religion results from an epistemological assumption, that 'religion' is an 'objective' fact and an 'indivisible entity' (Durkheim, 1995[1912], p. 33).

Many other studies of religion follow this Durkheimian approach of understanding religious phenomenon as strongly characterized by the dualism between religious experience and aspects of social structure (or the 'reification' and 'objectification' of religiosity). Quite often the way reli-gion is conceptualized reduces the significance of either its subjective or its structural aspects and moreover, degrades these aspects, of terms of their independent properties. The first tendency would be recognized by Edward Evans-Pritchard as psychological definitions of religion which include intellectualist and emotionalist theories, and the second as socio-logical definitions of religion (Evans-Pritchard, 1965, p. 4). Edward Bailey associates this dualism with the distinction between institutionalized and experienced religion (Bailey, 1997, p. 22).

A paradoxical situation in the sociological study on religion is the fact that the tendency to study religiosity as an 'objective' phenomenon and in terms of 'structural facts', which goes back to the Enlightenment, has been accompanied by the ongoing inclination to reduce religiosity to subjective aspects. According to Rodney Stark and Finke (2000) the 'Enlightenment approach to religion' includes also the assumption that religion is a result of human creativity, which has little in common with objective reality. In this sense, Thomas Hobbes characterized religion as 'credulity' and 'ignorance' (Hobbes, 1887, pp. 56–63). As Voltaire advocated, in the social mission to enlighten and educate people, religion should be eradicated. 'Voltaire wrote endlessly of the need to attack religion in preparation for the coming triumph of philosophy.' (Stark and Finke, 2000, p. 3) For David Hume, religion should succumb to psychology because it represents no more than sentiments and feelings (2012[1748], p. 23-25). 'Hume's belief that psychology was the science to which religion must succumb was widely shared.' (Stark and Finke, 2000, p. 9) 'Not content with making psychology into a science, the Enlightenment made it [...] into a strategic science. It was strategic in offering good, "scientific", grounds for the philosophers' attack on religion.' (Gay, 1969, p. 167) Later works developed the idea that religion reflects ideas incorporated in the human mind. In his famous writings, Ludwig Feuerbach defined religion as a projection of human subjectivity. 'Man – this is the mystery of religion – projects his being into objectivity, and then again makes himself an object to this projected image of himself thus converted into a subject [...] God is the highest subjectivity of man abstracted for himself.' (1957[1841], p. 29-31) It is not well known that the critique of Christianity included in the writings of Feuerbach does not imply atheism. For this German Hegelian philosopher, religion is in essence anthropological. God is 'a being of the understanding', a 'moral being' and 'love'. The way in which people understand themselves and the world is mediated by God (Williams, 1973). Through religious contemplation, humans become acquainted with themselves. 'The consciousness of the infinite is nothing else but the consciousness of the infinity of consciousness; or, in the consciousness of the infinite, the conscious subject has for his object the infinity of his own generic nature.' (Feuerbach, 1957[1841], p. 3) In other words, religion is a projection of a human being's inward nature.

At this point, I hope it is clear why social scientists who study religion are so reluctant to either 'subjectivize' or 'objectivize' religion. Until today this epistemological dualism between approaches which emphasize the 'subjectivity' of religious experience and the 'objectivity' of the social structure is typical of sociological studies of religion. Most often in sociology the distinction between religious experience and social structure is reflected in the division between institutionalized religion and shared religious values and ideas. Moreover, this dualism in the study on religion is evident in the sociological predisposition to distinguish different 'forms of religion' and results in the tendency to 'de-subjectivize' religion. The German sociologist of religion, Richard Toon, for example, pointed out two dimensions which facilitate his categorization of religion into four typologies. The first dimension refers to the level of organization of the religion. Religious phenomena presented on this organizational scale could be classified as more or less organized, including both non-organized forms of religion and those strictly organized. The second dimension includes the referential reality that is, focusing on what is the reference point of the religion. Religion may be linked to supernatural (non-empirical) reality – on the one side – or to empirical, mundane reality on the other (Toon, 2017, p. 7). Roland Robertson proposed the category of 'surrogate religion' (Robertson, 1970, p. 39 and 42) which includes organized forms of social life which play equivalent functions to those of 'conventional religions'. 'Surrogate religion' refers to organized equivalents to religion such as psychoanalysis, political ideologies or some pastimes without any personal relationship to transcendence. Robert Towler (1974) conceptualized 'common religion', a term which he used to represent non-organized forms of religion, including conventional supernatural realities such as a personal understanding of God, or divine grace, which often takes the form of magic or superstition. To underline the process of heterodoxy, that is, the growing distance between official beliefs and practices included in official religious systems (for instance, Christian dogmatics[1]), Michael Hornsby-Smith introduced the concept of 'customary religion' (Hornsby-Smith, Lee and Reilly, 1985). When religious beliefs and practices are distanced from their 'official' sources, trivialized and 'polluted', 'customary religion' emerges which is heterodox and unstructured. All such concepts detach religion from human subjectivity.

Even some of the most recent sociological concepts that have been used in studies of religion barely cope with the distinction between religious experience and social structure. Over many years, Cipriani has been developing his concept of 'diffused religion' (Cipriani, 2017). He understands this to be a form of religious beliefs and values, inherited from the pervasive culture, which has become detached from institutionalized religion but nevertheless preserves its generic religious character. Such a form of religion manifests in political attitudes and norms. In the process of secularization, institutional religiosity declines but 'diffused religion', he argues, 'seems to be regaining credibility or at least respect for values of the solidaristic, humanitarian, pacifist, liberal type: a sort of "lay religion" which "betrays" orthodox religious values but which adapts and reinserts itself into the contingent realities of political action' (Cipriani, 1984).

Other recent attempts to study religion seem to follow the same path. Peter Staples distinguishes between 'official religion', 'folk religion' and 'popular religion'. 'In his formulation, 'popular religion' includes religious ideas and customs produced by commercial interests and accepted as consumer goods (Staples, 1979). A more sophisticated approach is presented by Hubert Knoblauch who reformulates the relationship between individual and collective aspects of religion and studies the field which emerges between the private and public spheres as part of the religious domain. He claims that popular culture is a field of distribution for religious elements and points out that in modern societies communication media disseminate references to transcendence. Knoblauch identifies this penetration of religion into the public sphere as a new form of religion (2008). Knoblauch's conceptualization is strongly influenced by the social ontology formulated by the functionalist and systemic approach of Niklas Luhmann (1995) according to which religion is integrated into society not only by religious institutions but also in the form of various everyday elements. In a formal 'Gestalt' approach, the understanding of religion is changed and religious institutions are replaced by more ideational and 'fuzzy' forms. Knoblauch pays special attention to communication as the foundation of society, and claims that religion in a particular society is especially shaped by the forms of communication pervasive in that society. In traditional societies religion was communicated orally, which implies the integration of religion with everyday life. The traditional form of religion was essentially configured by religious institutions, especially churches. The invention of the printing press by Gutenberg in the mid-15th century diametrically changed the way religion was communicated and resulted in new cultural divisions. According to Knoblauch (2000), since the 16th century European culture has been divided into two independent sectors, namely the 'sacred' and the 'profane'. Thus, modern societies entail a strict distinction between the 'public' and 'private' spheres.

Knoblauch is however fully aware that the growing popularity of new communication technologies such as radio, television and above all, the Internet, results in the deep reconfiguration of this public-private distinction. The sharp boundary between private life and the public sphere has been eroded and religion becomes a popular topic in public discussion. In modern societies the role of religious institutions is declining but they persist in the public sphere through visible reference in the media of communication. According to Knoblauch, the concept of 'popular religion', as a phenomenon of the interrelationship between modern culture and religion, implies the existence of a 'new spirituality' in modern society. In this way, religion 'breaks down the boundaries between "privatized" and "public" religion' (Knoblauch, 2008). Gordon Lynch expresses a similar attitude towards the connection between religion and culture. He claims that new forms of the sacred emerge from such social fields as the marketplace, human rights, gender and nature (Lynch, 2012).

A more theoretically refined approach is presented by Pierre Bourdieu, who opened up a new perspective for the understanding of the relationship between religious experience and religious institutions, within his social critique of the judgement of taste. In doing so the French sociologist deconstructed Kantian aesthetics as based on the reductionist opposition between the 'taste of sense' and the 'taste of reflection' (Bourdieu, 1984). In Kantian philosophy, two general kinds of art can be distinguished. The first, based on the facile pleasure of the senses, delivers some gratification, purpose or interest. In its popular aesthetic form, art is subordinated to its function. 'Popular taste applies the schemes of the ethos, which pertain in the ordinary circumstances of life, to legitimate works of art, and so performs a systematic reduction of the things of art to the things of life.' (Bourdieu, 1984, p. 5) The second type of art, which is based on the 'pleasure purified of pleasure', is 'predisposed to become a symbol of moral excellence and a measure of the capacity for sublimation' (Bourdieu, 1984, p. 6) and represents 'disinterestedness' and pure contemplation (Bourdieu, 1984, p. 41).

It may seem that Bourdieu put the sociological study of religion on a more subjective path. However, for him, the opposition of popular aesthetics to elite aesthetics results from social distinctions and creates, as well, the experience of social inequality. Differences between popular and elite aesthetics should be understood as practices determined by *habitus*.[2] The popular dimension of aesthetics is related to social and structural conditions which override human consciousness and language and go 'beyond the reach of introspective scrutiny or control by the will' (Bourdieu, 1984, p. 466). In such an approach the background of religious experience is reduced either to aesthetics or to human *habitus*.

Highlighting subjective aspects of religious experience implies the question of what is the relationship between human experiences and religious institutions in general? Thomas Luckmann gives a modern response to this question. He proposes the concept of 'invisible religion' which is a 'subjective system of "ultimate" significance' (Luckmann, 1967). This definition of 'invisible religion' implies both a reference to institutionalized religion and to a subjective human system of meaning. 'Invisible religion' is implicit rather than overt (Astley, 2017, p. 91). A subjective system of ultimate significance may also be organized and still not belong to the sphere of institutionalized conventional religion. With this conceptualization, Luckmann opens up a new perspective for the sociological study of religion and delivers tools to study new religious phenomena in the modern world. For him, the 'institutional specialization of religion, along with the specialization of other institutional areas, starts the development that transforms religion into increasingly "subjective" and "private" reality' (Luckmann, 1967, pp. 85–86). Thus, Luckmann opens up the sociology of religion to the possibility of focusing on new forms of subjective experience. However, such an approach to religious experience has in fact no specific difference from the approach to other forms of human experience. Religion could easily be reduced to any moral or ethical meaning system. The question arises as to what is the difference between morality and religion? In the case of Polish society, centuries old Christian and Catholic society, the question is very important.

Peter Berger delivers more sophisticated insights into the tension between the individual and the social structure in the context of religion when he studies the distinction between objective religious culture and religious experience in terms of phenomenological dialectics. His constructivist approach describes religion in terms of the dialectic process of constructing meanings including externalization, objectivization and internalization (Berger, 1967). The link between subjective religious experience and culture is described in the category of 'legitimation'. Berger highlights the 'multiple worlds' inhabited by the individual and in studying religion gives attention to the problem of alienation. 'Alienation is an overextension of the process of objectivation, whereby the human ("living") objectivity of the social world is transformed in consciousness into the non-human ("dead") objectivity of nature.' (Berger, 1967, pp. 85–86) I will partially follow Berger's sociology of religion and his approach to the distinction between religious experience and social institutions, highlighting important progress which has been made in the sociology of religion, thanks to his phenomenological approach. However, when I study traditional religiosity in the next part of this chapter, I will clarify how the phenomenological approach, in attempting to comprehend the processes by which religious identity is shaped, also implies some elements of reductionism.

Traditional religiosity

The discussion of human experience versus social structure in the context of religion has outlined the limits to our understanding of what religion is and has highlighted the tension between the notions of subjectivity and religious institutions. The central issue of the interrelationship between structure, agency and culture becomes even more obvious when studying the concept of traditional religiosity, as it is commonly acknowledged that the view of traditional society has been strongly dominated by the idea of the nation and a linear approach to history. Members of traditional society shared a common history and language. This common history had a cosmic and universal dimension and encompassed all individuals. History was experienced as a teleological process. Individual fates were subordinated to common destiny. In that sense religiosity in traditional societies was not a matter of reflexivity, but instead was mechanical and ritualistic. Traditional religiosity has often been described in terms of 'folk' or 'popular' religiosity, and was habitually understood as a form of religiosity characterized by low levels of knowledge and theological wisdom. It was seen as ritualistic and even non-rational.

The sociological approach to 'folk religion' was inspired by Max Weber, who juxtaposed the 'religious anxieties of the masses' with the rational religion of the 'elites'. The sociological phenomenon of the so-called 'masses' [*Volk*] is derived from such elements as common language, customs and historical experiences and is manifested in such factors as race and ethnicity. 'Religion of the masses' [*Volksreligiositaet*] or 'popular religion' is based on social domination which codifies individual experience and transforms it into everyday routines (Weber, 1978[1922], p. 252). The 'religion of the masses' is especially characteristic of peasants. Peasant piety in comparison with bourgeois religiosity is not concerned with salvation but rather with practical outcomes and is oriented to magical effects. Agrarian piety is dia-metrically opposed to 'prophetic religion', represented by gifted individuals who proclaim existential or ethical teachings. A prophet embodies a mis-sion, which contravenes existing religious traditions. Peasants on the other hand are oriented against 'intellectual rationalism' and are

> so strongly tied to nature, so dependent on organic processes and nat-ural events, and economically so little oriented to rational systematiza-tion that in general the peasantry will become a carrier of religion only when it is threatened by enslavement or proletarianization, either by domestic forces (financial or seigneurial) or by some external political power.
>
> (Weber, 1978[1920], p. 422)

The term 'religion of the masses' was later developed by Gustav Mensching, who used the concept of '*Volksreligion*' to distinguish between universal and ethnic religions. The difference between both these forms of religion consists in the essential character of their beliefs. Universal or 'world religions' include a transcendent vision of God which is not lim-ited to a specific social group (Mensching, 1972, p. 286). '*Volksreligionen*' are represented by social groups such as the nation, tribe or other inte-grated communities. Mensching claims that, '*Der einzelne lebt hier aus dem Kollektivum*', which means that the individual is subordinated to the primary group. Religion is a manifestation of an integrated socio-cultural system. Transcendence in 'folk religions' cannot be distinguished from the social order because the 'sacred' is limited to a given and specific social form. The social subordination of followers of 'folk religion' is rooted in their emotional and irrational belief in spirits. Peasants in opposition to bureaucratic officials are influenced and even manipulated by traditional beliefs. The term 'folk religion' has also been used in a historical sense to depicted religion in the past in a general way. In this context, the historical studies of Urs Altermatt on Catholicism have been very influential. For him, 'folk Catholicism' was represented mainly by the lower social classes and was a normative approach towards faith (Altermatt, 1989). In later literature, the category of 'folk religion' was implied occasionally until the 1980s, when 'popular piety' started to play a central role in the sociolog-ical study of religion (Drehsen and Morel, 1982, p. 99). François-Andre Isambert defined 'popular religion' as characteristic of the 'popular layer' (Isambert, 1982). 'Popular religion' for him was related to liturgical prac-tices which were integrated with daily life. He admitted that the concept takes up theoretical and practical tensions between the dichotomies 'elite-masses', 'traditionalists-innovators' and even includes the 'sect-church' dichotomy (Isambert, 1975).

A vision of tradition, shared by contemporary social thinkers, reveals many similarities with Weber. I will only mention two very popular theorists of modernity: Anthony Giddens and Ulrich Beck. The former points out that tradition generally is about rituals and solidarity, that is, about action and social structure.

> Tradition [...] is an orientation to the past, such that the past has a heavy influence, over the present. Yet clearly, in a certain sense at any rate, tradition is also about the future, since established practices are used as a way of organizing future time. The future is shaped without the need to carve it out as a separate territory. Repetition, in a way that needs to be examined, reaches out to return the future to the past, while drawing on the past also to reconstruct the future.
>
> (Giddens, 1994, p. 62)

Tradition organizes the past in the present; it is an 'organizing medium of collective memory'. It includes some elements of endurance and continuity, which resist change. People recall tradition as members of a collective, practising 'collective memory'. Tradition is actively constructed and needs to be continually interpreted. However, tradition is based on a 'formulaic notion of truth' and relates to no other reality than the collectively constructed world. Important from our perspective is the fact that, for Giddens, tradition includes moral and emotional content and is related to human memory, which is rather unconscious and unreflexive. Tradition and rituals are interpreted only by 'elites' because 'elites' have access to 'formulaic truth'. The guardians of tradition inherit a special status in traditional society; they interpret tradition and tend to ritually reconstruct tradition. According to Giddens, knowledge of the meaning of rituals is not widespread, but is limited to a narrow group of people (Giddens, 1994, p. 64). Mediated by 'traditional elites', tradition binds together the past and the present by acting as a medium for interpreting the present and delivering normative content concerning the present. From a structural perspective, tradition delivers a sort of 'ontological security' and a set of mechanisms to control emotions, especially anxiety. Emotional attachment delivers, rather, moral authority and that is why tradition is bound up with authority. Holding authority includes having power over others and being a reference point for knowledge.

Ulrich Beck, points out that in the history of societal development, the relationship between the individual and the social system has been redefined (Beck and Beck-Gernsheim, 1996, p. 25). According to him, social institutions integrated traditional society. Individuals belonged to a social class, their actions were informed by gender roles and their identities defined by such structures as neighborhood or family. In other words, social structures 'automatically' defined the identity of individuals. Human being was born into a set of social preconditions. Life biographies were predefined and humans did not experience the almost coercive possibility of 'free choice' that modern people experience. Cultural habits liberated people from the necessity of making decisions. Culture discharged people from responsibility. In pre-industrial society, human life was ruled by 'internalized natural law'. Rules and norms were sanctioned by traditions which included religion. Beck refers to the example of marriage as a typical aspect of social life observed to undergo significant cultural change in modernity. Marriage was understood as part of a wider moral and legal order, a kind of duty which individuals must obey and follow, subordinating their own will to the newly emerging family after the marriage. Social duties were rooted in religion and they manifested as moral order. This moral order was not abstract but rather, strictly correlated with the biological nature of human beings. Moral rules were reinforced and stimulated by the fact that it was efficient to live according to them and resulted in a successful life. Social institutions were sanctioned by their economic effectiveness. Women specially were not able to survive economically outside the institution of marriage. Both authors – Giddens and Beck – quite profoundly identify traditional society with the predominance of social structure over individual agency.

In such a perspective, individuals were so deeply immersed in traditional culture that there was no space for their subjectivity. Culture did not let them elaborate upon or exploit their reflexive powers. Miklos Tomka claims that although traditional cultural ideas represented 'simple cognitive systems, expressing popular reasoning and feelings', the reflexivity of individuals in traditional societies was reduced to group reactions to threats, which resulted in 'xenophobia, fundamentalism, and similar responses'. Religion in traditional society was uncritically accepted even if some of its elements did not follow general logical rules. It was impersonal and should be defined as unreflexive cultural belonging, rather than as an experience of the sacred.

> Religion is indistinctly embedded in general socio-cultural identity, related rather to existential and emotional than to intellectual qualities and is actualized in all aspects of life; in special individual and social, official and unofficial symbolic expressions. Individual religiosity does not require manifest substantiations. Special confirmations of religiosity, whether personal or social, are out of place.
>
> (Tomka, 2006, p. 257)

A perspective that is often ignored is that the concept of 'folk religion' includes an element of normative evaluation when it describes religious beliefs and practices which transgress those of institutional religion as represented and codified by church institutions (Bailey, 1998). Moreover, only a few sociologists refer to 'traditional religiosity' as a private and subjective religious experience resulting in social agency (see Parker, 1998). The strong opposition between structure and agency is implied in Robert

Bellah's research on traditional religiosity. In an interesting essay regarding religion in Italy, Bellah (1980) delivers a stimulating understanding of religious traditions and popular ways of feeling. He cites the famous Italian artist Carlo Levi who, in one of his novels – *Christ Stopped at Eboli* (1970) – characterizes the traditional peasant mentality. According to the historical descriptions in Levi's work, people attribute double meanings – literal and spiritual – to animals, plants and objects. Objects of everyday reality embody a kind of soul. In other words, peasants share pantheistic attitudes towards the material sphere. In a traditional mentality there is no place for abstract ways of thinking. Peasants do not understand well-defined and clear rational, historical or even religious categories. 'Peasants live at a level of "subterranean" intensity beneath the "clear-cut meanings" of reason, religion, and history' (Bellah, 1980, p. 89). Such a form of religiosity is emotional which means that it is not ascetic (Levi, 1970, p. 117) but represents opposition to the universalism of ascetic rationalism of high Italian culture. What is more, religious institutions in Italy, especially Catholic, embody obligations and require loyalty. Catholicism incorporates habits, which are devoid of 'religious sentiments', do not require reflexivity and which stimulate mechanical action rather than subjective agency. 'Catholic identity has often been more of a shield for particularistic loyalties than an expression of deep inner faith.' (Bellah, 1980, pp. 86–118) That is why traditional religion differs from 'legal' or institutional religion and is particularistic or shared within the strict limits of a social group. Bellah recommends the term 'religious ground bass' for such a form of traditional religion embedded in the social structure.

Despite some oversimplifications in his characterization of traditional and post-traditional societies, Tomka has well discerned the specificity of Western Christianity in comparison with its Eastern counterparts. He claims that in the West, religion was strongly institutionalized and reified. The model of religiosity was controlled and objectified by Church institutions. This form of religion 'became autonomous from its historical origins and from individually diverse, genuine religious experience' (Tomka, 2006, p. 259). In Eastern and East-Central Europe, religion is characterized by different socio-cultural circumstances. What is more, the French sociologist, Michel de Certeau, noticed the process of domination of cultural aspects of Christianity in Western Europe and as a consequence, the reduction of religion to a cultural dimension. Thus, institutionalized Christianity has become detached from faith and more tied to culture. Such a process results in the 'folklorization' or 'aesthetization' of religion (De Certeau and Domenach, 1974).

Peter Berger in his phenomenological approach to religion highlights the considerable difficulties inherent in attempting to include both subjective and structural aspects of tradition, in recent developments in sociology. For him religious rituals and mythology serve to 'recall' tradition and to legitimate religion. Rituals 'restore ever again the continuity between the present moment and the societal tradition, placing the experiences of the individual and the various groups of the society in the context of a history (fictitious or not) that transcends them all' (Berger, 1967, pp. 40–41). However religious activity is dialectically separated from 'religious ideation'. Tradition 'maintains the socially defined reality by legitimating marginal situations in terms of an all-encompassing sacred reality' (Berger, 1967, p. 44). Berger's constructivist ontology integrates 'objective' social structures and 'ideational' aspects of the culture. That is why reflexivity is 'hibernating' in traditional religiosity and 'activates' when a strong tension between tradition and human experience occurs. Reflexivity plays an important role when tradition declines:

> When the external (that is, socially available) authority of tradition declines, individuals are forced to become more reflective, to ask themselves the question of what they really know and what they only imagined themselves to know in the old days what when the tradition was still strong. Such reflection, just about inevitably, will further compel individuals to turn to their own experience.
>
> (Berger, 1979, p. 33)

The case of 'traditional religiosity' highlights how difficult it is, not only to study the religion but also to study the society, with their dual aspects of being both individual and social, of including both experience and the link to social culture. Before I move to my concept of religious identity from the perspective of social morphogenesis I will present a detailed study of religious change from the perspective of agency which will facilitate our understanding of the need for a dynamic vision of religion.

Dynamism in religious life

Emil Durkheim claimed that in traditional societies religion pervades all dimensions of social life. Beliefs and sentiments are collective, and the collective has a religious character. His concept of 'common conscience' denotes a state of transcendence. However, in the process of social change, the association of religion with various areas of social life tends to decrease. 'God, who was, at first present in all human relations, progressively withdraws from them; he abandons the world to men and their disputes' (Durkheim, 1964[1893], p. 169). In Durkheim's theory the transition from traditional to modern society does not consist in the simple change from a society structurally based on reference to transcendence, into a society without such a reference. He admits that the change is more sophisticated. Religion may still play a role but

> it is from on high and at distance, and the force which it exercises, becoming more general and more indeterminate, leaves more place to

the free play of human forces. The individual really feels himself less acted upon; he becomes more a source of spontaneous activity.

(Durkheim, 1964[1893], p. 170)

This classical approach corresponds well with the sociological characterization of 'late modernity'. Anthony Giddens defines modern culture as 'a time of endings' (Giddens, 1994, p. 56). Giddens has no doubt that civilization has experienced the end of traditional society and the transition to post-traditional society. In traditional society, power and social structure were legitimized by socialization within families and the maintaining of 'relatively passive subjects'. Post-traditional society emerges when modern institutions are globalized and intentional radicalization takes place. People are influenced by general tendencies and their decisions have global implications. 'This extraordinary, and still accelerating, connectedness between everyday decisions and global outcomes, together with its reverse, the influence of global orders over individual life, forms the key subject-matter of the new agenda' (Giddens, 1994, p. 58).

But does this mean that modernity is more reflexive? Modernity is experimental and, in that sense, implies risk. Technology is changing people's everyday lives. The enactment of bureaucratic rules elevates authorities and 'rational-legal' authority dominates modern societies. Modernity is 'compulsive', in the sense of modern psychology because behaviour is undertaken without understanding. An example of compulsive behaviour is addiction, which is the repetition of behaviour without reflection.

> In pre-modern societies, tradition and the routinization of day-to-day conduct are closely tied to one another. In the post-traditional society, by contrast, routinization becomes empty unless it is geared to processes of institutional reflexivity. There is no logic, or moral authenticity, to doing today what one did yesterday; yet these things are the very essence of tradition. The fact that today we can become addicted to anything – any aspect of lifestyle – indicates the very comprehensiveness of the dissolution of tradition [...] in its traditional form.
>
> (Giddens, 1994, p. 71).

The fact of importance here is that in modern society human beings lead lives of their own choice. People's biographies are not 'given' or 'ascribed' but must be 'elective'. 'The do-it-yourself biography is always a "risk biography", indeed a "tightrope biography", a state of permanent (partly overt, partly concealed) endangerment' (Beck and Beck-Gernsheim, 1996, p. 25). Human beings must take responsibility for their decisions and may fail, make mistakes and experience frustration. People are forced to choose between life opportunities in an active way. They must negotiate, calculate and plan. The necessity of making decisions causes fear and stress. Humans tend to escape from the 'tyranny of possibilities' and reduce risk. As examples of such tendencies, Ulrich Beck points to the advice literature, new religious movements and psychotherapy. Human freedom and decision-making are deified. 'Questions that went out of use with God are re-emerging at the centre of life. Everyday life is being post-religiously "theologized"' (Beck and Beck-Gernsheim, 1996, p. 31).

Such a process of individualization does not mean the disintegration of social forms only. The process of individualization imposes new forms on individuals. Beck refers to Parsons' notion of 'institutionalized individualism'. In new social forms such as education, bureaucracy or the job market, an individual 'has to do something, to make an active effort' to gain social advantages (Beck and Beck-Gernsheim, 1996, p. 25). Individuals escape from old institutional rules and orders but, simultaneously, are confronted with new constraints. In this way, individualization theory focuses on the individual and describes society from the perspective of the individual. Beck claims that individuals in post-traditional societies require self-interpretation and reflexivity to survive. People need to be critical of this modern social condition and understand it.

Such an approach to social change implies the concept of 'religious individualization'. Bryan Wilson claimed that secularization is stimulated by science which replaces the 'holy cosmos' and thus churches cease to have an important role in socialization and social control. He claims that the process of secularization is accompanied by a process of socialization (Wilson, 1982, p. 154). 'My thesis is that secularization is the decline of community: secularization is a concomitant of societalization' (Wilson, 1976, pp. 256–266). Social change consists in moving away from a society based on small and closed local communities, towards a society of large and systemically organized organisms. Such changes result from the development of communication techniques as well as the dissemination and unification of the education system. This leads to a transformation in social needs. One such need in traditional communities was for a 'common' and 'local' identity in which religion played an important role. Individuals' departure from these communities corresponded to the disappearance of religion-related needs. The development of technology resulted in rationalization and the transition from 'substantive values' 'to 'procedural values' (Wilson, 1976). The rise of social security, the changes in lifestyles and the degree of individual freedom also affect the character of religious experience. In this context, Bryan Wilson distinguished between the 'faith of an individual' and that of 'religious institutions'. Individual faith is something given and relatively constant, in contrast to that which is influenced by the economy and the culture of a religious institution. In the so-called modern, 'I-society', religiosity is not the result of imposed norms and principles, but rather, an arbitrary choice of values available 'on the market', where religion competes with secular values (Stolz, Konemann, Cheneuwly Purdie, Engelberger and Kruggeler, 2014).

Also, for David Martin, the transformation of social bonds plays an important role in shaping religious experience. The outcome of contemporary social changes is the depersonalization of relationships and an emphasis on technical rationality. The disappearance of the community transforms traditional, moral and religious institutions into technical and bureaucratic forms of social control (Martin, 1978, pp. 83–88). Religious life becomes an aspect of 'private life', and church institutions can no longer count on gaining support for their own goals from social institutions in the most general sense. In such a perspective secularization means a modification of the reference point in life biographies and the transformation of the transcendent universe of norms and values. Institutional changes to religious life are rooted in the transformation of the orientation of individuals. Traditional 'reference points' are eroded. Religion, which could be described previously in terms of ideology, is now transformed into a more practical and experiential dimension, which could now be defined as lifestyle. In modern social science, secularization is no longer understood as a deterministic and one-dimensional process that leads to 'rational disappointment', but as a process primarily involving individualization and religious pluralization. From the point of view of religious institutions, this implies a kind of 'institutional deregulation' (Hervieu-Leger, 1999). Religion is no longer inherited and linked to historical identities, but results from the conversion process of individuals, is deregulated and becomes the basis for the re-establishment of new forms of communities. For example, religious organizations such as congregations still affect life projects by providing contexts, 'imaginative options', and relationships. However, humans are increasingly preoccupied with their personal concerns (Marti, 2015, p. 9).

As we can see, the categories of subjectivization and individualization dominate in some of the recent theories of religious change. However, this approach assumes a strong dualism between religious experience and social structure and may lead to the dissolution of transcendence as an element of religiosity. From the perspective of Thomas Luckmann, religious change is related to the opposition between what could be considered to be 'private' or 'public'. The private sphere of religion signifies an autonomous individual who approaches religion as a consumer and is able to follow his own subjective preferences. 'He may choose from the assortment of "ultimate" meanings as he sees fit – guided only by the preferences that are determined by his social biography [...] A certain level of subjective reflection and choice determines the formation of individual religiosity.' (Luckmann, 1967, p. 99) This subjectivization of religion implies the process of detachment from traditional and official religiosity. Religion is reduced to the construction of 'sub-worlds' and 'fragmented universes of meaning' encompassing no more than nuclear families (Berger, 1967, p. 133).

Karel Dobbelaere lists the following results of such a process:

> The polarization of the sacred (religion) and the secular (society) brought about by laicization, is the result of changes described: traditional versus complex, pragmatic, and modern societies; magical and religious versus rational and empirical orientations; an overarching

sacred cosmos versus institutionally specialized ideologies; incalculable magical powers and forces versus calculable and controllable actions and situations; traditional values versus secular law; moral habits versus legal routines; a religious ethic versus instrumental technical control; community versus *Gesellschaft*; total personal relationships versus specialized anonymous roles; face-to face relationships with known people versus social interaction between unknown players; affective versus contractual, formal, and utilitarian relationships; horizontal and vertical bonds versus anomie and social class; small workshops and offices versus large factories and bureaucracies; the church as a total and official organization versus churches as voluntary associations

(Dobbelaere, 1981, pp. 21–22)

The well-known shift in Berger's attitude towards secularization resulted from his highlighting of the growing role of pluralism within the religious world (Berger, 2014). In modern societies, individuals are forced to reflect upon religion due to cultural pluralism and competing non-religious ideas. Religious beliefs require 'constant individual and social confirmation and cultivation' (Tomka, 2006, p. 258). Individuals elaborate their identity in confrontation with opposite opinions and views. That is why 'within the post-traditional social system, to be religious indicates a more or less reflected, conscious, personal choice' (Tomka, 2006, p. 258). In post-traditional culture, social commonalities are reduced to economic, social or geographical categories. Social order is rooted in formal laws and legalistic rules. 'Mobilization for common tasks uses an enforced conformity to laws and formal prescriptions, the fulfillment of which is more of a pragmatic than a moral matter.' (Tomka, 2006, p. 257) Tomka claims that in post-traditional societies, reflexivity is emancipated from 'popular reasoning'. 'In the differentiated social organization, religious views and teachings are organized into a complex rational system partly independent of and partly controlling popular reasoning and feelings, attempting to preserve their independence.' (Tomka, 2006, p. 257)

The sociological quest for religious individualization is developed by taking human identity as the starting point in sociological inquiry. For Martin Riesebrodt, capitalism represents a revolutionary force that 'creates new subjects, transforms the traditional life-chances of people, their structure of needs and their relations to others' (Riesebrodt, 2014, p. 7; 2010). From such a perspective, religion remains an alternative to the secular state and still embodies an important resource for criticism of the social order. With reference to Riesebrodt (2010), I wish to highlight the need for the categorization of religion within a wider perspective, within the culture, and include the changing relationship between the individual and society as a whole. Religious changes should be understood from the perspective of the formation of individual identities. Thomas Nipperdey in his historical inquiry claims that: 'Modernity normally is connected with the making

of the nation and that individuality, culture, and nation are intertwined.'
(Nipperdey, 1988, p. 6)

> At the end of the eighteen century traditional ties began to loosen
> and the living and visible presence of tradition (norms, loyalties, and
> meanings) had weakened. The regional-local segmentation of society,
> estates, and professions, the primarily personal relationship between
> people and the personal organization of power – all these factors began
> to fade. 'Society' assumes the place of 'community'. Inner directed-
> ness, gradually of course, takes the place of following the norms of
> tradition, and thus each person becomes more of an individual, more
> independent. But embedded in abstract, large groups and structures
> like the state, the individual's life becomes more isolated and less
> immediate. Norms and values become increasingly objects of reflec-
> tion and discussion, and the cultural media that convey this reflection
> and discussion – as well as the processes of communication – gain
> more importance, as a result enabling the individual to find his unique
> and collective identity.
>
> (Nipperdey, 1988, p. 6)

Hans Joas argues that modernity should not – as is conventionally
assumed – be defined as the opposite alternative to religion. Both religion
and modernity are able to coexist and can even be mutually enriching
(Joas, 2014). Daniele Hervieu-Leger proposes the concept of 'religious
products of modernity' (2000). According to her, religion should not be
identified with tradition, defined as 'past times'. Human beings inherit
some kind of inner tendency to obey 'external order' (Hervieu-Leger,
2000, p. 133).

These perspectives for studying religious change unlock the concept of
'individualization' and direct our attention to the fact that religious transformation emerges in the relationship of agency to structural and cultural
changes. From the perspective of 'post-traditional' society, as noted by
Giddens, the agential aspect of religion is often eclipsed and its analytical
independence from social structure and culture is not assumed (Giddens,
1994, p. 78). That is why it is worthwhile to recall the theories of Ernst
Troeltsch. In his inquiry into Protestantism, Troeltsch (1912) sheds new light
on the relationship between religious structures and agency. He claims that
religious communities and organizations are established in the interplay
between new ideas and social interactions. The new religious movement of
Protestantism began not only as the result of class conflict but also as a 'religious novelty', that is, as a set of new cultural ideas. Troeltsch claims that
religious communities and organizations are inspired by 'naïve revelation',
which is 'absolutized' and 'deified' by a group. 'Revelation' for Troeltsch
means some kind of social impulse which affects a group of people through
'strong' and 'deep' emotions. These emotions represent a form of social

'energy' which emerges from commitment to the transcendental order. The formation of a new religion includes emotional and unreflexive commitment to new and innovative religious ideas, which Troeltsch does not hesitate to label as 'phantasy', 'emotional life', 'intransigence of certitude' and 'neediness' (Troeltsch, 1912, p. 27). In his view, such unreflexive dimensions of religion are characteristic of the 'lower classes'. These emotional dimensions of religion contribute to the social strength of religion. However, the development of religious organizations requires the involvement of its adherents in a 'culture of reflection'. Religion is integrated into society through this reflexive process. Reflection,[3] understood as critical deliberation upon philosophical and dogmatic ideas, plays an important role in the creation of new religions (Troeltsch, 1912, p. 26). Moreover Troeltsch asserts that Christianity, in the beginning, represented popular and folk religion [*Volkstümlichkeit*] but by the 2nd century, it had integrated a 'culture of reflection'. As a result, in this process of social change, a new 'reflexive culture' was formed (Troeltsch, 1912, p. 27).

This approach corresponds well with the sophisticated insights into the relationship between religious tradition and religious identity proposed by Slavica Jakelic. She points out that the simple identification of late modernity with growing religious individualism tends to result from Protestant theological ideas that are not an adequate description of what is going on in Southeastern Europe. In her book on 'collectivistic religions' she demonstrates that being part of publicly manifested, institutionalized and historically embedded religions is not necessarily in opposition to religious choice. Even religions whose membership is based upon being born into their religious culture are founded on the basis of choice and are 'individualistic in the locus of experience and absolute in personal commitment' (Jakelic, 2016, p. 1). 'Collectivistic religion' is embedded in specific histories and in belonging to a religious community. As one example of such 'collectivistic religion', Jakelic evokes Polish Catholicism which has developed in a very specific historical context. 'Being Polish for centuries has meant being a Catholic, just as being Catholic in such a geo-political context meant being Polish' (Jakelic, 2016, p. 2), despite the fact that the understanding of both being Polish and being Catholic has changed over time. Jakelic protests against the claim that social identities shaped by religious traditions will disappear in late modernity and she maintains that religious pluralization may indeed sustain ascribed religious identities. Her study parallels my research on agency within Polish Catholicism, as her concept of 'collectivistic religions' includes the idea that group identity actively shapes religion and attributes a certain agency to religion.

Conclusions

The wide range of sociological theories and perspectives presented above concerning the relationship between religious experience and socio-cultural background in which religious experience is found leaves no doubt that the issue is very complex. I have presented a variety of theories concerning the link between religion and agency and mentioned some basic assumptions concerning the definition of religion as formulated by different sociological schools and traditions. Overall, I have attempted to show how central the problem of 'structure and agency' is for the sociology of religion, and how the concept of religion has been defined with reference to human subjectivity and social structure accordingly.

This part of the book has presented some basic and common understandings of traditional forms of religiosity as being rather unreflexive and embedded in the social structure. It has been demonstrated that the study of religion in western sociology until now has been characterized by strong tendencies towards dualism. This became especially clear when I examined the sociological understanding of traditional religiosity. Theoretical assumptions about religion from the perspective of traditional society omit sufficient consideration of agency. On the one hand, a religious phenomenon is regarded as a subjective, emotional or cognitive aspect of social life; on the other, religious experience is often reduced to a structural aspect of society without direct reference to human subjectivity. This means that, in the terminology of Margaret Archer, some 'conflation' tendencies are observed in the sociology of religion. As it stands, the concept of religiosity scarcely addresses the issues of 'structure' and 'agency' and does not handle them as different kinds of emergent entities, with different properties and powers. Sociological concepts and theories relating to religion represent instead 'upwards' or 'downwards' conflations, what results in one-dimensional theorizing of the relationship between structure and agency. Conflations do not pay attention to the dynamics of agency and structure but reduce one to the other, thus 'depriving the two of independent properties, capable of exerting autonomous influences, which would automatically defy one-dimensional theorizing' (Archer, 1995, p. 6).

The changing relationship between the individual and social structure alerts us to the fact of religious change. The modernization perspective leans toward a specific vision of the link between subjectivity and social structure. Theories of secularization have strongly influenced the modern discourse on religious change in Europe and in the world. All the theories reviewed in this chapter, and their associated authors, have opened up to me ways of thinking about a new conceptualization of religion in terms of 'religious identity'. This will be presented in the following chapter. My overall conclusion, based on this necessarily brief summary of theories is that an ontological foundation is necessary for a better understanding of the dynamics of religion and religious change. Therefore, the book presents a historical description of religious change in Europe, using Polish Catholicism as a case study, to demonstrate the centrality of the relationship between individual and social structure for the study of religious change.

My central assumption is that if the researcher wishes to avoid the concepts of religion and religiosity becoming oversimplified or misunderstood, due to some ambiguous and unrigorous theoretical assumptions, he or she needs a solid theoretical foundation for the study. Studying religion in its cultural context involves ontological assumptions which must be explained and defined to achieve a logical and precise sociological study. In my opinion the wide range of existing theories suggests that a higher degree of ontological conceptualization is necessary to grasp the true nature of religion, in this case, Polish Catholicism. In my modest aim to shed some light on Polish Catholicism and some stages of its development, I wish to start with the conceptualization of religious phenomena which I will later try to describe and explain in the Polish context. The understanding of both traditional religious beliefs and practices and religious identity in a changing cultural context needs the underlying ontological assumptions to be better understood and explained. Thus, to tease out these theoretical concerns, the book explores with empirical data/case material, what happens when traditional Polish Catholicism moves into the Polish Communist era and beyond the Solidarity reforms of the modern era, and how it functions in the Polish diaspora of migrants to Ireland.

Notes

1. In Christian tradition, a dogma is an element of official doctrine.
2. *Habitus* is a term proposed by Pierre Bourdieu and central to his work. For him *habitus* is a concept which designates the very complex sphere of an individual's tendency to behave in a certain way, from such things as posture to schemes of perception, feeling or mental habits, based on his or her social origins.
3. German: *Reflexion.*

References

Altermatt, U. (1989). *Katholizismus Und Moderne. Zur Sozial – Und Mentalitaetsgeschichte Der Schweizer Katholiken Im 19. Und 20. Jahrhundert.* Zuerich: Benziger.

Archer, M. S. (1995). *Realist Social Theory: the Morphogenetic Approach.* Cambridge: Cambridge University Press.

Astley, J. (2017). *Ordinary Theology: Looking, Listening and Learning in Theology.* Lo̶᷄ ᷄ and New York: Routledge.

B᷄᷄ ᷄997). *Implicit Religion in Contemporary Society.* Leuven: Peeters.

᷄᷄8). Folk Religion. In: W. Swatos Jr. ed., *Encyclopedia of Religion and* ᷄ut Creek: Alta Mira Press. Available at: http://hirr.hartsem.edu/ ᷄Accessed 1 June 2020].

᷄sheim, W. (1996). Individualization and 'Precarious Freedoms': ᷄ntroversies of a Subject-Oriented Sociology. In: P. Heelas, S. *Detraditionalization. Critical Reflections on Authority and* ᷄xford: Blackwell Publishers, pp. 23–48.

Bellah, R. (1980). The Five Religions of Modern Italy. In: R. Bellah and E. Hammond ed., *Varieties of Civil Religion*. San Francisco: Harper and Row, pp. 86–118. Available at: https://www.religion-online.org/book-chapter/chapter-4-the-five-religions-of-modern-italy/ [Accessed 1 June 2020].

Berger, P. (1967). *The Sacred Canopy. Elements of a Sociological Theory of Religion.* Garden City, NY: Doubleday.

Berger, P. (1979). *The Heretical Imperative. Contemporary Possibilities of Religious Affirmation.* Garden City, NY: Doubleday.

Berger, P. (2014). *The Many Altars of Modernity. Toward a Paradigm for Religion in a Pluralist Age.* Berlin: De Gruyter. DOI: 10.1515/9781614516477.

Bourdieu, P. (1984). *Distinction.* London: Routledge and Kegan Paul.

Cipriani, R. (1984). Religion and Politics. The Italian Case: Diffused Religion. *Archives de sciences sociales des religions,* 58, pp. 29–51.

Cipriani, R. (2017). *Diffused Religion: Beyond Secularization.* Cham: Palgrave MacMillan.

De Certeau, M., Domenach, J.-M. (1974). *Le Christianisme Eclate.* Paris: Editions du Seuil.

Dobbelaere, K. (1981). Secularization: A Multi-Dimensional Concept. *Current Sociology,* 29(1). London: Sage Publications.

Drehsen, V., Morel, J. (1982). The Phenomena of Popular Piety. *Social Compass,* 2–3, pp. 99–101.

Durkheim, E. (1964[1893]). *The Divison of Labour in Society.* London: The Free Press of Glencoe, Collier-MacMillan Limited.

Durkheim, E. (1995[1912]). *The Elementary Forms of the Religious Life.* New York: The Free Press.

Evans-Pritchard, E. (1965). *Theories of Primitive Religion.* Oxford: Oxford University Press.

Feuerbach, L. (1957[1841]). *The Essence of Christianity.* New York: Harper Torchbooks.

Gay, P. (1969). *The Enlightenment. The Interpretation,* vol. 2: *The Science of Freedom.* New York: Knopf.

Giddens, A. (1994). Living in a Post-Traditional Society. In: U. Beck, A. Giddens and S. Lash, ed., *Reflexive Modernization: Politics, Tradition and Aesthetics in the Modern Social Order.* Cambridge & Oxford: Polity Press.

Hervieu-Leger, D. (1999). *Le Pelerin Et Le Converti. La Religion En Mouvement.* Paris: Flammarion.

Hervieu-Leger, D. (2000). *Religion as a Chain of Memory.* New Brunswick, NJ: Rutgers University Press.

Hobbes, T. (1887). *Leviathan: or The Matter, Form and Power of a Commonwealth, Ecclesiastical and Civil.* London: George Routledge and Sons.

Hornsby-Smith, M., Lee, M., Reilly, P. (1985). Common Religion and Customary Religion: A Critique and a Proposal. *Review of Religious Research,* 26, pp. 244–252.

Hume, D. (2012[1748]). *An Enquiry Concerning Human Understanding.* Chicago: Maestro Reprints.

Isambert, F. (1975). Autour Du Catholicisme Populaire. Reflexions Sociologiques Sur Un Debat. *Social Compass,* 22(2), pp. 193–210.

Isambert, F. (1982). *Le Sens Du Sacre. Fete Et Religion Populaire.* Paris: Editions de Minuit.

Jakelic, S. (2016). *Collectivistic Religions: Religion, Choice, and Identity in Late Modernity*. Abingdon: Routledge.

Joas, H. (2014). *Faith as an Option. Possible Futures for Christianity*. Stanford: Stanford University Press.

Knoblauch, H. (2000). Die Populaere Religion, Markt, Medien Und Die Popularisierung Der Religion. *Zeitschrift für Religionswissenschaft*, 8, pp. 143–161.

Knoblauch, H. (2008). Spirituality and Popular Religion in Europe. *Social Compass*, 55, pp. 140–153.

Levi, C. (1970). *Christ Stopped at Eboli*. New York: Noonday Press.

Luckmann, T. (1967). *The Invisible Religion. The Problem of Religion in Modern Societies*. New York: MacMillan.

Luhmann, N. (1995). *Social Systems*. California: Stanford University Press.

Lynch, G. (2012). *The Sacred in the Modern World. A Cultural Sociological Approach*. Oxford: Oxford University Press.

Marti, G. (2015). Religious Reflexivity: The Effect of Continual Novelty and Diversity on Individual Religiosity. *Sociology of Religion* 76(1), pp. 1–13. DOI: 10.1093/socrel/sru084.

Martin, D. (1978). *A General Theory of Secularization*. New York: Harper Colophon Books.

Mensching, G. (1972). *Die Weltreligionen*. Darmstadt: Carl Habel Verlagbuchhandlung.

Nipperdey, T. (1988). Religion and the Center: Reflections on German History. In: L. Greenfield, M. Martin eds., *Center: Ideas and Institutions*. Chicago: University of Chicago Press, pp. 1–17.

Parker, C. (1998). Modern Popular Religion: A Complex Object of Study for Sociology. *International Sociology*, 12(2), pp. 195–212.

Riesebrodt, M. (2010). *The Promise of Salvation: A Theory of Religion*. Chicago: University of Chicago Press. DOI: 10.7208/chicago/9780226713946.001.0001.

Riesebrodt, M. (2014). Religion in the Modern World: Between Secularization and Resurgence. Max Weber Lecture. Available at: https://www.semanticscholar.org/paper/Religion-in-the-modern-world-%3A-between-and-Riesebrodt/b7ff1630fd635da81452ddaf063779b692101bb2 [Accessed 1 June 2020].

Robertson, R. (1970). *The Sociological Interpretation of Religion*. Oxford: Basil Blackwell.

Staples, P. (1979). Official and Popular Religion in an Ecumenical Perspective. In: P. Vrijhof, J. Waardenburg eds., *Official and Popular Religion*. Mouton: The Hague, pp. 244–293.

Stark, R., Finke, R. (2000). *Acts of Faith. Explaining the Human Side of Religion*. Berkeley and Los Angeles: University of California Press.

Stolz, J., Konemann, J., Cheneuwly Purdie, M., Engelberger, T., Kruggeler, M. (2014). *Religion Und Spiritualitat in Der Ich-Gesellschaft*. Zurich: Theologisher Verlag Zurich.

Tomka, M. (2006). Is Conventional Sociology of Religion Able to Deal With Differences between Eastern and Western European Developments? *Social Compass*, 53, pp. 251–265.

Toon, R. (2017). *Methodological Problems in the Study of Implicit Religion*, Religious Research Paper 3. Leeds: Department of Sociology, University of Leeds.

Towler, R. (1974). *Homo religiosus: Sociological Problems in the Study of Religion*. London: Constable.

Troeltsch, E. (1912). *Die Soziallehren Der Christlichen Kirchen Und Gruppen.* Tubingen: J.C.B. Mohr.

Weber, M. (1978[1920]). Religious Groups (Sociology of Religion). In: G. Roth, C. Wittich eds., *Max Weber. Economy and Society. An Outline of Interpretative Sociology.* Berkeley: University of California Press, pp. 399–634.

Weber, M. (1978[1922]). Types of Legitimate Domination. In: G. Roth, C. Wittich eds., *Max Weber. Economy and Society. An Outline of Interpretative Sociology.* Berkeley: University of California Press, pp. 212–301.

Williams, R. (1973). Schleiermacher and Feuerbach on the Intentionality of Religious Consciousness. *The Journal of Religion*, 53(4), pp. 424–455.

Wilson, B. (1976). Aspects of Secularization in the West. *Japanese Journal of Religious Studies*, 3, pp. 259–276.

Wilson, B. (1982). *Religion in Sociological Perspective.* New York: Oxford University Press.

2 Religious identity from the perspective of critical realism

In Chapter 1, I have argued that understanding the link between agency and structure is the foundation for the study of religious identity and religious change. When agency is neglected in the study of religious identity, the resultant characterization of religious forms ignores the link between individual and structural aspects of social life. There is a real risk in the tendency to overlook or deny either the structural or the subjective aspects of religion. Agency is especially pivotal in the study on traditional religiosity, where the dominant focus on structural aspects seems to overshadow human subjectivity on the one hand and culture on the other. I wish to emphasize that the study of religious identity needs not only practical research questions but requires also a social ontological framework which delivers adequate concepts and presents the relationships between them.

In this chapter, I will present my understanding of religious identity. My vision is not an original concept of what religion is. On the contrary, this book stands on the strongly established and ontologically grounded approach of critical realism. Critical realism offers a systematic and well-justified theoretical approach for studying social life. It reformulates the relationships between reality, experience, knowledge and causal mechanisms, and challenges epistemological postulates which are often taken for granted in the social sciences. Critical realism establishes a new perspective for studying religion, avoiding the positivistic understanding of religion which was previously dominant (Archer and Tritter, 2000).

The critical realist way of thinking in social science was initiated by the philosopher Roy Bhaskar in 1975, when he published the influential book *A Realist Theory of Science* (2008[1975]). In this work, he examined, from the perspective of the philosophy of science, the epistemological status of natural science. Bhaskar deployed a 'Kantian' transcendental procedure to explain the nature of modern science, namely by asking 'What needs to be the case for X to exist'. He gave 'Christmas shopping' as his example. In later books, entitled *The Possibility of Naturalism* (1998[1979]) and *Reclaiming Reality* (2011[1989]), he developed his realist perspective. He moved from the concepts of 'transcendental realism' and 'critical naturalism' to 'critical realism' as a reluctant compromise, as others had started using the other two terms. Among critical realist scholars, I have chosen Margaret Archer and her morphogenetic approach as the most appropriate for my research field. Archer has elaborated a clear and consistent vision not only of culture and structure but also of the human person in social life (esp. 1988; 2000). In her ontology, she often refers to transcendence and provides a solid theoretical basis for a critical realist approach to the sociology of religion.

In this second chapter, I will introduce the ontological foundations of the sociology of religion. The concepts and theories presented here, mostly inspired by Margaret Archer's writings and my personal discussions with her, should not be understood as a theoretical framework which limits and restricts the exploration of religious life. Rather, they deliver a systematic platform for our general understanding of the fundamental elements of social life, and the relationship between these elements and social processes. My central purpose is not to repeat the most general assumptions of critical realism and morphogenesis: primarily my work is devoted to the exploration of religion. However, in this chapter, I will outline the work of some of the most representative critical realist scholars in order to integrate their understanding of religion into my study. Moreover, the concept of 'reflexivity', which is central to Margaret Archer's work, when applied to the religious arena opens up a new perspective for studying religious experience in the context of different cultures and social conditions. I will guide my investigation carefully, avoiding ontological failures and considering both the subjective and structural properties in the religious phenomena. Based on some ontological assumptions postulated by critical realists, I want to transcend the approach in which religious identity is seen as representing either subjective or structural aspects of social life. I am searching for a new approach to religious identity from the perspective of agency and hope also to elaborate a particular vision of religious identity which will allow me, not only to highlight some subjective and idiosyncratic aspects of Polish social life, but also permit me to study Polish Catholicism in a systematic and methodical way.

The human person and experience

Critical realism opens up new perspectives, especially for an integrated approach to the study of social structure, culture and agency. In positivist sociology, the rudimentary elements of society are depicted most often as 'individuals' and studied as independent observable facts between which casual relations may be found. Critical realist ontology transforms this formal approach into something more relational, processual and dynamic. Social agents are no longer observed as individuals, but rather as relational beings – human persons. At first glance, such categories may seem too philosophical or personalistic and insufficiently sociological. However, as an epistemological approach, that is, as a theoretical paradigm, critical realism sheds light on realities which have not been conceptualized before in sociology. In his formulations, Christian Smith shows that there is space within sociology for such a term as the 'human person' (Smith, 2010). Any restrictions against using the category of 'a person' in sociology are a consequence of taking for granted some epistemological paradigms, especially naturalistic positivism. As a result, there is no space in social science for what is not directly observable, nor for what is not material. Abstract concepts such as personhood or even culture are dismantled under pressure from positivism. Christian Smith knows very well the positivistic and empiricist approach in studying social facts. He is one of the most eminent representatives of empirical approaches to the sociology of religion in America (see Smith, 1996a and 1996b; 2000; Smith and Lundquist, 2005). The 'personalistic shift' in his sociology can be understood, not as a revolution, but rather as an evolutionary development. Smith's realist shift within his approach to the sociology of religion has been inspired not only by critical realism, but also by personalism and anti-naturalistic phenomenological epistemology. Smith does not presume that human beings have a specific and identifiable 'nature', which is rooted in the natural world and apprehensible through rational discourse. This 'quiddity' ('whatness') about the human person is a theoretical assumption within the realist approach to sociological study (Smith, 2010, p. 9).

The key concept in a realist understanding of social reality is that of 'emergence' which explicates the stratified character of social reality. Debates concerning the nature of emergence have quite a long history.

> Emergence refers to the process of constituting a new entity with its own particular characteristics through the interactive combination of other, different entities that are necessary for the creation of the new entity but which do not contain the characteristics present in the new entity.
>
> (Smith, 2010, p. 26)

For instance, the physical and chemical worlds are emergent in nature. Well-known substances such as oxygen (O_2) or water (H_2O) are emergent structures consisting of more basic elements but which in combination represent new entities. Some roots of the concept of 'emergence' within social science can be traced to the theories of classical scholars, including both philosophers such as Wilhelm Hegel, Karl Marx, August Comte, John Stuart Mill, and later Alfred Whitehead and Karl Popper, and sociologists such as Thorstein Veblen or even Talcott Parsons. Recently, the philosopher Roger Scruton developed such an approach to the human person in his study on sexual desire (Scruton, 1986). Emergence brings to mind the classical dialectic schema of social constructionism formulated by Peter Berger and Thomas Luckmann but links socially constructed human knowledge with the biological background of cognitive processes. While Smith designates these latter two sociologists as 'proto-emergentists', he notes that the realist conception of emergence should be differentiated from a dualistic way of thinking. Instead of assuming parallel elements which intermingle and result in synthesis, emergence underwrites the existence of 'lower' and 'higher' levels of stratified reality that represents not only autonomous entities but also their different qualities. Emergence as a theoretical framework explains how is happens that human persons are equipped with powers and capacities which make them social beings. Human consciousness, aesthetic sensitivity, creativity, symbolization or moral awareness could all be explained as emergent phenomena which are 'sources' of social structures. Human subjects as real, embodied selves, plunged into their biological nature, equipped with self-awareness and the ability to reflect upon their experiences, are much more than a product of social forces (Smith, 2010, p. 72).

This view has tremendous consequences for the concept of society as it establishes a new dimension for thinking about social life. The theory of emergence establishes the link between cognitively constructed society and the natural world. Critical realism assumes the dialectic between the human being (self) and the realistically understood natural world, as human beings are constituted by their relationship to nature. Human consciousness emerges from the biological nature of human beings (their personal emergent properties), which in critical realism are given priority over social relations. Relations to the natural and environmental (biological and physical) world are sources of the human sense of self. The human self is regarded 'as an emergent relational property whose realization comes about through the necessary relations between embodied practice and the non-discursive environment' (Archer, 2000, p. 123). While the 'sense of self' is universal and autonomous from socially rooted linguistic relations, the 'concept of self' depends upon social interactions and is shaped by linguistic relations. Human proprieties and powers emerge from the interplay between the self and the realistically understood world. In comparison with a modernist point of view, human beings are not only reference points for the whole of reality but, as well, are subordinated to natural and objective reality. This implies that society is attributed with *sui generis* properties. Both individuals and society as a whole have their own autonomous power.

Margaret Archer in her morphogenetic approach is especially interested in the interplay of human subjects and social structure in terms of agency. Archer discusses this point with reference to what she calls 'downwards' and 'upwards' conflation. She sees both as problematic. The former dissolves human agency by explaining the nature of human beings in terms of society as a whole. On the other hand, upwards conflation, as an approach, is mistaken, 'for it is some property of people (usually their in-built rationality, though sometimes modified by social additives such as normativity) which is held to account for the entirety of the social context – by a process of aggregation' (Archer, 2000, p. 21). There remains also the third possibility, which is 'central' conflation, where the autonomy is withheld from both social structure and human subjects, because they are held to be mutually constitutive. Both levels are inseparable and neither the 'parts' nor the 'people' are epiphenomena of one another. The 'central' conflation implies conjunction between structural and subjective properties (Archer, 1995, pp. 93–134).

A key element of Archer's morphogenetic approach is her delineation of four orders of reality in the 'human world', including not only the social, but also the natural, practical and transcendental orders (Archer, 2000). All four orders are essential for human beings. Orders of reality represent intentional objects and are related to three different clusters of emotions. Although individuals are confronted with the reality of the orders simultaneously, each order of reality is related to a distinct type of concern. The natural order bestows concern about physical well-being and generates emotions that are stimulated in encounters with the natural environment. Concerns related to the natural order are embodied in the physical constitution of human beings. The practical order is represented by human labour and practical engagement with the world of material culture and relates to performative concerns. The social order includes the participation of individuals in the social realm and represents the discursive environment. The transcendental order was explicitly distinguished by Archer three years later and will be described below.[1]

The way Margaret Archer distinguishes between the natural, social and practical orders on the one hand and transcendental order on the other corresponds well with the work of Peter Berger when he, following Alfred Schutz, juxtaposes what he labels as the 'life-world', or 'paramount reality' on the one hand with 'the other realities'. Berger assumes that despite the fact that 'the reality of everyday life is dramatically deprived of its "paramount" status [...] the specificity of religious experience, then, is not to be sought in its breaching of the "paramount reality", but rather in the characteristics that structure its "finite province of meaning"' (Berger, 1974, p. 130). Similarly, for Archer, Berger's understanding of transcendent experience is not religious *per se*. He claims that, for example, humour 'may be understood as a "signal of transcendence"' (Berger, 1974, p. 131). When Berger follows the approach of Rudolf Otto in this way, he shows that his understanding of 'numinous' is a starting point in the search for a sociological understanding of religious experience, as he strongly distinguishes between the phenomenological experience and the social structure. Significantly, Berger shares this perspective with critical realism. In fact, the perspective of Margaret Archer corresponds well with Berger's point of view that religious experience transforms how people perceive the reality of everyday life and that religious experience radically 'relativizes' and 'trivializes' everyday life (Berger, 1974, p. 130). 'Religion introduces an additional dimension to experience; once this has happened, there continues to be the awareness that the stage of everyday action is "hollow", that there is another level "beneath" it, and that the figures located there may "surface" at any moment. Needless to say, this awareness (even if at times it is only held dimly) accentuates the precariousness of everyday life and all its works' (Berger, 1974, p. 131). Berger also affirms the role of rituals in this 'relativization of everyday reality' and the fact that there are great variations in intensity in this experience, as the 'power' of religious experience is relative to individual experience. The most crucial difference between the approaches of Margaret Archer and Peter Berger is the fact that Berger in his study on religion is trapped in the 'phenomenological cage' of human experience and does not make allowance for the study of reflexivity and agency.

In a realist perspective, humans undergo a multiplicity of experiences when interacting with the four orders of reality. These experiences deliver in turn a wide range and variety of emotions to the individuals concerned. Despite the fact that human experiences may be illusory, generally people believe in what they experience, and experiences appear to be rational. Emotions play an important role for humans as embodied beings. Emotions are commentaries upon our concerns and are emergent from relationships with the natural, practical and social (discursive) orders of natural reality. They regulate relations between a person and the orders of reality, involve a sense of their situation and are affective modes of awareness of a situation. Emotions are relational, that is, they are emergent from the relationship between human embodiment and the environment. What is very important to note, in comparison with the positivist perspective, is that in a realist approach, emotions do not operate in the human body as stimuli which automatically generate behavioural reactions. Rather, emotions require cognition of their intentional object and are related to personal expectations or 'action readiness'. This means that emotions depend upon 'human concerns', which attribute values to that which is experienced by human persons. These concerns represent a constellation which defines the personal identity of a person.

> The emergence of persons from selves is also the work of this middle ground, where we uniquely define ourselves by virtue of our constellations of concerns about the world. Yet, to arrive at a definition of such concerns entails considerable experience of the natural, practical and social orders of reality, in which none has any automatic precedence.
>
> (Archer, 2000, p. 190)

Emotions within the social order emerge from the relationship between a social subject and normative order rooted in the social structure. 'The most important of our social concerns is our self-worth which is vested in certain projects (career, family, community, club or church)' (Archer, 2000, p. 219). Concerns about self-worth, related to social commitment, generate judgements of approbation or disapprobation. Humans evaluate their conduct in relation to social norms. Norms should not be understood in a Kantian way, as does Max Weber. Norms represent much more than a transcendental voice of duty. Norms fuel human commitment and have an affective component. The emergence of emotions within the social order is dependent upon: (1) the subject's status in society; (2) the receipt of moral evaluations from the social order and (3) the conjunction between the subject's personal concerns and the nature of society's norms.

According to Archer's definition, '"reflexivity" is the regular exercise of the mental ability, shared by all normal people, to consider themselves in relation to their (social) contexts and vice versa' (Archer, 2007, p. 4). Reflexivity is the emergent property of persons, which generates personal identity because humans are not passive in their encounter with emotions, but rather are equipped with a 'second-order' capacity to reflect upon emotions and to transform them. Emotions represent the 'fuel of our internal conversation' (Archer, 2000, p. 194) which constitutes human reflexivity. Reflexivity transforms emotions of the so-called 'first-order' into 'second-order' emotions. First-order emotions, or 'affects', represent no more than a commentary upon human concerns. Such a transformation requires human acts of commitment. Reflexivity reviews emotional commentaries, elaborates upon them, shapes emotionality itself and develops the sense of self. That is why people are able to shape concerns in a deliberative way. Emotions are reflexively elaborated; human concerns can be re-ordered through 'internal conversation' and 'ultimate concerns' can be disengaged. 'These are concerns that are not a means of anything beyond them, but are commitments that are constitutive of who we are – the expression of our identities.' (Archer, 2004, p. 65) Ultimate concerns[2] are configured as acts of human will which subordinate but do not necessarily repudiate other concerns (Archer, 2006, p. 277). 'Persons debate with themselves what importance they will attach to a given import: asking and answering how much they are prepared to suffer physically in relation to their ultimate concerns.' (Archer, 2000, p. 209) The disengagement of ultimate concerns entails two elements: (1) cognitive judgement about their inherent worth and (2) deep emotional attachment to them (affect or love) (Archer, 2006, p. 277). '"Ultimate affirmation" is made after evaluating the consequences for the self, by taking account of the positive and negative costs to be borne and establishing how we are.' (Archer, 2004, p. 74) In this way, reflexivity is exercised through inner dialogue (internal conversation) with the use of language – a symbolic medium, but also through visceral sensations and visual imagery. Interior conversation elaborates a *modus vivendi* when concerns are integrated and unified, and emerge as a way of life. Reflexivity is both grounded in individual identity and shapes personal identity by regulating emotions and ordering concerns which are translated into 'life projects'.

Human beings are 'encultured' in the world and their lives by reflexivity. Reflexivity, or the process of self-monitoring, can be explained with the use of Archer's 'DDD scheme' (Archer, 2007, p. 20) which refers to the three phases of internal conversation and internal experimentation: discernment, deliberation and dedication, and which includes both thoughts and feelings.

Discernment is a moment of sifting or negative classification. Within her inner dialogue, a person compares and contrasts some desiderata related to her concerns. Desiderata may be in response to satisfactions or dissatisfactions with her current way of life and emphasize positive concerns (What do I really want?). Archer describes this process as 'book-marking', in which important items are highlighted for further elaboration. Deliberation consists in exploring some implications of the concerns already selected. In this process, a hierarchical structure of concerns is generated. Imagination delivers visual projections which provoke emotional commentaries. Finally, dedication is the culminating moment of decision-making which involves human will. The decision is very often difficult to make, because the agent is forced to abandon some concerns (Archer, 2007, pp. 20–21). The focus on human reflexivity in relation to social structure is an exploration of the relationship between the human subject and the social context. The process of shaping human biographies includes: (1) accepting or rejecting relationships with the environment; (2) developing concerns through relations with the context of the subject; (3) elaborating social networks; (4) reshaping concerns through social exchanges and (5) establishing a *modus vivendi* within the social context (Archer, 2007, pp. 147–148).

Reflexivity should not be seen as opposed to religious rituals because reflexivity derives from human embodiment (embodied practices) in the world and should not be understood as something idealistic, detached from the four orders of reality. Reflexivity refers to the context, which is changing and is associated with the capacity to affect human consciousness, commitment and moreover it causally influences agents within social relations. People reflexively shape themselves; they form specific *modus vivendi* and become agents in society. Reflexivity shapes not only personal identity but also provides a basis for life projects and personal biographies (Archer, 1995, p. 124). Reflexivity refers not only to particularly personal and unique life projects but also to universal human projects that are generated as collective life projects, especially when a group of people live in similar circumstances.

The personal relationship to transcendence

In a critical realist approach, as has been mentioned above, human persons stay in touch with four basic dimensions (orders) of reality: (1) natural, which refers to the natural environment; (2) practical, which includes their relationship to practical skills and knowledge; (3) social, which includes their social interactions and (4) transcendental. Although discussion of the transcendental order only appeared in the more recent works of Margaret Archer (2004 and 2006) and she did not elaborate upon it to the same extent as the other orders of reality, it is nevertheless a crucial aspect of social life for my study. In my understanding, the transcendental order is based on culturally transmitted religious beliefs but the relationship with transcendence is conditioned by personal commitment. Culturally integrated ideas concerning God, theological concepts and shared knowledge represent a medium for a personal relationship with the transcendental order. One's personal commitment to the transcendental order is relevant to transcendence as an ultimate personal concern. The relationship between transcendental concerns and transcendental reality generates (emergently) emotional commentaries. Transcendental concerns are reflexively elaborated; the configuration between transcendental concerns and ultimate concerns is shaped in internal conversation. It is a matter of will that a believer struggles to prioritize transcendental concerns and to subordinate other 'naturalistic concerns'. Transcendent ultimate concerns arise as the religious believer ventures into 'religious experience'.

Transcendental concerns have a powerful capacity to reconfigure human concerns and unite other concerns into an integrated whole. Emotions elevated by transcendental experience, as a 'commentary on' religious concerns, incorporate the capacity to shape human commitment and action. Such commitment is manifested in 'disinterested involvement' (Archer, 2004, p. 80), when some humanistic or universal concerns, referring especially to those relating to the common good, and which are not culturally integrated with religion, are dominant. Archer labels commitment to transcendental concerns 'theosis', a theological term meaning the transforming effect of the relationship to the transcendence. Such transcendental commitment shapes human identity and 'acts as a new sounding board against which old concerns reverberate; the emotional echo is transformed' (Archer, 2006, pp. 275–276). Transcendental commitment revaluates and re-orders other concerns which are associated with other orders of reality, giving priority to religious concerns, that is, shaping ultimate concerns of a religious nature. This process is called 'affectual transformation' and includes a kind of interior 'struggle' between concerns belonging to different orders. Transcendent emotions and commitment to transcendental concerns involve the experience of 'love', 'sinfulness' and 'detachment'. Reflexively determined emotions entail pragmatic potential, because they have the power to reevaluate life projects and shape life expectations.

> This is what makes us moral beings. It is only in the light of our 'ultimate concerns' that our actions are ultimately intelligible. None of this caring can be impoverished by reducing it to an instrumental means-ends relationship, which is presumed to leave us 'better off' relative to some indeterminate notion of future 'utility'.
>
> (Archer, 2004, p. 65)

What is very important here is that the transcendental order does not refer only to religion. Transcendence is not only 'supernatural' in the traditional meaning of the word. It denotes the 'human capacity to overcome some existing state or level of consciousness, including knowledge' (Archer, Collier and Porpora, 2004b, p. 27) which cannot be reduced to any other order of reality: neither social nor natural, or even to pre-existing knowledge or tradition. Transcendence manifests itself in three different forms of human relations: (1) subject-object; (2) subject-subject and (3) subject-transcendent. In the first form, people transcend their relations to things and ideas with creativity. Such creative activity allows people to overcome problems by adopting new ideas, technical innovations and other forms of inventiveness. Subject-subject relations refer to interpersonal relations and constitute a form of transcendence which transforms normative expectations of emotionality or commitment. Subject-transcendent relations include 'personal awareness of God as the ultimate reality' (Archer, Collier and Porpora, 2004b, p. 27) and hence this form of transcendence surpasses knowledge concerning divinity accumulated within religious traditions. This last form of transcendent relations gives rise to affective and cognitive outcomes different from human love and cannot be understood as only the extrapolation of subject-subject relations. That is why Archer does not hesitate to assign universal meaning to the transcendental order. Transcendental experience is not reserved for believers only. Non-believers do not include a positive 'cognitive judgment' about the existence of God but find love in other orders of reality (for instance, in nature), 'sustaining dedication to an ultimate concern within the triad [of] naturalistic concerns' (Archer, 2006, p. 277). Furthermore, she claims that the denial of transcendence has damaging consequences for human well-being. This is so because the transcendental order rises a form of love which is presented by Archer as having a particular and indispensable role in human life. Transcendental concerns may involve, as well, disinterested engagement in such domains as ecology, culture or humanity.

Critical realism integrates the transcendent order with both subjectivity and cultural contexts. Religious experience is shaped by social forces but is not to be reduced to them. The way people report the experience of transcendence varies. The human relationship to the transcendental order encompasses a wide range of possibilities, from the total negation of transcendent reality (atheism), through the acceptance of mutually contradictory concepts and schemes of transcendence, to a variety of mystical experiences. But to the critical realist, 'Absence of religious experience is itself a kind of experience' (Archer, Collier, Porpora, 2004a, p. 4). The distinction between believers and non-believers is based upon two criteria: (1) some people experience transcendence and others do not; (2) some people interpret the transcendence which they experience as religious, whereas others do not.

In terms of critical realism, 'religion', a traditional and ambiguous concept within the sociology of religion (Orsi, 2003), is epistemically relative and conditioned by personal concerns and modes of reflexivity, as well as by structural and cultural contexts, including prevailing norms and the cultural dissemination of religion. Religious experience surpasses interpersonal relations; the religious elements included in human culture should not be perceived as part of an idealistic sphere but as part of 'descriptive tradition', which is legitimized and authorized by prior human experience (Archer, 2004b, p. 28). Religious tradition, including theological knowledge and concepts, is animated by human experience. People are categorized as 'religious' (i.e., believers), not only because they have experience of the transcendental order but also because they interpret their experience in terms of a culturally contextualized concept of religion. People define themselves as religious because of the emotions which accompany transcendental experience (such as love), which are related to the transcendental order, and which they interpret as religious. People experience love within the transcendental order, find themselves being loved within this transcendental reality and associate this emotion with the reality which is described in tradition as a personal God or another form of supreme being. Religious experience delivers confirmation of transcendence and allows a believer to find, in transcendence, 'an ultimate concern that is cognitively of supreme worth, if they are justified in their beliefs' (Archer, 2006, pp. 261–283). The experience of transcendence incorporates cognitive content and is a learning experience (a clarification or illumination), but with a distinct meaning, and includes (1) the experiencing subject; (2) the content of experience and (3) the object of experience. The content of experience refers not only to the subject but also to the object. 'In any true experience, the object of experience contributes something to the content of experience.' (Archer, Collier, Porpora, 2004a, p. 13) An emotional reaction to transcendental experience accompanies emotional attachment to the experienced object. The experience of transcendence is the discovery that 'God is, by his nature, inherently worthy of the highest loving concern' (Archer, 2006, p. 274).

Religious commitment is not necessarily accompanied by strong personal affects, which are essentially described by Archer as love. People also declare themselves as religious when their personal concerns 'are satisfied' with the many theological arguments accumulated within religious traditions. Such religious commitment is an outcome of a 'teaching tradition' (which contextualizes religious experience) rather than of emotion. However, the acknowledgement of religious tradition is also associated with emotional attachment to the experienced reality (Archer, 2004a, p. 4) because the experience of transcendence exceeds the frame of culturally conditioned language. Common language and symbols are not relevant for capturing the nature of profound transcendental experience, as is expressed in the lives of religious mystics such as St John of the Cross and St Teresa of Avila (Archer, 2007, p. 66). Language, which could be used to express what has been experienced, is not sufficiently broad and deep. That is why mystics often use metaphors to overcome the limitations of language. 'Equally, the tradition of religious symbolism and imagery could constitute the equivalent for the Western contemplatives, who relied heavily upon metaphorical extrusion when they reached the limits of (natural) language.' (Archer, 2007, p. 67)

Shaping religious identity reflexively

The application of critical realism and the concept of reflexivity to the sociological study of religion require new conceptualizations. The conceptualization of religion from the perspective of reflexivity shares some similarities with the Weberian approach to religion. The most common characteristic of this approach is the study of religious identity from the perspective of subjectivity. As Weber notes

> The external courses of religious behavior are so diverse that an understanding of this behavior can only be achieved from the viewpoint of the subjective experiences, ideas, and purposes of the individuals concerned – in short, from the viewpoint of the religious behavior's «meaning» [*sinn*].
>
> (Weber, 1978[1922], p. 399)

What is more, Weber is aware that religious identity is oriented to 'this world' and everyday life: 'Even human sacrifices, although uncommon among urban peoples, were performed in the Phoenician maritime cities without any otherworldly expectations whatsoever' (Weber, 1978[1922], p. 400). Weber assumes also that religious identity is rational in the sense that it follows some rules of experience. The understanding of religious identity in terms of reflexivity includes some similarities with the Weberian term 'charisma'. From such a perspective religious identity is a very personal characteristic because charismatic powers are accumulated within the dynamics of personality (Weber, 1978[1922], p. 401).

The concept of reflexivity opens up new perspectives for the understanding of religious identity. Reflexivity plays a crucial role in shaping human identity and a person's commitment to religion. Religious persons integrate transcendental concerns with natural, social and performative ones. From such a perspective, it is necessary to study the relationship between transcendental concerns and other orders of reality. The transcendental order should not be understood as independent from other orders. From the perspective of the sociological study of religion, what is crucial is not the ontological status of the transcendental order but how transcendental concerns are integrated with other concerns in the makeup of the human person. In this sense, transcendental concerns relate to the order of reality which is transcendence but are implied in the experience of natural, social and performative concerns. Religious people, in light of the morphogenetic approach, are committed to the transcendental order through their special relationship to nature, and their commitment to social relations, which shapes also their relationship to the performative order. What is meant here could be described by the philosophical expression: *Sub specie aeternitatis* [from the perspective of eternity]. Religious people shape their relationship with nature, performative achievements and other people, with reference to transcendence. When people are religious, reflexivity encompasses transcendence also and the reflexivity of religious people shapes their relationship with transcendence. Such a form of reflexivity, which denotes transcendence, could be called 'religious reflexivity' but should not be understood as a different mode of reflexivity. 'Religious reflexivity' is rather a practical application of reflexivity to the transcendental order. The term suggests that reflexivity *binds* [Latin: *religio, -are*] a person to the transcendental order.

In this way, the category of 'religious reflexivity' shares common elements with the sociology of everyday life proposed by Nancy Ammerman (2014) and Meredith McGuire (2007 and 2008) and is especially useful for overcoming the distinction between institutional religion and spirituality. The roots of sociological inquiry on religion from the perspective of 'lived religion' go back to the work of David D. Hall (1997) who defines this point of view as the historical study of religious practices in the context of everyday life. Ammerman realized that the rational choice perspective for studying religious attitudes imposes strong restrictions within the sociology of religion. Ammerman's initial assumption is that 'institutional boundaries are porous […] individuals carry frameworks and expectations and practices from one part of life to another, and organizations often learn from each other' (2014, p. 6). That is why she claims that the study of religion should include 'a range of ideas, memberships, and practices that bring the spiritual and the mundane world into conversation with each other' (Ammerman, 2014, p. 5). She later goes on to emphasize, 'What happens in religious communities is not an otherworldly sacred retreat but a place where mundane concerns mix freely with spiritual realities' (Ammerman, 2014, p. 19). Research on 'lived religion' reestablishes the relationship between the actual experience of religious persons and institutionally defined beliefs and practices. Robert Orsi introduced the concept of 'lived religion' (2002) as an alternative to the misleading – according to him – concept of 'popular religion', which I discussed in Chapter 1.

The concept 'religious reflexivity' has already been used by Gerardo Marti (2015) to analyze religious phenomena within the frame of modernity. Marti defines 'religious reflexivity' as a 'deliberative and problem-solving dynamic' (2015, p. 3) which applies transcendental concerns to new circumstances and life situations. 'Religious reflexivity therefore involves continual self-critique in evaluating the distance between the desire to actualize ultimate concerns and the visible progression evident in behavior so far' (Marti, 2015, pp. 3–6) and hence, how humans exercise agency in living out religious imperatives in the world. The concept serves not only to characterize anthropological mechanisms of religious experience but also to explain the presence of religion in modern cultures. The religious pluralism dominating many modern cultures challenges individual identities and affects 'stable identity packages' (Marti, 2015, p. 2). Marti claims that modern pluralistic culture stimulates the development of subjectivity in religious experience and the need for religious reflexivity. Julian Schaap and Stef Aupers define 'religious reflexivity' as an 'open-ended process of meaning-making' (2017, p. 1747).

The concept of 'religious identity' in the critical realist perspective implies a specific understanding of religious rituals. Reflexivity plays an important role at the stage of rites, when the individual stands on the threshold between her previous and her new identity. In such an understanding, 'liminality' is a stage of reflection (Turner, 1967, p. 105). Conscious reflection results from the experience of events, the presence of alternative worldviews, ritual actions and the transmission of religious ideas, including ritual language (Hjobjerg, 2002, p. 1). Philip Mellor and Chris Shilling even use the 'reflexivity' concept to re-conceptualize the theoretical category of *habitus* as proposed by Pierre Bourdieu in the field of religion (2014). They supplement this new theoretical category with the notion of 'instauration', proposed by Bruno Latour (2006 and 2011). For them 'religious *habitus*' is 'a reflexive crafting of a mode of being that locates human action, feeling and thought at the embodied intersection of worldly and other-worldly realities' (Mellor and Shilling, 2014, p. 280). Individuals and groups actively remake their bodies through the reflexive mediation of religious ideas stored within religious traditions. Kimberley Patton, from a historical and ethnographic point of view, presents 'divine reflexivity' as a self-reflexive and self-expressive action, which is generative because it instigates and inspires human religious activity (2009).

Furthermore, the phenomenon of religious conversion cannot be understood without reference to religious reflexivity. A person who is distanced from previous habits and even social bonds by the conversion process actively shapes new commitments and intentionally crafts new life priorities and a new biographical trajectory. The process of a paradigm shift, such as in the case of conversion, implies reference to the transcendental order. The convert goes beyond the conventional and, to some extent, his expected life trajectory, and shapes a new biography. In the process of conversion, reflexivity shapes new life dynamics and actively shapes a new stage of socialization.

To sum up, religion, as a social institution which operates within the social order of reality, is a specific form of integration between the transcendental and the social orders. The characterization of a 'religion' from the perspective of religious identity must include the individual's internal conversation and religious experience which are socially shaped. Religious identity is composed not only of religious behaviour or instrumental knowledge, but also of the person's 'reflexive disposition'. Religious identity is influenced to some extent by human concerns. Transcendental order is integrated with other orders, but not in the same way as the other orders are integrated with each other. The relationship between religious concerns and concerns belonging to other orders shapes the process of reflexivity. However, the dominating form of reflexivity is shaped not only by the configuration of human concerns but also by the social context.

Performing transcendence

Religion in a critical realist perspective encompasses both reference to religious experience which surpasses the social order and ought not to be reduced to human language, and to the culture in which it is embedded, which denotes a set of ideas and *intelligibilia*. From such a point of view, religious identity not only denotes transcendental experience and ultimate concerns, but is linked also to cultural ideas, symbols or general knowledge. Embodied religious experience transcends the simple distinction between reason and emotions. Emotions, however, are not the opposite of knowledge. Without affects, discursive knowledge would not represent a motivation for any sort of human action. 'This means that feelings are not just felt, they relate to the nature of their object and what makes an emotion appropriate or inappropriate is nothing self-referential, but the nature of the emotion's object.' (Archer, 2000, p. 184) As Archer clarifies: 'When cold, we extend our hands towards the fire, but excessive heat leads us to withdraw them, and it is upon these prior physiological signifiers that our language of feelings is built and our emotional expressiveness is born' (Archer, 2000, p. 155).

Realist ontology attributes priority to practical order. Human practice should not be reduced to the nominal use of the language, but it should be related to some form of reality which can be experienced and which has the potential to evoke emotions. The natural order regulates human practice without 'verbal intermediaries' (Archer, 2000, p. 155). 'Artifactual reality' represents powers and properties which cannot be reduced to linguistic and subjective knowledge. In the 'practical interaction' between nature and subjects, non-linguistic and embodied knowledge, such as skills, know-how and tacit information, emerge. According to Archer, there is no religion which is not practical.

In her realist explanation of the religious tradition, Archer protests against a 'logocentric view of human beings' (Archer, 2000, p. 185); for her, religion represents 'a codification of practice' and belongs to the practical order. Religious knowledge is relatively non-discursive and based on 'feelings' but is nevertheless practical because it 'entails experience, illumination and ecstasy rather than explanation' and includes 'spiritual know-how' (Archer, 2000, p. 184). Liturgical rituals, together with paintings, sculpture and other artistic objects, represent the practical order. Religion could be transformed into discursive knowledge, but the practical dimension is fundamental in the religious domain. The transformation of religion into discursive knowledge is labelled by Archer as the 'consolidation of religion' and consists of the systematization and dogmatization, that is, the 'codification', of religious practice. The religious rituals of a religion's 'founding fathers' constitute religious normative models. Anamnesis, that is, symbolic remembrance, 'sustains the vibrancy and salience of the pro-phetic life-practice' (Archer, 2000, p. 184). Religious persons, in conducting religious rituals, generate sacred objects in a practical sense, thus building elements of a religious cultural system and also constituting a socio-cultural system, through the interactions based on religious rituals.

The 'codification of religious practices' refers directly to the social order. There are no religious practices without social bonds. Religious practices require and imply a community. Even the etymology of the word 'commu-nity' relates to both the social and performative orders. The English term 'community' is derived from Greek and includes two elements: a prefix '*con*' indicating a state of being or bringing together of several objects and '*munus*' which means office or service. The performative, social and tran-scendental orders are intertwined with religion. Religion implies also the existence of the natural order.

> [The] practical religious order cannot and does not remain self-contained. On the one hand, its catechetical impulse impacts upon the *natural order* because its very aim is ineluctably tied to the tran-scendence of the incarnational – formalized as *metanoia*, the change of mind-set in the Christian tradition, or as *kenosis*, the self-emptying of Buddhism, or the *karma* of Hinduism.
>
> (Archer, 2000, p. 185)

Religious tradition cannot be understood in terms of logical deductions or propositional and instrumental normativity. Tradition is normative to the extent that it is practical and 'aimed at lived practice'. Archer initiates the formulation of her morphogenetic approach by discussing the so-called 'myth of cultural integration'. She claims that this myth was initially elab-orated by anthropologists especially, who neglected the analytical study of what culture consisted of and focused on an 'inner sense' of culture, offering some kind of 'aesthetic' hermeneutics. Early anthropological works read-ily contrasted traditional society with modernity. Later, functionalists such as Pitirim Sorokin and Talcott Parsons presumed that culture is strongly coherent and consistent. The 'myth of cultural integration' found its place in Marxist sociology as well, with the concepts of 'hegemonic culture' and 'dominant ideology'. According to this myth, culture exemplifies a per-fectly integrated system, 'the perfectly woven and all-enmeshing web' and 'a community of shared meanings' (Archer, 2000, pp. 2–4). Archer claims that the 'myth of cultural integration' is embedded in the sociological image of traditional society, because traditional cultures were frequently studied from the perspective of their external consistency and an examination of their internal logical consistency was relatively neglected. 'Almost automat-ically [...] the durability of routine was attributed to its enmeshment in an all-pervasive perfectly integrated cultural system which had imposed itself as the printed circuit of the primitive mind.' (Archer, 1988, p. 7)

Traditional culture represents much more than just instrumentally accepted norms and procedures. The social ontology of Margaret Archer represents an attempt to overcome the reductionism of the myth of cultural integration and to grasp culture in a more comprehensive way. In this sense, traditional culture shapes also the way people define their social situation and the emotions which emerge in their contact with the natural, performative and transcendent orders. According to 'analytical dualism', two different aspects of culture should be distinguished, namely 'ideational elements', such as beliefs, knowledge, norms, which represent logical consistency; and 'causal consensus' which characterizes the 'distribution' of ideational elements within the social structure, as mentioned above. 'Causal consensus' refers to relations of power within a culture.

With regard to our topic, analytical dualism opens up a new perspective for the conceptualization of traditional culture. According to the 'myth of cultural integration', in such 'old and cold' societies all action was routine. Traditional practices are assumed to be non-discursive and based upon tacit knowledge and embodied skills. It is claimed that human beings in traditional society were equipped with 'second nature', which was non-discursive and enabled them to act in a mechanical way. In opposition to such claims, Archer assumes that reflexivity is an essential attribute of human beings and if there is no reflexivity, there is no society. 'Normal people' are self-aware, and their sense of self is necessary for their identity as human beings. Human capacities emerge from the natural, social, practical and transcendent realities but cannot be reduced to any one of them, neither the biological nor social order. The human 'continuous sense of self' cannot be dissolved into any social structure. The quality of reflexivity, understood as characteristic of a person ('reflexive first-personhood'), along with the human beings themselves, constitutes society, both traditional and modern. Reflexivity includes their relationship to the practical order, including interactions with artefacts. Traditional culture contains internal contradictions and humans deal with cultural inconsistencies by reflexive decision-making. Traditional society would not have been able to function if humans were not able to cope with these cultural disjunctions. Being human implies reflexivity when encountering cultural novelty. As Marti has argued, even upholding religious tradition requires reflexivity because the self must monitor whether behaviour corresponds to traditional guidelines. Stated differently, the legitimacy of being 'traditional' requires competent performance. Given the desire for self-assurance and social testimony to others, there is inherent to tradition a need for 'reflexive accounting' (Marti, 2015, p. 7).

The understanding of human action formulated by Margaret Archer shows, to some extent, common elements with Max Weber's theory of behaviour. Both claim that human action should be interpreted from the perspective of 'sense' and 'meaning'. The sociological study of human action must include 'self-consciousness' as formulated by Weber, or 'reflexivity' in an Archerian perspective. However, both Weber and Archer formulate their theories of human action within distinguished philosophical perspectives. As Archer notes, Weber defined the human person in the frame of Kantian philosophy. Archer blames the Kantian roots of Weber's sociology for his misunderstanding of human emotions. 'The stern voice of duty has the task of overriding our passions, [Weber] also makes Calvinists of us all in our lifeworlds.' (Archer, 2000, p. 80) For Weber, religion represented a somewhat rational rather than affectual mode of action. Behaviour which was religious or magical was goal-oriented in the sense that it was purposive. The purpose of religious behaviour included a wide range of 'utilities' from the most transcendent, such as salvation, to economic considerations (Weber, 1978[1920], p. 400). Religious rituals were viewed with the belief that there existed a causal relationship between devotion and some transcendental impact on human reality. For Weber, Christianity was an 'ethical religion of salvation' which was dedicated especially to personal devotion. Weber also described the character of rural religiosity as exemplified by peasants. He claimed that peasants were so strongly committed to the natural order of reality that they started to reflect upon the transcendental order only in times of existential threat, such as their experience of financial problems or fear of the ruling political power (Weber, 1978[1920], p. 468). In rural areas, religiousness was shaped by 'feudal powers' in the direction of ritualism and formalism. That is why, for Weber, the true nature of Christianity would tend to manifest in urban environments especially (Weber, 1978[1920], p. 472). Weber challenged the primacy of human emotions by contrasting 'affectual' action with 'traditional' and 'value-rational' action. He argued that emotions were not controllable forces and, as such, were not subject to deliberation. When deliberated upon, they were immediately transformed into rational utility in the process of rationalization.

To sum up, Archer tries to reinstall '*pathos* alongside our *logos*' and advocates 'letting the "passions" back in to give us the shoving-power to make our commitments' (Archer, 2000, p. 81). According to Archer, human beings are neither imprisoned and constrained by the structural powers of tradition nor is their behaviour determined by some set of external emotions. Tradition in the perspective of morphogenesis conditions human action but also leaves space for human subjectivity. People reflect not only upon the instrumental ends of their actions but make reference as well to affects in their internal conversations. Some similarity to the understanding of traditional religion represented by critical realists is evident in Martin Riesebrodt's distinction between 'religion' and 'religious practices' (Riesebrodt, 2010). He delineates three components within religious systems: (1) the religion itself; (2) religious tradition and (3) religiosity. A religion designates a system of practices in time and space. Religious tradition is the 'intellectual construction of symbolic continuities across time and space'. Religiosity represents 'the subjective appropriation of religion' (Riesebrodt, 2014, p. 6).

Morphogenesis in 'late modernity'

Margaret Archer's great contribution to the understanding of structure and culture and their mutual relationship consists in the fact that she situates both culture and structure in the broad frame of so-called morphogenesis and the process of shaping personal and social identity. Culture is made up of a system of ideas or *intelligibilia*: beliefs, conceptions, theories, etc., which could be identified as Popper's third world of knowledge, including the ideal and comprehensible components. Metaphorically, the system of human culture could be presented as akin to the amount of knowledge accumulated in libraries. What individual elements of this knowledge have in common is 'a language' which is a comprehensible way of representing cultural items. This 'language' does not refer to a specific ethnic or national language, but rather to a logical system of symbols, which is a means for people to express, transfer and comprehend ideas. Invariant logical principles which provide patterns to make the cultural system transitive, exist in parallel with the cultural system which is socially constructed.

In Archer's formulation, the cultural system is a time-related and time-conditioned reality (Archer, 1995, p. 89). A specific form of culture exists at a given moment of time. The cultural system which existed previously is no longer identifiable as that identical culture in the following moment of time. Time passes and culture is unceasingly subject to change. All beliefs, ideas, values and preferences are in the process of constant change. This unstable character of the cultural system refers especially to the non-material dimension of culture, because culture, when materialized into artistic objects, is not so variable, although these are influenced by time as well. Archer builds her theory of morphogenesis by distinguishing analytically between the cultural system and the socio-cultural system. The socio-cultural system is composed of causal relations and refers to interactions and relationships between agents. Action in the socio-cultural system takes place within the context of the cultural system. This cultural system influences the socio-cultural system (conditioning) that results in cultural interactions. Cultural interactions result in cultural elaboration. Such a process is cyclical in a sequential sense, but not in the repetitive sense. The 'cultural system logically predates the socio-cultural action(s) which transform it; and that Cultural Elaboration logically post-dates such interactions' (Archer, 1988, p. XXIII). Modification of the cultural system is unintended in the sense that it is a consequence of the sum of the uncontrolled action of individuals and groups. Action undertaken is often met with opposing action; real conflicts and acts of cooperation are difficult to plan or even to intend.

Cultural elaboration is a cyclical process in the sense that the end point of one cycle is the starting point for another one, which may be conditioned by a different cultural context. In terms of the classical distinction between structure and human action, action is conditioned by social structure and operates over different periods of time. Properties of a structure emerge from human actions and, as the aggregate and emergent characteristics, exert casual influence upon actions or 'interactions'. In other words, social structure influences human action by 'endowing' actors with interests related to their social positions. Structural systems and the agency of actors are mediated by mechanisms which support or negate actions. Through these mechanisms, groups of different situational interpretations are conditioned; rewards and motivations are experienced, which result in retaining the action, or, the structure distributes exigency to eradicate the action. Actors are equipped with autonomous emergent powers; they reflect upon the costs and benefits of their action, which is rooted in the social context (Archer, 1995, p. 90).

The morphogenetic approach is contrasted with the concept of 'social hydraulics' which assumes that social action may be explained in a mechanical way, without reference to human subjectivity (Archer, 2007, p. 6). It opposes as well the so-called 'Two-Stage Model' (Archer, 2007, p. 13) which grants the individual a set of subjective and personal motives but 'from outside', from the perspective of an external observer. To avoid such an 'external' and 'objectivist' approach to human agency within the social dynamic, Archer offers an alternative 'Three-Stage Model' (2007, p. 16). Theoretical analysis of human action opens with the question of the objective proprieties of the cultural system. Structural and cultural proprieties 'possess generative powers of constraint and enablement' (Stage 1). These structural powers refer to actors' subjective constellation of concerns in relation to the four orders of reality (Stage 2). Through reflexivity, practical projects are evaluated in relation to the social context and a course of action is produced (Stage 3) (Archer, 2007, p. 17).

From the more practical perspective of human beings, social actors are situated in a paradoxical situation. Human beings in society are both free and constrained. What is more, actors are reflexive; this means they are aware of being in such contextualized situations. Human reflexivity does not mean that actors are perfectly aware of the whole complexity and predispositions of cultural conditioning. Social changes are not intentional, but rather unpredictable consequences of human activity. However, some knowledge about actors' limits and opportunities in relation to the social structure are cognitively available to actors. Reflexivity opens up the space for personal creativity and innovation in their response to the social structure and in interpreting its contextual culture. 'The subjective powers of reflexivity mediate the role that objective structural or cultural powers play in influencing social action and are thus indispensable to explaining social outcomes.' (Archer, 2007, p. 5)

The morphogenetic approach represents more than just a theoretical perspective for points of view within sociology. In addition, it includes methodological and practical implications for the study of society and the role of individuals within society (Archer, 1995, p. 5). Its focus on 'reflexivity' is also a fruitful point of view to describe the modern character of social life. However, Margaret Archer, in contrast to Ulrich Beck, Anthony Giddens and Scott Lash (1994), avoids using the term 'reflexive modernization' to label the modern character of social life. She points out that the term 'modernization' as used by Giddens refers instead to the 'runaway society', or the 'juggernaut out of control' or, as Beck suggests, to 'a cluster of globally dangerous and uncontrolled side effects'. 'Reflexivity' on the other hand means self-monitoring and self-control. This is why Archer claims that the term 'reflexive modernization' is to some extent contradictory (Archer, 2007, p. 30). Archer labels the modern forms of social life as 'late modernity', which is a more neutral and methodologically accurate term.[3]

In the new globalized culture dominated by 'meta-reflexivity', instrumental rationality is rejected. Ultimate human concerns are no longer subordinated to social mobility and stratification. Moreover, the process of globalization affects whole societies, not just the individuals within society, but also its forms of government and its institutions of education, social services and civil society. Thus, in the end, the culture of 'late modernity' can be defined in terms of globalization, as 'contextual discontinuity' and the 'logic of opportunity'. Although the principal assumption Archer makes is that reflexivity is a persistent process throughout human history and, consequently, that human reflexivity shapes the culture today as it did in the past, nevertheless some elements of human subjectivity may well be more accentuated at some points in human history than at others. Human beings are not simply passively conditioned by social structure: they have causal influence on their culture. Modes of reflexivity affect action orientations, social mobility and, in a broader perspective as well, institutions. Globalized culture promotes the 'logic of opportunity' that privileges complementarities, combinations and synergies, and people only become successful if they are able to connect these different domains and disciplines, transfer skills and knowledgeably manipulate the possibilities available to them. This 'logic of opportunity' relates not only to occupational mobility but also to personal life projects (Archer, 2007, pp. 53–54 and 60–61). People deliberate how to avoid obstacles and take advantage of circumstances. They are committed to their concerns and are trying to sustain a *modus vivendi*.

Conclusions

My aim in presenting these two chapters at considerable length is to make the reader fully aware that critical realism delivers a solid ontological background for studying the phenomenon of religion within society. As mentioned above, this theoretical approach represented especially by the work of Margaret Archer opens up new perspectives for the study of religion. Central to this ontology are the concepts of transcendence and reflexivity.

Archer claims that reflexivity is a characteristic of persons. She agrees however that social structures may shape personal reflexivity. Society as a whole is able to put 'a pressure upon individuals to become more reflexive' (Archer, 2007, p. 32). Reflexivity is not only a process of producing information or generating a volume of new knowledge. As concluded by Pierpaolo Donati, 'Reflexivity is not merely a need induced in individuals or groups by a risky environment. It is not only a reactive process, leading people from one condition of uncertainty to another' (Donati, 2011, p. 21). Rather, it is an essential aspect of social and religious life.

The transcendental order as defined by Margret Archer should be fully appreciated and understood as a valid conceptual element in the discipline of sociology. In other words, it does not need to be seen as implying a theological way of thinking. The category of transcendence provides a new background for distinguishing between religious and non-religious aspects of social life. This means that by introducing the concept of transcendence, the sociological study of religion gains a new core which furnishes new levels of understanding of religious phenomena in society. In a critical realist perspective social life is not religious *per se*. Any element or dimension of social life becomes 'religious' through its relationship to transcendence. Social institutions, organizations or even social structures could be labelled as 'religious' through their relationship to the transcendental order. These relationships are mediated by human reflexivity and emerge from personal relationships to transcendence. That is why the focus on human subjectivity in the context of the transcendental order is the key element in the sociological study of religion.

Religious identity, understood as the concerns of the individual emerging in his or her relationship to the transcendental order, implies also their relationship to the social, practical and natural orders. Therefore, religious identity cannot be understood only in terms of the individual and subjective characteristics of a person. At the centre of social life is human subjectivity, which cannot be separated from social structure. Reflexivity designates much more than a merely rational or conscious way of logical thinking. Reflexivity is the link between the individual and the social context. That is why religious identity should be understood also in the context of social agency. There are some similarities between phenomenology and the morphogenetic approach to religion. However, critical realism opens up new perspectives beyond phenomenology, especially in terms of the relationship between the individual and social structure.

As is always the case, a theoretical vision of social life is not easily operationalized and implemented within an empirical study or fieldwork project. However, the concept of reflexivity and the morphogenetic approach to social life inspired me to conduct this empirical study of religious dynamics, the results of which are presented in this book. That is why subsequent chapters present my necessarily brief study of Polish Catholicism from the perspective of agency and the configuration between the transcendental, social, practical and natural orders of reality. My focus on the relationship between the latter three orders of reality and transcendence, each one approached independently, allows me to characterize the changing forms of religion within Polish society over time and in all their complexity. Going beyond the frequently highlighted 'relationist'[4] aspect of religious identity in the field of the sociology of religion, I emphasize not only the relationship between transcendence and the social order but I also include a focus on the practical aspects of religion. I include reflexivity and the morphogenetic approach in my study of religion, to the extent which is endorsed in current methodologies within the sociology of religion and existing empirical data, and I include also agential aspects of religion within Polish society.

This new theoretical perspective of critical realism brings much benefit to the empirical study of religion in Polish society. My inquiry into Polish Catholicism is divided into three parts representing different stages of its development, from its traditional form in Poland's premodern era, through the post-Communist transformation in recent decades, to some effects of recent migration on the religious identity of members of the Polish diaspora. In every stage, my focus will be on reflexivity, agency and transcendence. Furthermore, I will present how the shaping of religious identity has changed in different cultural contexts. By concentrating on the basic characteristics of Polish Catholicism at the different stages of its social development and focusing mainly on the relationship of believers to transcendence, I am able to elucidate the relationship between the transcendental, social, practical and natural orders. By adopting such a structure for the study of religious identity, I am able to stress the central category of transcendence in human identity. What is more, this allows me to study the link between different orders of reality, and to pinpoint transcendence as central to the character of religious identity. I will include a discussion of the agential aspect of Polish Catholicism in the three contexts: the traditional society; the modern post-Communist transformation; and the migration era, in the sense that agency results from the reconfiguration between individual and social structure in each case.

Notes

1. As Margaret Archer noted during my private conversation with her: 'This time gap was deliberate in order to "avoid" the whole argument being dismissed by the "anti-religious" – as I anticipated. This savage attack was born out when Bhaskar started to write about "Meta-Reality" at the end of his life'.
2. The Archerian concept of 'ultimate concerns' shares many similarities with ultimate concerns as defined by Paul Tillich (1957).
3. Margaret Archer uses the term quite often, for example, in the title of her book *The Reflexive Imperative in Late Modernity* (2012).
4. I use here the term proposed by Pierpaolo Donati, which could partly be defined as reducing social life to a process of transaction (Donati, 2017).

References

Ammerman, N. (2014). *Sacred Stories, Spiritual Tribes*. New York: Oxford University Press.

Archer, M. S. (1988). *Culture and Agency. The Place of Culture in Social Theory*. Cambridge: Cambridge University Press.

Archer, M. S. (1995). *Realist Social Theory*. Cambridge: Cambridge University Press.

Archer, M. S. (2000). *Being Human: The Problem of Agency*. Cambridge: Cambridge University Press. DOI: 10.1017/CBO9780511488733.

Archer, M. S., Collier, A., Porpora, D. (2004b). What Do We Mean by God. In: M. Archer, A. Collier, D. Porpora, eds., *Transcendence. Critical Realism and God*. London and New York: Routledge, pp. 24-40. DOI: 10.4324/9780203420683.

Archer, M. S. (2004). Models of Man: The Admission of Transcendence. In: M. Archer, A. Collier, D. Porpora, eds., *Transcendence. Critical Realism and God*. London and New York: Routledge, pp. 63–81.

Archer, M. S., Collier, A., Porpora, D. (2004a. Introduction. In: M. Archer, A. Collier, D. Pourpora, eds., *Transcendence. Critical Realism and God*. London and New York: Routledge, pp. 1-23. DOI: 10.4324/9780203420683.

Archer, M. S. (2006). Persons and Ultimate Concerns: Who We Are Is What We Care About. Conceptualization of the Person in Social Sciences. Pontifical Academy of Social Sciences. *Acta*, 11, pp. 261–283.

Archer, M. S. (2007). *Making Our Way Through the World: Human Reflexivity*. Cambridge: Cambridge University Press. DOI: 10.1017/CBO9780511618932.

Archer, M. S. (2012). *The Reflexive Imperative in Late Modernity*. Cambridge: Cambridge University Press. DOI: 10.1017/CBO9781139108058.

Archer, M. S., Tritter, J., eds. (2000). *Rational Choice Theory: Resisting Colonization*. London and New York: Routledge. DOI: 10.4324/9780203133897.

Beck, U., Giddens, A., Lash, S. (1994). *Reflexive Modernization: Politics, Tradition and Aesthetics in the Modern Social Order*. Cambridge: Polity Press.

Berger, P. (1974). Some Second Thoughts on Substantive Versus Functional Definitions of Religion. *Journal for the Scientific Study of Religion*, 13(2), pp. 125–133.

Bhaskar, R. (1998[1979]). *The Possibility of Naturalism. A Philosophical Critique of the Contemporary Human Sciences*. London and New York: Routledge.

Bhaskar, R. (2008[1975]). *A Realist Theory of Science*. New York: Routledge.

Bhaskar, R. (2011[1989]). *Reclaiming Reality. A Critical Introduction to Contemporary Philosophy*. London and New York: Routledge.

Donati, P. (2011). Modernization and Relational Reflexivity. *International Review of Sociology/Revue Internationale de Sociologie*, 21(1), pp. 21–39.

Donati, P. (2017). Relational Versus Relationist Sociology: A New Paradigm in the Social Sciences. In: E. Halas, P. Donati, eds., *The Relational Turn in Sociology: Implications for the Study of Society, Culture, and Persons*. Special issue *Stan Rzeczy [State of Affairs]*, 12(1), Warszawa: Instytut Socjologii UW, pp. 15–66.

Hall, D., ed. (1997). *Lived Religion in America. Towards the History of Practice*. Princeton NJ: Princeton University Press.

Hjobjerg, Ch.. (2002). Religious Reflexivity. Essays on Attitudes to Religious Ideas and Practice. *Social Anthropology*, 10(1), pp. 1–10.

Latour, B. (2006). Efficacite ou instauration? *Vie et lumiere*, 270(2), pp. 47–56.

Latour, B. (2011). Reflections on Etienne Souriau's Les Modes d'existence. In: G. Harman, L. Bryant, N. Srnicek, eds., *The Speculative Turn: Continental Materialism and Realism*. Melbourne: Re.press, pp. 304–333.

Marti, G. (2015). Religious Reflexivity: The Effect of Continual Novelty and Diversity on Individual Religiosity. *Sociology of Religion,* 76(1), pp. 1–13. DOI: 10.1093/socrel/sru084.

McGuire, M. (2007). Embodied Practices: Negotiation and Resistance. In: N. Ammerman, ed., *Everyday Religion: Observing Modern Religious Lives.* New York: Oxford University Press.

McGuire, M. (2008). *Lived Religion: Faith and Practice in Everyday Life.* Oxford and New York: Oxford University Press.

Mellor, P., Shilling, C. (2014). Re-Conceptualising the Religious Habitus: Reflexivity and Embodied Subjectivity in Global Modernity. *Culture and Religion,* 15(3), pp. 275–297.

Orsi, R. (2002). *The Madonna of 115th Street: Faith and Community in Italian Harlem, 1880-1950.* Newhaven, CT: Yale University Press.

Orsi, R. (2003). Is the Study of Lived Religion Irrelevant to the World We Live in? Special Presidential Plenary Address, Society for the Scientific Study of Religion, Salt Lake City, November 2, 2002. *Journal for the Scientific Study of Religion,* 42(2), pp. 169–174.

Patton, K. (2009). *Religion of the Gods: Ritual, Paradox, and Reflexivity.* Oxford, New York: Oxford University Press.

Riesebrodt, M. (2010). *The Promise of Salvation: A Theory of Religion.* Chicago: University of Chicago Press. DOI: 10.7208/chicago/9780226713946.001.0001.

Riesebrodt, M. (2014). Religion in the Modern World: Between Secularization and Resurgence. Max Weber Lecture. Available at: https://www.semanticscholar.org/paper/Religion-in-the-modern-world-%3A-between-and-Riesebrodt/b7ff1630fd635da81452ddaf063779b692101bb2 [Accessed 1 June 2020].

Schaap, J., Aupers, S. (2017). 'Gods in World of Warcraft exist': Religious Reflexivity and the Quest for Meaning in Online Computer Games. *New Media & Society,* 19(11), pp. 1744–1760.

Scruton, R. (1986). *Sexual Desire. A Moral Philosophy of the Erotic.* London: Weidenfeld and Nicholson.

Smith, Ch., ed. (1996a). *Disruptive Religion: The Force of Faith in Social Movement Activism.* New York: Routledge Publishers.

Smith, Ch. (1996b). *Resisting Reagan: The U.S. Central America Peace Movement.* Chicago: University of Chicago Press.

Smith, Ch. (2000). *Christian America? What Evangelicals Really Want.* Berkeley: University of California Press.

Smith, Ch. (2010). *What Is a Person? Rethinking Humanity, Social Life, and the Moral Good from the Person Up.* Chicago and London: University of Chicago Press. DOI: 10.7208/chicago/9780226765938.001.0001

Smith, Ch., Lundquist, D. (2005). *Soul Searching: The Religious and Spiritual Lives of American Teenagers.* New York: Oxford University Press.

Tillich, P. (1957). *Dynamics of Faith.* New York: Harper & Row.

Turner, V. (1967). *The Forest of Symbols: Aspects of Ndembu Ritual.* Ithaca, NY: Cornell University Press.

Weber, M. (1978[1920]). Religious Groups (Sociology of Religion). In: G. Roth, C. Wittich, eds., *Max Weber. Economy and Society. An Outline of Interpretative Sociology.* Berkeley: University of California Press, pp. 399–634.

Part 2
Empirical

3 Traditional Polish religiosity

Photo 1 Procession in Lichwin (South Poland) in the 1930s. Photo: Author's Family
Archive.

A classical book by Joseph Stein which inspired the creation of the famous
musical 'Fiddler on the Roof' tells the story of a Jew, Tevye the Milkman,
and his five daughters. Tevye attempts to maintain Jewish tradition as outside
influences encroach upon his family life in a small village in a historically
Polish area. In one of the most significant parts of the musical Tevye states:

> Because of our traditions, we've kept our balance for many, many years.
> Here in Anatevka we have traditions for everything… how to eat, how
> to sleep, even how to wear clothes. For instance, we always keep our
> heads covered and always wear a little prayer shawl… This shows our
> constant devotion to God. You may ask, how did this tradition start? I'll

tell you - I don't know. But it's a tradition... Because of our traditions, everyone knows who he is and what God expects him to do.

(Fiddler on the Roof, 1964)

Another cinema masterpiece, which is relevant to this chapter is the well-known film directed eight years later by Francis Ford Coppola, and based on Mario Puzo's novel entitled The Godfather (1972). The story chronicles an Italian family who gradually become committed to crime. In a famous scene the main character, Michael Corleone, is speaking with Cardinal Lamberto. The cardinal, who will soon become the pope, retrieves a pebble from under the water. 'Look at this stone' he says. 'It has been lying in the water for a very long time, but the water has not penetrated it'. He then strikes the rock on the side of the fountain. The stone breaks. The cardinal says: 'Look... perfectly dry'. The water on the outside had not seeped in. And Lamberto adds: 'The same thing has happened to men in Europe. For centuries they have been surrounded by Christianity, but Christ has not penetrated. Christ doesn't live within them'. Both scenes help us to capture the unfathomable character of religion in social life.

From such a point of view, the traditional, and especially peasant [*chlopi*],[1] worldview in predominantly Catholic, Polish peasant society, was monolithic, that is, the whole of social life was subordinated to the religious and universal vision which was the common history of the community, but despite this, it could be said that the individuals themselves were not penetrated by religion. General social changes in Poland, at least since the 19th century, when educational reforms and social emancipation were inaugurated, show evidence for the justification of such a claim that traditional society was not sufficiently 'enlightened' and self-aware for being wisely religious. Significantly, some notable Polish authors, who will be cited in this chapter, share a similar understanding of the nature of life in traditional Polish society. Tradition is quite often presented negatively, as a context which limits individual human agency. The famous Polish writer Witold Gombrowicz exemplifies this attitude towards tradition most expressively in his novels. In 1937 he published one of his best-known books entitled *Ferdydurke*. The novel tells the story of Jozio Kowalski who is transported back in time to his school days. Being in school, he is strongly influenced by the educational system, which limits his freedom and devastates his subjectivity (Gombrowicz, 2012[1938]).

In this chapter I will focus on the character of religious identity within traditional Polish society. Traditional religiosity was grounded in local communities and dominated rural areas in Poland before the Second World War. Despite strong waves of industrialization and urbanization in the postwar Communist era, traditional social forms continued to exist in local rural communities in Poland till the socio-political transformation of the 1990s. I will answer the question of whether it is justified to claim that traditional Polish Catholicism was unreflexive and that Christianity did not affect human beings. Did religion in Poland flow down within social life like water, without penetrating the deep structure of human personality and subjectivity? In this chapter I examine the social phenomenon which has been termed 'traditional Polish Catholicism'. In doing so, I analyze the nature of religious tradition in the context of human reflexivity using theoretical categories proposed by Margaret Archer. In other words, I will study dynamics of religion within traditional Polish society from the perspective of the interrelationship between structure, agency and culture. It is not my intention to trace the traditional form of religiosity in a historical way; rather I use it as a sociological 'ideal type' of Polish religiosity.

Traditional culture and religious identity

Polish society in the so-called Second Republic of Poland (1920–1939) was strongly dominated by rural communities. In 1921 most of the population (63.8 percent) declared agriculture, forestry or gardening to be their main sources of income (Ambroch, Czermak, Lisiak and Szydlowska, 2018, p. 17). In 1931, 73 percent of the general population of 31 million Polish residents dwelt in rural areas (Statistics Poland, 1939, p. 18). In 1938, exactly 50 percent of the population of the Republic of Poland consisted of peasants. Among the other groups, the most significant were workers (30 percent), petit bourgeoisie (11.8 percent) and intelligentsia (5.7 percent) (Zarnowski, 1973). The religious structure of Polish society was more pluralized than it is today. Apart from the 75 percent of Catholics (made up of 86 percent Roman Catholics and 14 percent Greek Catholics[2]), the Polish population included 12 percent Orthodox, 10 percent Jews and only 3 percent Protestants. In some administrative regions or provinces (the so-called *Voyevodenship*[3]) the representation of non-Catholic Polish citizens exceeded 80 percent. This was especially the case in the rural areas of the Wolynskie Voyevodenship, as presented in Table 3.1 below.

As a consequence of the Yalta Conference (1945) the borders of Poland were newly demarcated. Vast territory in the east was separated from the Polish state. Moreover, due to the terrible extermination of the Holocaust, Jewish people were almost eradicated from Polish society. That is why, since the 1950s, more than 90 percent of the Polish population are Roman Catholic. For instance, in 1971 Roman Catholics represented 93.4 percent of the 32.7 million Polish citizens, (Marianski, 1991b, p. 50). Thus, Polish society after the Second World War became very homogeneous in terms of religious affiliation. Catholicism was highly dominant and strongly integrated with peasant culture especially in the rural areas. The majority of Catholic parishes were situated in the rural sector. The earliest statistical data available on parishes comes from 1972 and shows that, among 6692 Catholic parishes, only 9 percent were located in cities. Another 18 percent of parishes straddled both urban and rural areas and 72 percent represented strictly rural areas (Zdaniewicz, 1978).

Systematic, quantitative research on religiosity in Poland began in the 1960s, so it is almost impossible to reconstruct the nature of religiosity in

Table 3.1 Religious affiliation in some Eastern Polish Voivodeships in 1931 (census data in units of 1000)

Voivodeship	Total	Roman Catholic	Greek Catholic	Orthodox	Protestant	Other Christian	Jewish	Other non-Christian	No-data
Poland in general	*31 915.8*	*20 670.1*	*3336.2*	*3762.5*	*835.2*	*145.4*	*3113.9*	*6.8*	*45.7*
Wilenskie	1276	797.5	1	324.7	3.5	34.7	110.8	2.8	1
Urban	2613	159	0.3	19.6	2	3	76.2	1	0.2
Rural	1014.7	638.5	0.7	305.1	1.5	31.7	34.6	1.8	0.8
Wolynskie	2085.6	327.9	11.1	1455.9	53.4	28	207.8	0.1	1.4
Urban	252.5	63.8	1	59.3	3.5	0.6	1.4	0.1	0.2
Rural	1833.1	264.1	10.1	1396.6	49.9	27.4	83.8	0	1.2
Lwowskie	3126.3	1447.7	1305.3	9	13.1	4.1	342.4	0.1	4.6
Urban	775.7	371.4	138.2	1.9	4.9	0.6	257.8	0	0.9
Rural	2350.6	1076.3	1167.1	7.1	8.2	3.5	84.6	0.1	3.7
Stanislawowskie	1480.3	246	1079	0.9	12.5	0.6	139.7	0.2	1.4
Urban	295.2	86.8	99.6	0.4	5.1	0.2	102.8	0.1	0.2
Rural	1185.1	159.2	979.4	0.5	7.4	0.4	36.9	0.1	1.2

Source: Glowny Urzad Statystyczny [Statistics Poland], 1939, p. 24.

Poland at the beginning of the 20th century up until the immediate postwar era, using the quantitative indicators so well-known in Polish sociology of religion circles. However, there is no doubt that traditional peasant culture was highly religious. The realm of religion permeated the lives and daily circumstances of Polish peasants. Even working the land and daily tasks were experienced as religious action. Religious indifference, if it existed, resulted more from specific events, such as an individual's conflict with a priest rather than from a spontaneous choice to distance oneself from religious experience (Marianski, 1983, p. 263). In 1976, farmers represented the most religious social category in Poland (Marianski, 1983, p. 265–267). Tradition represented a sort of moral universe which shaped different aspects of human life.

According to Barbara Bukraba-Rylska, Polish popular religiosity characterized not only the lives of the rural population but to some extent could be attributed to the whole of Polish society also (Bukraba-Rylska, 2008). She describes how peasant traditional values contrasted with the traditions of the Polish nobility, which were much more secular. Members of the nobility adopted a pluralistic approach to social life and participated in religious rituals without special commitment, for the main events of an individual's life cycle, birth, marriage and death. But in cities and among the upper classes, individuals were emancipated from the values dominating traditional religious culture. Daily life and work were largely separate from religion. Especially internal migrants from rural areas could be characterized as having weaker bonds with the Church and their parish in the city.

At the outset, it should be mentioned that traditional Polish society was also strongly affected by international emigration. Polish citizens have been leaving their home country *en masse* at different times in its history and for different reasons. In the past Poles were often forced to migrate due to political persecution. Members of the Polish nobility escaped the country due to increasing oppression after failed national uprisings in the 19th century. Most of them moved to France, Great Britain and North America. In the second half of the 19th century, Polish workers migrated to France, Belgium and Germany to find jobs in the mines and the developing industrial sectors in those countries. According to Stefan Kieniewicz the first group of Polish labour migrants was recruited during the Prussian partition[4] in the second half of the 19th century. At that time 0.6 million Poles moved to West Germany. A comparable number of Polish migrants left the country at the beginning of the 20th century. Resulting from the Russian partition at the end of 19th century and at the beginning of 20th century about 1.3 million people moved to East Germany, USA and Brazil. From the Austrian partition Poles emigrated especially to the USA, Canada and Brazil (Kieniewicz, 1968, pp. 293–394). Peasants motivated by poverty, especially from South Poland (Galicja) joined great waves of immigration to North and South America. Between 1871 and 1913 about 3.5 million people fled the territory of Poland. During the First World War, together with Italy and Czechoslovakia, Poland, with about 2 million emigrants, belongs to the group of countries with the highest rates of emigration. Then, in the 1920s and 1930s half a million people emigrated from Poland to France (Dzwonkowski, 1988). During the Second World War many people, including Polish-Jewish citizens, left the country. In the 1980s during the era of Communist persecution Polish citizens took refuge principally in France, Western Germany and Great Britain.

Despite the fact that there was mass migration from the rural areas to the cities, especially after 1945, and hence levels of individual religiosity were confronted with the process of industrialization and urbanization, it can still be said that traditional religion in Poland demonstrated a far-reaching continuity into the 20th century (Piwowarski, 1983, p. 10). As will be discussed below both the character of local peasant Polish communities and Polish emigrant communities in the past reflected the traditional character of social bonds.

The reflexive elaboration of religious identity

Polish traditional religiosity has been described by some authors as not intellectually grounded and to some extent as 'fideist'. There is almost no recognition of the role of reflexivity for believers in studies of traditional religion. Surprisingly, Albert Wierzbicki claimed, with reference to the writing of Stefan Czarnowski, that Polish 'traditional religiosity' was without reflexivity (Wierzbicki, 1979). Also Edward Ciupak readily contrasted the view of the religious life centring on ritualistic religiosity with one based on reflexivity in his writing. He claimed that:

> The development of religiosity among peasants was mainly channeled into the field of rituals; there was no phenomenon of 'religious awareness' that could result in the person's reflection on the nature of his or her worldview (Ciupak, 1968, p. 2) [...] This nature of external and habitual religiosity, fixed in gestures, words and institutions – relatively permanent elements – is the typical cultural background of traditionalism.
> (Ciupak, 1968, p. 24)

Ciupak claimed that the attachment to Catholicism among peasants resulted from unreflexive sensualism:

> Of great importance were the habits and specific culture of the village, fused with Catholicism in its folklore. A new and different approach to faith, the social effects of which the peasant could have no control over, would deprive him of something most essential, namely – experiencing the sensual feelings provided by the Catholic rite.
> (Ciupak, 1968, p. 8)

Such an attitude towards traditional religiosity could be explained by the simplistic assumption that religiosity was generally grounded in religious knowledge rather than in religious experience (Ciupak, 1968, p. 140). On the other hand, paradoxically, Ciupak in his attitude towards Catholicism, has suggested that the best way for 'de-Christianization' to happen is through the transformation of 'dark, fanatical and intolerant' Catholics into tolerant and enlightened ones (1968, p. 157). For Ciupak, it was not clear in which direction traditional Polish Catholicism would develop: either traditional religious forms would penetrate modern social life or Catholicism would become more 'aware' and intellectual (1968, p. 158).

The relatively stable discrepancy between religiosity in rural and urban areas confirms such statements. In the 1960s Polish sociologists observed strong negative correlations between reading books, 'participation in the culture' and the level of religiosity (Pawelczynska, 1969, pp. 56–59). As Anna Pawelczynska has noted, the more 'open' the social milieu, the more discernable was the decline in religiosity among young people (1964, p. 52–53). The specific interpretation of traditional religiosity in Poland was also amplified by some indices demonstrating that believers who readily declared attachment to Catholicism did not necessarily share the moral values representative of official theology. Alongside this approach the view that popular religiosity consisted of archaic or even pagan and Proto-Slavic traditional and magical beliefs and rituals are highlighted. From the modern perspective, traditional religiosity was partly based on fatalism and referred to that area of social life which today has been replaced by medicine or science. As Franciszek Bujak explained:

> Not only all phenomena in nature, but also almost all human actions explain and announce themselves as the will of God. Everything is happening, because it pleases the Lord Jesus, so you should agree with every fact and accept it with resignation, with the conviction that despite suffering and harm in this life, God will reward you in the future, or else here on earth will avenge the wrongdoer. The people of the Ujanowice parish are still a great testimony to the fact that even the Christianization of concepts and the application of the Christian philosophy of life does not elevate or ennoble the little spirits, because it gives a real degree of intellectual development without which the highest standards [of Christian values] will be misunderstood and result in dead formalism.
>
> (Bujak, 1903, pp. 140–141)

Wincenty Witos, born a peasant, later People's Party leader, and three times prime minister of Poland from 1920 to 1926, recalled in his memoir that people prayed unreflexively, that is, prayers were repeated automatically without understanding or reference to experienced emotions. However, this does not mean that the habitual and repetitious way of praying was not reflexive in our understanding. The habitual way of praying reflected strong 'concerns about God's protection' and being 'guarded by transcendence' (Witos, 1998, p. 76). Even a deep belief in the teachings of the Church and what seemed to be an uncritical approach to the sermons which people heard during Sunday Holy Mass were accompanied by criticism. When priests preached that stealing was a heavy sin, generally people did not worry about thieving wood from the forests because they justified their behaviour with the reasoning that forests represent a common good (Witos, 1998, p. 73). As an example of reflexivity linked to transcendental concerns, Witos described in his memoir that peasants in their spiritual development were able to apprehend that Jesus and Mary were Jews, and hence members of the same social group that they knew in their neighborhood (Witos, 1978, p. 44).

Even if traditional Polish religiosity has been characterized by Stefan Czarnowski, one of the best-known researchers of Polish traditional culture, as very practical and ritualistic, this does not mean that he defined peasant religiosity as unreflexive. On the contrary: 'Personal experience and experience transmitted by peasant generations of former times, are intertwined with religious content' (Czarnowski, 1956, p. 101). Thus, traditional Polish religious culture as presented by Czarnowski shares many common elements with critical realism. According to Czarnowski, humans 'are generated' by culture which transcends the natural order. Human consciousness, or the interior life, should be distinguished from both the religious and material environments. The social context differs from the 'psycho-physical' configuration of human beings (Czarnowski, 1956, p. 15). 'We experience ourselves, directly ourselves, when we feel strong desire and when we relinquish our desire, when we are delighted by beauty and when we are disgusted, when we are full of emotions and when we control our passions by the strength of our will' (Czarnowski, 1956, p. 15). Emotions for Czarnowski are subjective commentaries on our relationship to reality. He specifically criticizes the idealism of some German authors who oppose the dichotomy of a subjective culture represented by spiritual growth and an objective culture manifesting in the material and organizational aspects of human civilization. 'The fact that we experience something as our own and original, does not mean that this is integrated within us, exists outside of ourselves' (Czarnowski, 1956, p. 16).

Czarnowski's understanding of human culture fully corresponds with critical realism when he claims that our subjectivity entails both a relationship to the experienced object and an emotional commentary on this reality. Czarnowski focuses intentionally on the socio-cultural aspect of religion, that is, to what extent and how do social groups assimilate the Catholic cultural system into everyday life. The author argues that it is not justified to contrast psychical with material facts (Czarnowski, 1956, p. 17) and in the religious domain, he distinguishes between religion and the religious cultural system, which corresponds with the Archerian distinction mentioned many times in this book. In his approach to religion Czarnowski criticizes the distinction between 'pure' and 'practical' religion and the separation between 'real', 'conscious' and 'lived' religion.

This is why, according to Barbara Bukraba-Rylska, both the 'romanticized approach' and 'positivist empiricism' failed to capture the nature of Polish popular religiosity (Bukraba-Rylska, 2008). Ludwik Stomma claims that a 'romanticized approach to religion' in fact overlooks the spiritual character of popular religiosity (Stomma, 2002, p. 246). Pragmatic and theoretical concepts, which dominate the empirically focused sociology of religion in 20th century Poland, were used to criticize popular religiosity as primitive and not sufficiently intellectually grounded (Stomma, 2002, p. 246). Ryszard Tomicki, in referring to Polish traditional religiosity, proposes a way to overcome the simplistic and ambiguous distinction between religion and superstition. 'Folk religiosity emerges as a deep interrelationship between the institutional model of religiosity and the cultural heritage of local communities.' (Tomicki, 1981, p. 50) He claims that 'lived religion' is not directly related to an institutional model of religiosity but 'is determined by the distinction between empirical and super-empirical reality' (Tomicki, 1981, p. 30).

The well-known Polish anthropologist, Anna Niedzwiedz, expresses her critical attitude towards the ethnographic understanding of 'folk religiosity'. As she notes, 'folk religiosity' is most often described through the perspective of 'folk culture' or 'traditional peasant culture'. In fact, however, 'folk religiosity' represents such a diverse and polyphonic human experience that any reduction of traditional religious forms to one general model represents a methodological mistake. What is more, Niedzwiedz claims that ethnographic sources and original publications concerning 'folk religiosity', especially in relation to Polish peasant communities, are rather limited. That is why the most common presentations of this phenomenon are rather selective, value-laden, even ideological (Niedzwiedz, 2014, p. 328), and based on superficial distinctions between official and popular religion. 'Folk religiosity' includes not only peasant characteristics but also noble and baroque forms of religiosity and is too ambiguous to be referred to as 'Polish religiosity'. The most common approach to 'folk religiosity' in Polish publications ignores the fact that traditional forms of religiosity included strong bodily experiences of the sacred, representing a kind of embodied experience. That is why Niedzwiedz advocates the replacement of the term 'folk religiosity' with the category 'lived religion' (Niedzwiedz, 2014, p. 334).

By the 1980s, some Polish sociologists of religion were already advocating a description of Polish religiosity in terms of *religion vecue* [lived religion] rather than 'folk religion' (Piwowarski, 1983, p. 10). Jozef Majka claimed that Catholicism was a 'life religion' and that the German concept of *Volkreligiositaet* should be replaced in the case of Polish society with 'folk faith' or 'the religion of life' (1980, p. 39–40). Majka protested against using the term 'popular religion' in describing Polish religiosity, because he claimed that the term refers to primitive religion (1980, p. 40). Moreover, Majka suggested that, thanks to this lived nature of Polish religiosity, Catholicism in Poland was generally resistant to secularization of the religious cultural system and religiosity preserved its 'authentic' and transcendent character. Polish beliefs could be distinguished from both humanistic naturalism and ideological sectarianism. In this way beliefs were integrated with ethics and moral obligations. Dominating religious ideas were separated from a revolutionary or messianic approach to history. A supernatural dimension of epistemic realism characterized religious ideas and beliefs.

Over its history Polish religiosity has integrated many dimensions of Catholic Christianity, such as Eucharistic, Christological, Marian, sacramental and eschatological elements. Christian beliefs were perceived as real, Christian rules and norms were seen to solve morals problems. Catholics used to accept religious ideas on trust rather than as intellectual knowledge (Majka, 1980, p. 35). Religious beliefs represented real local social relationships and rural customs. For example, belief in eternal life corresponded with the image of the rural manor house. In this way abstract theological concepts were adapted to the rural mentality and imagination. The role of Polish religiosity was particularly displayed in times of social crisis and danger. When Polish independence and freedom were under threat, faith acted as a motivation in the struggle for liberation. In this way, Catholicism provided essential ideas for reflexivity not only in relation to the transcendental but also to the social and practical orders (Majka, 1980, p. 35).

According to Wladyslaw Piwowarski, Polish 'popular religiosity' should neither be reduced to 'the religion of the masses', according to the well-known Marxist expression that 'religion is the opiate of the masses', nor compared with the 'religion of the elites'. Despite the fact that Piwowarski directly labelled Polish religiosity as 'popular', he clarified this claim by saying that Polish religiosity was popular because it referred to subjective experience. In his view, Polish 'popular religion' means neither magic nor superstition and should not be reduced to any ritualistic or formalistic types of religion (Piwowarski, 1983, p. 10). Instead, 'popular religiosity' should be understood as the 'lived religion of the social masses, who participate in a religious community' (1983, p. 10). This 'lived character' of religion in Poland manifested mainly during holiday times and festivals. Poles were committed to religion especially during exceptional moments in the annual religious cycle such as Advent, Christmas and Easter. As a 'festival religion' Catholicism in Poland was actively experienced but was still rather separate from such daily life involvements as one's occupational career (Piwowarski, 1983, p. 16). Religion provided ideas and emotions for establishing a personal *modus vivendi*. Piwowarski claimed that Polish Catholicism expounded not only a specific form of devotion but also a particular Polish form of spirituality. General characteristics of this spirituality included not only devotion to the Mother of God but also the generally strong emotional and experiential dimensions of a life of faith (Piwowarski, 1983, p. 10). He makes a strong case that Polish religion was popular because it was 'enculturated' into everyday life.

Stanislaw Grygiel and Tischner (1960), claimed that the nature of traditional religiosity should not be understood as manifested by charitable activity or moral virtue alone. The principal goal of religious activity in its traditional form was the experience of transcendence.

> Religious manifestations include external prayer, processions, participation in religious services, living a moral life, individual sacrifices of a religious character [such as fasting], etc. All these numerous and dynamic manifestations of rural religiosity are characterized by a common feature that defines their significance to a village resident. In the rural consciousness, only these acts are regarded as a manifestation of religiosity, which are intentional and directed specifically to God. In the first instance, "religious acts" are such phenomena as: prayer, participation in worship, pilgrimage, buying indulgences,[5] fasting, and sacrifice on behalf of the church. Secondly, 'religious acts' are actions directed towards helping others, showing further diligence, honesty, veracity, sobriety etc. And this, it seems, explains why in the countryside some manifestations of the religious life are joyous and at the same time others continue to inhibit the lives of the peasantry; one gets the impression that [an individual's] shortcomings on one level are compensated by zeal on another.
>
> (Grygiel and Tischner, 1960, p. 1458)

It is also interesting to note that the text cited above, written by the young philosopher Jozef Tischner, later one of the most famous Polish philosophers, and his friend Stanislaw Grygiel, was strongly criticized by Edward Ciupak (1968, pp. 140–150).

Janusz Marianski has added the view that 'popular religiosity' in the countryside was strong enough to resist the laicization activities during the Communist era. In comparison with such Central European countries as the Czech Republic, or even to some extent Hungary, Polish Catholicism was not affected by Communist atheistic propaganda (Marianski, 1983, p. 263). Instead Michal Luczewski has argued that Polish folk religiosity is a personal phenomenon. In a convincing way he proposed the view that Polish 'folk religiosity' is rational (2007). For him people who represent popular religiosity are driven by instrumental motives such as maximizing profits through the use of religious means. When taking part in folk rituals, such individuals may be strongly affected by emotions or even mystical experiences. According to Luczewski, 'As a result, this leads to the representation of the Polish peasant as a traditional-instrumental-emotional being without good reasons behind his values' (2007, p. 9). Luczewski tries to identify traditional folk religiosity with rational actions based on values [*Wertrationalitaet*] as classified by Weber, or within the category of axiological rationality formulated by Raymond Boudon (1994).

Religion continued to represent a context of reflexive human concern when Polish Catholics migrated from traditional rural areas to other countries. As noted by Florian Znaniecki and William Thomas, in the past, religiosity came under threat in a situation of social disorganization such as emigration because only a few Polish migrants were able to conceptualize and elaborate upon some kind of religious mysticism. But for Znaniecki and Thomas, the beliefs of Polish peasants were very eclectic and included belief in magic. People believed in the spiritual dimension of nature and readily identified Catholic saints with animals; they referred to the cycle of agrarian work through the seasons as sacred. Their worldview was dominated by the duality of the material and spiritual world. In religious terms, Polish migrants defined themselves as Catholics. In letters addressed to the Emigrants Protective Association in Warsaw, aspiring Polish migrants praised God and deliberately inquired about religious issues; for instance, they expressed anxiety about 'losing faith' once in the new social context. As one letter quoted by Znaniecki stated:

> Meanwhile I have heard that in America there are enough churches and our faith will not get lost. So please, respected society, advise and explain to me where most of our brothers are, what kind of soil there is, what customs, what climate, the price of one desiatina[6] [*dziesiecina*] and whether it is worth the trouble, so that I may not lead my wife and my children to destruction and lose my fortune, for which I am responsible and must give an account to our Lord God.
>
> (Thomas and Znaniecki, 1920, p. 30)

In America the initial attitude of Polish immigrants to church buildings and properties was that the parish was the property of the priests and bishops. In terms of belief, Polish peasants were completely respectful to the institutional Church. In the Polish diaspora, the Catholic parish played an important role not only in religious life but also in education and the maintenance of the Polish language (Chalasinski, 2013[1934], p. 212–213). The need for new social organizations encouraged people to create new forms of association consciously. The American 'Polish colonies' were composed of uneducated groups, with such exceptions as priests and a group of 'moral refugees' who were forced to leave the country due to the ethical crisis of identity they experienced.

> The Polish institutions have, indeed, imported Polish cultural values, but they made a reflective or unreflective selection of them for their own local purposes and gave them a new meaning suited to the specific forms and conditions of Polish-American life, just as they did with American cultural values.
>
> (Thomas and Znaniecki, 1920, p. xv)

These results from research imply a strong correlation between traditional Catholicism and people's readiness to participate in and stay within localized ethnic communities.

Integrating social and religious concerns

Traditional religiosity is most often characterized by a strong relationship between social ties and religious experience. As was presented in the first chapter, Emile Durkheim had already described religion as a system of beliefs and practices which binds individuals into one moral community (Durkheim, 1995[1912], p. 44). Charles Taylor, in homage to these critical insights of the father of sociology, has labelled the strong relationship between national identity and religion as 'neo-Durkheimian'. Taylor claims that 'the marriage of Christian faith and modern civilization' transformed Christian theology from the dominance of the transcendental order exclusively and opened the way for the 'anthropomorphic turn'. New anthropocentric cultural patterns relativized traditional civilizational values and also Christian values. According to Taylor there were in fact some exceptions in these civilizational processes: Poland and Ireland. 'Elsewhere, the civilizational crisis of the First World War was a body blow to established faiths, from which they have never recovered' (Taylor, 2007, p. 418). This is why, even in the second half of the 20th century, the religious situation in Poland could still be characterized as 'neo-Durkheimian'. Polish religiosity has emerged substantially from the specific relationship between Catholicism and the 'state ideology' arising from Poland's experience of occupation by adversary political powers since the 18th century and later by the Communist regime. As a result, from the situation 'between Church and state' there emerged a sphere of values and attitudes embodied in the concept 'folk religiosity' (Piwowarski, 1968, p. 75).

Moving to the insightful contributions of Polish authors, Stefan Czarnowski claimed that, in the traditional form of religiosity, the social aspect was dominant (1956, p. 90). And according to Barbara Bukraba-Rylska, the key characteristic of traditional Polish culture was that one's religiosity was mediated by one's membership in primary and secondary social groups such as the family, local community or parish. Different social groups practised religion in specific ways. For instance, families and villages possessed their own patron saints (Bukraba-Rylska, 2008) and individual aspects of religion were subordinated to their social aspect. As Czarnowski claimed, 'An individual subjectively affects his religious life but only as part of a social environment' (1956, p. 90). Being Catholic manifested and was included as being part of a local community such as a parish or village. 'The spatial and annual organization of religious worship is the background for organizing the life of local society' (Czarnowski, 1956, p. 91). Hence members of local communities manifested deep affection and attachment to local religious symbols such as chapels, sculptures or sacred pictures. The individual in traditional society served the community and completed tasks representative of that society. Religion and shared moral values, manifesting as forms of social control, activated and mobilized the individual through engagement with traditional social institutions such as the family, neighborhood or parish. Traditional social control mechanisms spanned a wide spectrum of social life, encompassing different social dimensions such as religion, economics and leisure.

The sense of belonging to the local parish and community was stronger than the sense of national belonging that was beginning to emerge at that time. The popular ethos was largely based on religious moral principles, and the parish and the church were its institutional advocates. Moreover, punishments for public crimes included donations to the parish and even prayer or public confession in the church (Bujak, 1903, p. 22). Moral behaviour was assessed in accordance with the Church's commandments. Christian values represented a moral basis for children's education (Wierzbicki, 1963, p. 145). In traditional Polish culture, the social and transcendental orders were integrated into the institution of the local parish. The parish encompassed nearly all dimensions of human life. As noted by Stefan Znaniecki and William Thomas:

> The parish is a kind of great family whose members are united by a community of moral interests. The church building and the cemetery (originally always surrounding the church) are the visible symbols and the material instruments of this unity. It is the moral property of the parish as a whole, managed by the priest. We say 'moral property', because economically it does not belong, in the eyes of the peasant, to any human individual or group; it is first God's, then the saint's to whom it is dedicated.
>
> (Thomas and Znaniecki, 1927, p. 275)

The parish priest and other priests in the parish, often labeled as 'catechists', held an important role in the life of the parish. Because of his office, the parish priest had great social capital of trust among the parishioners and was respected in his official capacity by the faithful. However, they also expected him to be personally involved with them and to be fatherly.

> A priest, a person who is surrounded by veneration almost to a degree of idolatry, if he is not accessible and gentle in evading them, if he does not want to talk to everyone at every opportunity, and especially if he rebukes from the pulpit, not only will he never gain recognition, but he will surely be hatred and will provoke revenge. Nothing hurts peasants more than [a priest] 'offending their honour' by openly disregarding them.
>
> (Bujak, 1903, p. 144)

The social role of the parish was strengthened by religious education. According to the Constitution of the Second Republic of Poland, from 1921, religious education in public schools was obligatory (1921, p. 44) and it was mostly delivered by parish priests. In this way, a priest stayed in touch with his local community members from their early childhood and played the role of the 'father of the community':

The role of the priest is modified in the same way. From a magician he becomes a father of the parish, a representative of God (Jesus) by maintaining the moral order, a representative of the parish by leading the acts of common worship. From his representation of Jesus results his superior morality, implicitly assumed wherever he acts, not as a private individual, but in his religious, official character. Therefore also his teaching, his advice, his praise or blame, whenever expressed in the church, from the chancel, or in the confessional, are listened to as words of Jesus, seldom if ever doubted, and obeyed more readily than orders from any secular power.

(Thomas and Znaniecki, 1927, p. 285)

At the end of the 1960s, Wladyslaw Piwowarski noticed that the clergy were no longer the privileged social class they had been before the war. His studies of rural parishes show that the social and cultural role of priests was declining, especially among young people. However, the role of priest gained new spiritual significance. There was still a deep respect for the clergy, which grew primarily from the fact that priests were regarded as intermediaries between God and man. Yet the authority of the clergy went beyond the liturgical sphere. Every third parishioner surveyed by Piwowarski said he or she would like to have a priest in the family due to their social prestige (Piwowarski, 1968). In popular opinion of the post-war era, the authority of priests in local communities was maintained, although its religious character predominated much more than previously, and its importance was weakened in the non-religious sphere. Such a rupture with cultural traditionalism and folklore gave scholars an opportunity to focus on the parish's activity in the religious sphere. The Church also made pastoral efforts in this direction. As the state surveys from that period indicate, parish communities became the only pervasive counterbalance to the effective atheization of Polish society (Kosela, 1996). Aleksander Wat was even convinced that the religiousness centred on the local community carried an extraordinary social force capable of defending the nation against Stalinism (1990).

In the first decades after the Second World War the general attitude toward religion was stable. According to the traditional Polish way of thinking, at least after the war, being a Pole was equated with being a Catholic.

For many of our peasants, especially of the older generation, Pole and Catholic are the same, similar to the way German and Protestant are identical. The peasant knows that there are other Catholic nations, but he thinks that they are, however, not so strongly integrated with the Church, that they are more peripheral to the Catholic community, that they are more distanced from God and holiness, which – according to his imagination – belong to the domain of the Polish language.

(Ciupak, 1973, p. 91)

Religious changes in Poland after the Second World War can be explained primarily in terms of the transformation of the Polish countryside and the decline of social cohesion (Ciupak, 1968, p. 141). At that time, despite the fact that secular institutions were taking over the functions previously performed by parishes (Ciupak, 1965), in fact, the parish continued to integrate the local village community (Wieruszewska-Adamczyk, 1978). Although in the late 1960s liberalization especially affected the moral attitudes of rural residents, particularly in the field of sexual and matrimonial codes of behaviour (Marianski, 1983, p. 277), still, in the parish, the private and public spheres overlapped. Although not as strongly as before, the parish continued to shape the local community through 'correctional-punishing' mechanisms.

> Transformations of the social ties between the parish and residents refers, rather, to secondary features, and result from the weakening of traditional "face-to-face" social ties and personal contacts and the cultural distinctiveness of the village. If the parish ceased to be the most viable institutional form of participation in culture, if its control functions decreased somewhat, at the same time its educational functions (catechization) and strictly religious functions increased.
>
> (Marianski, 1983, pp. 272–273)

In traditional Polish religiosity the relationship between the transcendental order and national identity is especially complicated. In popular understanding, Catholicism in Poland was strongly linked to national belonging. Being Polish and being Catholic were interrelated. In other words, Polish culture was essentially calibrated to Catholicism. Polish customs and even language corresponded to Catholicism. In his description of this phenomenon Czarnowski even suggested the term 'confessional nationalism'. As an example of the strength of this relationship between Catholicism and Polish nationality, he mentioned the tension which could be observed between Polish and Irish migrants in the USA (Czarnowski, 1956, p. 91). Edward Ciupak searched for the roots of the link between Catholicism and Polish national identity in the Reformation era:

> The Reformation and Counter-Reformation made a lasting impression on Polish Catholicism. Almost all social strata were affected except the peasantry. The very passivity of the peasantry during the Reformation period impacted on the future of Catholicism generally and allowed this social stratum to develop such forms of religiosity, which gave it a national stigma.
>
> (Ciupak, 1968, p. 1)

Due to official restrictions on religion in the public sphere during the Communist era, religion was relegated to family life. As forms of religious commitment, holidays and festivals were accentuated by the fact that Catholicism was practised instead in the private domain. The strength of

Polish Catholicism resulted from the fact that it resisted simple social categorization. Polish Catholicism was neither political nor separated from current politics. Even during the interwar period, the Church did not represent social dominance or a privileged social class (Majka, 1980, p. 39). Martin Conway confirms this claim, by pointing out that during the 1920s, the expansion of Catholic parties in Europe was evident with two exceptions: Poland and Ireland. Despite the fact that in both these countries Catholicism was inextricably bound up with national identity, no significant Catholic political parties emerged in them (Conway, 2008, p. 23). Polish Catholicism operated at two distinguishable levels of social reality, that is, individual or private, and social or national. On the one hand, the strength and stability of religion in Poland in the 1980s was especially associated with the social order, while in the private sphere, individuals manifested different levels of religiosity which was rather selective in its degree (Marianski, 1991a, p. 305).

Janusz Marianski characterized the Polish phenomenon of cultural religiosity at the end of the 1980s as the 'faith of the nation'. In his view, Catholicism integrated Polish society with its moral ideas and motivations. Catholicism represented some kind of 'common good' (Marianski, 1991a, pp. 302–309). Krzysztof Kosela claims that national identity in Poland is stronger than civic or religious identity (2003, p. 85). According to Bryan Wilson, in the 1980s some traces of 'religious nationalism' could be observed. As he puts it: 'Dominant religion [….] operate(s) quite explicitly as an agency of social and political criticism. (This may be seen very evidently in the case of Poland, although that is perhaps a special case.)' (Wilson, 1988, p. 200) However younger researchers such as Genevieve Zubrzycki (2015), following Riesebrodt, postulate the distinction between religion and religious tradition in Polish society. In Poland, as well as in Quebec, national identity has been historically constructed through the active role of religious tradition and religious institutions. Zubrzycki claims that faith and the internalization of beliefs in Poland should be distinguished from political processes concerning the role of religion in the public sphere (2015).

The specificity of the dynamics of religion in Polish society was based on the fact that people's lived experience of religion was consistent with institutional Catholicism, that it, with official Church teaching, at least in terms of beliefs. From this point of view, Polish Catholicism differs from many forms of popular religiosity especially in Africa or Latin America. Catholic institutions were identified with the transcendental order because they stimulated religious experience by supporting popular religiosity. Catholicism in the perception of members of Polish society was not burdened with a difficult and shameful history which included opposing scientific and technological progress. Polish Catholicism was preserved due to the sense of risk and danger which accompanied it within Polish society in the Communist era. Religion oppressed by Marxism gained extra significance as a repository of endangered values. The martyrdom of thousands of priests as a symbolic reference to the transcendental order is often neglected in the characterization of the dynamics of religion in Polish society during the Second World War and Communist eras (Datko, 2016).

The link between national and religious identity was also highlighted in the Polish diaspora, especially to North America. Although there was pressure for immigrants to assimilate and to become Americans in the 18th and 19th centuries, by the 20th century the American national ethos was much more tolerant and ethnic diversity was accepted. Migration to the USA in the first half of the 20th century was ethnic migration and immigrants built ethnic colonies in American cities. 'It was possible for the ethnic groups to continue and to develop an ideology which said they could be Irish, German, Polish or Jewish, and at the same time be as good Americans as anyone else – if not better' (Greeley, 1971, p. 42). Moreover, the role of religion as an important social factor in migration was highlighted in marriage patterns. Andrew Greeley observed that religious migrants tended to marry within religious groups (1971). Ruby Kennedy even formulated the metaphor of the 'triple melting pot' to express this tendency among Catholics, Protestants and Jews. If a married couple represented two different nationalities, it was more probable that both belonged to the same religious group (1944). People tended to marry within their own denominations and were less opposed to marriages across national borders. 'The German and Poles, who stand in the middle range of religious involvement, are not likely to encounter a spouse from a more devout family background, particularly since Poles are strongly disinclined to marry the Irish' (Greeley, 1971). Roman Dzwonkowski has described the role of the Catholic pastoral ministry in maintaining Polish identity among Polish migrants in France before the Second World War (1988). Catholicism supported the sense of community among Polish migrants to the UK also after the Second World War (Stachura, 2004).

The social organization in Polish-American groups was inspired by 'social spirit' which manifested especially at the parish level. Polish immigrants tended to associate with other Poles in America and to build up a Polish social milieu in American towns and cities. However, these new forms of social organization in the Polish diaspora did not compensate for the solid and coherent structure of traditional society in Poland itself. The underdevelopment of the social structure of Polish migrants in America influenced individual disorganization and social deviation such as delinquency, sexual immorality and poverty. The inner cohesion of Polish families in America was strongly reduced through the migration process. Usually only a few members of a family emigrated and quite often they were scattered throughout the new country. Despite the fact that Polish migrants actively participated in community and parish life, the integrative power of traditional norms was reduced in comparison with that of traditional communities in Poland. Even the impact of parish structures was limited due to the fact 'that the existence of the Polish-American church depends on the free will of the congregation' (Thomas and Znaniecki, 1920, p. 222). Thomas and Znaniecki observed that emotions and individual concerns such as sexual desire, maternal instincts and desire for security were not strong enough to protect the family structures of Polish migrants to the USA. For Polish migrants American society was 'practically unknown, usually indifferent, often contemptuous, sometimes even hostile' (Thomas and Znaniecki, 1920, p. 44). Polish culture was interpreted and deliberately and actively elaborated in the new social conditions. The two sets of values, the Polish traditional and the new American values did not exist independently in the new Polish communities in America but were combined and melded. In America, immigrants were deprived of their original social milieu and their social organization was quite weak and underdeveloped. Immigrants to America were not supported by social norms and rules and faced strongly demoralizing circumstances. 'The peasant immigrant is able to maintain his moral status in spite of the weakened social response and control only because of the power of mental habits' (Thomas and Znaniecki, 1920, p. 167). However Milton Gordon (1964) demonstrated that religious structures facilitated assimilation in America in the 1960s. That is why, many studies on Polish migration focus on the role played by congregations and local religious organizations in the social adaptation of the immigrants.

Embodying religion

Due to their life style, daily work and life conditions, people in traditional culture stayed in constant contact with what Archer defines as 'the natural order'. Whereas, generally speaking the fears and natural concerns which accompanied everyday life was integrated within the transcendental order. People experienced strong negative emotions and especially fear when, for example, things 'got off on the wrong foot' or a black cat crossed their path. As a result, when people observed some 'dangerous' signs they not only experienced fear but they may even have avoided activity in general (Witos, 1998, p. 82). Such behaviour demonstrated especially strong emotions related to human safety and well-being which should not be attributed only to traditional culture. However, what is specific to traditional Polish culture is the strong integration between natural and transcendental concerns. What is more, transcendental concerns were also accompanied by people's strong fear of becoming spiritually condemned because they believed that they could easily commit a sin. This sense of sin integrated transcendence with the social and natural orders. Sinfulness was accompanied by the fear of being punished not only after death but also in everyday life. 'When people sin, God punishes them to warn and protect them against eternal damnation.' (Witos, 1998, p. 74)

Stefan Czarnowski characterized Polish religiosity as 'sensualistic', that is, a strong reference not only to transcendence but also to the natural order was implicit in religious beliefs. For instance, even religious beliefs were influenced by specific rural and agricultural concerns and needs. Religious pictures, especially these brought from well-known pilgrimage destinations such as Czestochowa,[7] described below, were displayed in peasants' homes and accompanied the people in their everyday lives. The image of the Virgin Mary has been constructed according to peasant sensibilities. The Mother of God is characterized as a kind and merciful woman who protects and takes care of their children (Czarnowski, 1956, p. 101).

The relationship between well-being and religion has been highlighted in the context of past waves of Polish migration. Poles in America at the beginning of the 20th century were organized into informal 'societies', which took care of not onlytheir leisure and entertainment interests, but included also religious activities. Moreover, the state, in countries where Poles emigrated, was usually not able to support Polish families effectively because the public forms of support available did not harmonize with Polish traditions, as has been mentioned above. Thomas and Znaniecki (1920, p. 222) claimed that: 'As a result marriage almost ceases to be a social institution, and the old socially sanctioned attitudes upon which the strength and permanence of the conjugal bonds were based lose most of their practical influence'. Polish peasants were accustomed to thinking in a theological way; religious beliefs and ideas dominated their way of thinking. When such people arrived in the United States the process of adjusting their ideas to new conditions began.

> When the natural world, the former context of the peasant ideas, faded behind the transatlantic horizon, the newcomers found themselves stripped to those religious institutions they could bring along with them. Well, the trolls and fairies will stay behind, but churches and priests at very least will come. The more thorough the separation from the other aspects of the old life, the greater was the hold of the religion that alone survived the transfer. Struggling against heavy odds to save something of the old ways, the immigrants directed into their faith the whole weight of their longing to be connected with the past. As peasants at home, awed by the hazardous nature of the universe and by their own helplessness, these people had fled to religion as a refuge from the anguish of the old world.
>
> (Handlin, 2002[1951], p. 105)

Thus priests, pastors and rabbis served as moral and spiritual advisers. They organized not only spiritual and religious life but also built welfare institutions which delivered social services to the people. Religious structures were congregationally shaped. Parishes or religious communes delivered not only religious, but also social welfare services, and these were gradually transformed into 'denominations' (Smith, 1978, p. 1174). According to Timothy Smith, migration reinforced religiosity because migrants turned to religious institutions when faced with its challenges, such as the need for support and help in a foreign land (1978). From such a perspective, ethnic churches provided social networks which may have had a positive impact on immigrants (Guest, 2003). Parishes organized social life and represented, to some extent, a form of primary community.

Thomas and Znaniecki could theoretically assume that Irish-American parishes should have attracted Polish Catholics. This inclination could be expected because Irish priests represented higher moral and intellectual capacities and came from higher social classes. However Polish immigrants were not inclined to join Irish-American parishes because Polish parishes delivered not only religious, but also, and especially, social services. The construction of Polish parishes was initiated by 'average' people and manifested as a form of ethnic social capital. The parish structure was organized following a pattern, having devotional 'fraternities', associations for social activities and finally, a school. However, Thomas and Znaniecki claimed that religious interests, 'like all other traditional social attitudes, were weakened by emigration, though they seem to be the last to disappear completely' (1920, 41). When Poles were confronted with the lack of a Polish parish because of too few Polish people in the area, only some of them joined Irish-American churches. 'But in this case a large proportion—all those whose religious interests are not particularly strong – remain outside of all religious life' (Thomas and Znaniecki, 1920, p. 44). Thanks to their parish organizations Polish groups had both prestige and security. The parish was – according to these authors – the most important Polish-American institution as it played not only a religious but also a social role.

Polish immigrants in the USA found themselves without access to a social system which had economic activities familiar to them. The jobs which were available were often very different from their previous occupations. Moreover, in the American labour market Polish workers were faced with the need to change jobs quite often. They were menaced by debt to a much higher degree than in Poland. As a consequence, people started to live 'from hand to mouth', that is, unguided by any general plans or principles (Thomas and Znaniecki, 1920, p. 175).

These social dynamics of Polish migrants could be characterized not only by the decisive role of their ethnic identity but also by the challenges they faced in settling into their new life context and facing the social and existential risks of migration. First, Polish migrants faced insecure economic conditions. The social system of the Polish-American diaspora was oriented towards individual efficiency, and there was a strong tension, or even opposition, between social responsibility and individual efficiency (Thomas and Znaniecki, 1920, p. 343). Secondly, individual Poles could feel humiliation in social groups composed of other nationalities whom they perceived to be socially and culturally superior. The social structure of America with its new forms of organization did not cover all the social situations which challenged them. Therefore, they relied on the Catholic Polish parishes as an important source of support and spiritual comfort. 'In order to satisfy the social needs of its members and to reach the necessary minimum of cohesion, the immigrant groups must sooner or later resort to reflective social activity, must supplement the spontaneous reproduction of old social forms by a new conscious organization' (Thomas and Znaniecki, 1920, p. xiii). Polish Catholic structures both in Poland and abroad continued to respond to such natural needs until much later. Even into the 1980s, parishes in Poland still served as important distribution channels for charitable aid from Western Europe. For example, in 1988 about 70 percent of parishes in Poland organized charitable aid in the form of medicine, clothing and food to Polish citizens. (Firlit, 1990, p. 122).

Performing religion

In traditional rural communities in Poland it is true that the level of religious knowledge among congregations was very low and lectures on the Holy Bible were quite infrequent (Czarnowski, 1956, p. 100). However, following a critical realist approach, religious identity should not be reduced to cognitive elements; religious beliefs are seen as substantially connected to religious rituals. 'There is no culture which has no material elements and represents only "spiritual" aspects' (Czarnowski, 1956, p. 17). Within the culture even 'material culture' relates to human experience. Traditional Catholicism represented much more than merely ideas and abstract norms and included also practical forms and modes of action. This is why some authors have drawn attention to the sensualistic inclinations inherent in popular religiosity. The Polish mentality – in comparison with other nations – was, according to Czarnowski, especially dominated by sensualism. He understood the sensualism of traditional religiosity to be, for instance, devotion to visual representations of the sacred such as paintings or statues of saints, that is, some kind of embodiment, including emotionality, of the sacred. Religious sensualism resulted in the establishment of a firm association between transcendence and everyday life (Czarnowski, 1956, p. 101).

In saying that peasant religiosity was dominated by a practical dimension, this means that 'being religious' meant 'doing' rather than sharing some 'cognitive' beliefs. Especially such occasions as a parish feast allowed local inhabitants to 'make a covenant' within a group and with a sacred place. People participated in worship on behalf of the whole community not on their own account. Taking part in pilgrimages, despite being motived by individual and personal inspiration, included and manifested responsibility for other members of the community who entrusted the pilgrim with their intentions and spiritual demands. Thus, the spiritual benefits of religious worship were shared among members of the local community (Czarnowski, 1956, p. 93).

Edward Ciupak pointed out that the distinctiveness of religiosity in Poland was grounded in the fact that Polish Catholic observances were based not in philosophical concepts but in practical symbols and rituals.

> And this is probably some 'Polish way' of the development of Catholicism, which does not include strong intellectual support by the masses but adapts to the present day mainly by revealing the rich symbolism of external behaviour, rather than deep philosophical convictions.
>
> (Ciupak, 1968), p. 159)

The above mentioned Stanislaw Grygiel and Jozef Tischner highlight the element of 'visuality', the practical and factual dimensions as key characteristics of folk religiosity in South Poland (1960, p. 1458).

Traditional peasant culture was very pragmatic (Bartminski, 2015). Rituals which bound local communities together were related to local representations of the sacred. Pilgrimages and communal forms of devotion such as prayers or religious songs generated a stronger sense of community. Taking part in religious rituals transformed individuals into elements of the community. Individuals thus became members of the group and their individuality was suppressed. Participating in religious worship reflected social or even demographic distinctions between local groups. Of significance was the manifestation of the sacred, especially in the form of saints, but also of divine persons such as angels, who were represented as embodied and human. In terms of the relationship between the transcendental order and the natural or performative orders, they were so strictly united that it was as if there was no difference between the embodied or material representations and transcendence (Czarnowski, 1956, p. 100). Czarnowski, when he studied the issue of religious representation, pointed out the phenomenon of poor pilgrims who, upon receiving financial support from others, collected their spiritual demands and intentions and substituted themselves for the non-pilgrim's personal participation in the worship. Such pilgrims or poor people were recognized as more susceptible to transcendental states because of being in miserable and in economically depressed life circumstances. In this way pilgrimages bound people together spiritually.

Wincenty Witos highlights the strong relationship between religious rituals and the transcendental qualities of the pope, bishops and priests assigned to perform them. In traditional Polish Catholicism religious rituals were carried out frequently and in a very meticulous way. Men normally confessed once a year, while for women it was more often. Catholics who did not go to confession were forced to do so by priests or other administrators in the parish. During Sundays and religious feast days people did not work. People regularly prayed at home with their children. Religious practices formed a framework for everyday life (Witos, 1998, p. 74).

Moreover in the parish there was no place for spontaneity or unpredictability in the religious rhythm of life. Franciszek Bujak (1903) described how 'the order of a Holy Mass' was well organized, and depended strictly on the status of individual families in the village. Religious rituals also reflected the social structure of the local community. Especially in the case of peasants and noblemen, there were differences to some extent in their mode of participation in parish rituals. Such difference resulted from the obligatory financial or material charges for religious rituals. As Czarnowski notes, elements of religious belief corresponded with the social situation of the peasants and their feudal relationship with the manor houses in Poland (Czarnowski, 1956, p. 101). The most important celebration of the parish was the parish feast, which was celebrated once a year. The faithful from the parish also made pilgrimages to neighbouring parishes and shrines to obtain indulgences. 'Every adult person must go to Calvary every alternate or third year, and every year to any of the other pilgrimages. Negligence in this duty without an important reason rates as a sin' (Bujak, 1903, p. 140).

However, the ritualistic dimensions of parish life were not invariable. It would be inaccurate to argue that in rural parishes nothing changed for centuries and there was no place for specific liturgical innovation. For instance, in the repertoire of sung songs, new melodies and texts appeared quite often. The arrival of a new priest in a parish always resulted in changes. Parish life was also diversified by the arrival of the so-called missionaries, that is, folk preachers, who were first of all monks (Missionaries, Jesuits, Redemptorists), who conducted retreats and parish mission activities (Bujak, 1903, p. 144). In local parishes people celebrated the Church Holy Days together, and these merged with the rhythm of their work in the fields. In the Galician villages, as Bujak writes, people fasted for three days a week during Lent, which was in fact already a milder discipline. Indeed, the middle generation of peasants from the small village of Zmiaca remembered a time when they had been fasting, that is, abstaining from meat and dairy, during the entire 40-day period of Lent (Bujak, 1903, p. 121). The most important events in human life, the rituals at the time of one's birth, marriage and death, were celebrated in the parish. Franciszek Bujak wrote about the peasants in Zmiaca in this way:

> They perform all religious practices, without exception, they fast and rest on Sundays, everyone who is no longer a child, belongs to the scapular and rosary brotherhood and recites lace[8] and rosaries. They attend the parish church very diligently, more or less every Holy Day; everyone attends the whole service, that is, the mass and the sermon (...) When there are not very many farm activities, a few people in Zmiaca will attend weekday mass.
>
> (Bujak, 1903, p. 140)

In the 1960s it was observed that the level of religious practice in rural areas was high (Piwowarski, 1981, p. 12). The ritualistic aspect of Polish religious dynamism was strongly connected with Marian devotion (Bukraba-Rylska, 2008). An empirical study of pilgrims to Czestochowa in the late 1960s delivered very interesting results. This research demonstrated that participating in pilgrimage rituals resulted in the growth of both religious and national identity (Piwowarski, 1981, p. 17). Research conducted by Poland's Center for Research on Public Opinion and analyzed by Anna Pawelczynska showed that in 1960 about 26 percent of Catholics in the countryside and 19 percent in cities declared themselves to be 'deeply believing' while 58 percent in the countryside and 56 percent in cities were 'believing'. The proportion of people who declared that they were practising regularly was higher in the countryside and reached 47 percent, while in the city this was estimated at the level of 36 percent. The percentage of those who were non-practising represented 6 percent in the countryside and 12 percent in cities (Pawelczynska, 1970).

Between the 1950s and the 1970s, religious activity in parishes decreased (Adamczuk, Marianski and Zdaniewicz, 1991). With reference to this period, Janusz Marianski pointed out that 'if neglecting non-obligatory practices is the first symptom of dechristianization in relation to religious practices, many rural parish communities have already been through this stage' (Marianski, 1983, p. 267). He estimated the level of regular attendance on Sunday Mass in rural parishes in the diocese of Plock to be 54.8 percent in the years 1967–1976. In rural parishes 35 percent of the inhabitants attended May Service,[9] 17 percent attended rosary services, 34 percent, the Stations of the Cross, and 20 percent, the Gorzkie Zale [Bitter Lamentations] devotion.[10] Lent retreats, parish festivals and Corpus Christi processions, which involved massed gatherings, were much more popular (Marianski, 1983, pp. 265–267).

However, in the 1980s, religious life in Poland subsequently gained a new vitality parallel to the social dynamism taking place in the wider society. As Janusz Marianski claimed: 'The basic acts of Christian socialization show considerable resistance to the impact of industrialization and urbanization' (1983, p. 263). Wladyslaw Piwowarski explained this phenomenon with reference to religious rituals. Catholic celebrations, which had survived the pre-war period and constituted the manifestation of popular piety, now started to express also a sense of national belonging (Piwowarski, 1982). The Parish became a 'space of social freedom' in the era of Communist state oppression. Using the forces gathered in parishes, the Church became a partner in dialogue with the state authorities and a mediator in its conflict with workers. The pilgrimages of John Paul II to Poland became general social events which integrated religion with people's sense of national and social belonging. This topic will be studied in more detail in the next chapter. In conclusion, it is worth mentioning that, although no precise statistical data are available, but it is estimated that, even after emigrating, the majority of Polish migrants in the USA at the beginning of 20th century attended Sunday Mass regularly (Thomas and Znaniecki, 1920, p. 42).

Emerging mobility

Witos claims that religious concerns 'poisoned everyday life, reduced energy, diminished entrepreneurship and agency, and resulted in indifference and passivity' (1998, p. 75). However, it seems inaccurate to identify traditional Catholicism as a static socio-cultural system. In fact Catholicism in traditional Polish society represented very diverse and varied forms of social construction. For instance, Catholicism contributed to social mobility through the activities of priests who were not only advisers on moral and spiritual matters, but also organized a system of social services in the countryside.

As an example of such activity, the figure of Waclaw Blizinski can be mentioned. As a new priest in the rural parish of Liskow in Kalisz County, at the beginning of the 20th century he was already promoting education among his parishioners by organizing a school for children and subscriptions to newspapers. Using the parish as a base, he also organized a local cooperative society, an orphanage, a folk house, cooperative circles of farms, a dairy and savings and loan offices. Similar social welfare activities were led by the priest Antoni Tyczynski in the parish of Albigowa near Lancut in Podkarpackie Province. Moreover, many rural parish activists, including priests, were involved in political activities, mainly within the peasant movement. Bujak writes thus about the political role of priests: 'The influence of the clergy is of primary political importance, perhaps almost equal to the role of money; whomever the clergy allies with, that person has the greatest chance of winning peasant voices' (Bujak, 1903, pp. 132–133). Indeed, when he examined the diaries of members of the rural population, Stanislaw Siekierski noticed criticism of the priests' involvement in politics and cooperation with the richest groups of villagers (1995). According to Jozef Ciupak, Catholic institutions in traditional Poland were especially strong (1973, p. 42). In comparison with other countries in Europe the ratio of Polish priests to village inhabitants was very high and parish structures were well developed. The strong social role of priests and bishops affected the character of Church structures. For many years the hierarchical character of the Church was embodied in the role of the Primate[11]. As the Primate of Poland from 1948 until 1981, Cardinal Stefan Wyszynski, with his strong personality, actively influenced the structure of Polish Catholicism. The ecclesiastical reforms proposed by the Second Vatican Council were introduced and moderated in Poland according to his decisions.

But social agency within Catholicism in the context of traditional Polish Catholicism went beyond the role of the clergy. The agency of Polish laymen was relatively ineffective but it is essential to note that many similar programmes arising from the clergy's local parish social initiatives which emerged in the early 20th century subsequently gained legal recognition and autonomy after 1918 and thus their impact became even stronger. At that time, such individual initiatives were officially promoted by the Polish state authorities. At the parish level, these organizations mainly took the form of Rosary Crusades, Tertiaries,[12] and charities, the first of which was an organization called Caritas established in 1929. According to Zbigniew Wierzbicki, Catholic organizations in some parishes functioned more efficiently than agricultural organizations and institutions (Wierzbicki, 1963, p. 122). In Zmiaca in the inter-war period, the Catholic Youth Association was active, bringing together almost all male and female youth. Its activities consisted of organizing readings, choirs, orchestras and performances and exhibitions. In the first decade of its existence, the association organized 123 lectures, 38 performances and 40 celebrations, 20 national anniversaries, 2 hen breeding competitions, 3 beet cultivation competitions, and 1 flax cultivation competition (Wierzbicki, 1963, pp. 145–146).

It is important to mention that traditional Catholic institutions have also played an educational role and moreover that Catholic parishes injected a cultural dimension into the social life of local communities. Libraries, theatre groups, choirs and orchestras were created in parishes. In Ujanowice, a village described in detail by Franciszek Bujak, the vicar priest[13] led a band, which practised on holidays and on the days when people were not forced to work on the farms (Bujak, 1903, pp. 137–142). According to Wierzbicki, in the same small village in South Poland in the latter half of the 1930s 'there was a relatively well-stocked parish library with 758 books, which in 1936–1939 had 189 readers, and loaned out 2224 books' (Wierzbicki, 1963, p. 140). Moreover, his research shows that after 1918 the frequency of reading in Ujanowice increased. Religious reviews and magazines were the most popular items. There was also a parish kiosk, where residents could purchase newspapers and even receive copies free of charge (Wierzbicki, 1963, p. 141). In the 1970s Andrzej Swiecicki explained the higher degree of religious commitment in Poland in comparison with other Communist countries, in terms of the freedom of churches to organize religious education and publish religious materials (Swiecicki, 1977). The distinctiveness of the Polish socio-cultural system included also the fact that after 1945 Catholic communities in Communist Poland were not allowed to develop independent institutions of socialization such as state schools. Nevertheless, Catholic ideas, norms and beliefs continued to represent the principal reference points in the general formation of individual and social attitudes (Ciupak, 1973, p. 42).

Traditional religiosity was also accompanied by agency and social activity. People willingly contributed to the financial needs of their parishes. Many people participated in religious associations or small groups. The motivation for these affiliations was quite transcendental and resulted from a deep belief in eternal life and in God's protection in this world. For instance, it was believed that participation in a prayer group would be rewarded with divine protection in this life and in heaven (Witos, 1998, p. 76). According to Witos, it even happened that members of religious associations were sometimes manipulated by priests in their political struggle against 'enemies of the Church'. According to Bujak, religiosity interfered with the social mobility of peasants in Galicja. The parish was perceived to be an organization which could make a contribution to modernization and progress. Priests regularly organized rural educational and cultural activities, because they were often the best-educated inhabitants of the village. Similarly, Bujak writes about the economic role of the clergy:

> The main goal of the clergy's activity is not an economic one, they do not constitute a separate production class, although thanks to a significant part of their salary they may be able to run agricultural enterprises (priests' rectories may amount to a dozen acres of agricultural land),

but because of the characteristics of economic life in Galicya and the current cultural status of the vast mass of the population, the clergy have significant, even primary importance for the economic development of the country, as educators and leaders of the people in collective economic enterprises [*assocyacye*].

(Bujak, 1908, pp. 137–140)

The Polish sociologist and ethnographer Jan Stanislaw Bystron has even presented Catholicism as opposing traditional culture. He claims that the 'Church was combating old traditions' (1936, p. 168). Bystron asserts that the Church inspired the development of traditional literature, music and even theatre (1936, p. 183–199). The famous Polish historian and economist Franciszek Bujak, whose work has been mentioned many times above, also observed strong aspects of innovation in Polish traditional religiosity at the beginning of 20th century. In his acclaimed 'monographs' which study traditional villages in South Poland he protested against the simplistic understanding of 'tradition' as designating opposition to any change. 'It is a myth that in rural parishes there has been no change during past centuries and that there was no liturgical innovation', he wrote in 1903. When he made careful studies of historical developments in parish life he observed that new liturgical songs and melodies had been introduced. Moreover, whenever new priests arrived in a parish they introduced some elements of change (Bujak, 1903, p. 144).

Shifting the focus to Polish immigrants in America at the beginning of the 20th century, we can observe their dislocation from these rural peasant institutions and their installation in a situation of new economic and institutional bonds. The adaptation of the Polish peasant to the new culture should not be understood simplistically as the 'gradual substitution in his consciousness of American cultural values' (Thomas and Znaniecki, 1920, p. x). Polish immigrants arrived in America equipped with traditional values and attitudes but were separated from traditional Polish structures and organizations. Social groups of Polish immigrants 'have been partly drawn from Polish traditions, partly from the new conditions in which the immigrants live and from American social values as the immigrant sees and interprets them' (Thomas and Znaniecki, 1920, p. xi). Migrants were forced to place themselves in a new culture and to find their own new *modus vivendi*. Immigrants evaluated new cultures from the perspective of their own concerns and values. The question raised by them was what should be their point of reference for moving into the new culture? One option was traditionalism, which encouraged people to be guardians of the past. However, migration also released a wide range of emotions. The fact that they had left parents and relatives behind made them feel guilty. The past was idealized and romanticized. Migrants felt alone in the new American culture and the fact of being foreigners in a new land pushed them to search for a new identity and sense of community. Some symptoms of religious revivalism emerged, especially among Protestants. The Bible was interpreted in a straightforward, free and progressive way. Among Catholics, especially after the proclamation of the doctrine of papal infallibility (in 1870), appeals to Scripture were reduced. The folk religiosity that still dominated migrant congregations was progressive, full of innovation and impulses towards accommodation (Thomas and Znaniecki, 1920).

According to Timothy Smith (1978), migrating to America redefined the relationship between religiosity and ethnic identity. New ethnic awareness, mostly inspired by religious ideas, changed the boundaries of personhood. The process of migration exposed strong emotional feeling within a social group, which resulted in the intensification of theological reflexivity and religious commitment. Migration also generated ethno-religious ideologies such as millennialism or messianism, which focused on the creation of a universal human community or brotherhood. In this sense, migration was a 'theologizing experience'. Migrants were liberated from the moral constraints of their homeland's village culture. They were confronted with new languages, customs or even such ordinary but important things as new household appliances. American culture in the first half of the 20th century was dominated by materialism and pragmatism. Newcomers from Europe observed that American religious culture was much more focused on behaviour and ethical issues than on theological reflection. In the past, community leadership was strongly influenced by 'nationalistic, pretentious and selfish' ideology (Thomas and Znaniecki, 1920, p. 343). Later, Polish immigrants learned to regard Church properties from an economical perspective, according to the American mindset.

Being Catholic, in terms of Catholic tradition and faith, reinforced the migrants' strong 'national' identities. Ethnic groups organized substructures in American cities, which were characterized by specific life styles and generated 'mobility pyramids'. These enabled social promotion but also enclosed migrants in 'mobility traps' (Greeley, 1971, p. 50). An important character of religious life was that religion represented an influential moral force that strengthened modernization. Parishes, priests, rabbis, despite some traces of anticlericalism, were regarded as agents of progress. Among many examples of such mobilization was the temperance movement. Religiosity motivated people to clarify their ethnic identity and stimulated their autonomy, self-realization and mobility (Smith, 1978, pp. 1165–1166). Denominational understanding of religious groups as encompassing not only religious structures but also religious identity corresponded with 'cultural awakenings'. As the result, religious and ethnic identity started to become mutually interrelated. Smith claimed that 'ethnic mobilization' was not a result of migration to America but had been inaugurated before in homelands as an outcome of complex cultural and economic competition. 'The customs and beliefs of particular varieties of faith and the traditions of loyalty to them seem, then, to have been the decisive determinants of ethnic affiliation in America' (Smith, 1978, p. 1174).

Piotr Taras who studied Polish migration in Detroit claims that social bonds within Polish families and among Polish immigrants generally in the

USA were stronger than they were among other nationalities (Taras, 1989, p. 57). In his very interesting study in the 1970s he notes that:

> Every parish, as was formerly the center of social life for immigrants, later became the cultural heritage of their ancestors. The Church was and still is the place where deep emotions were experienced, where important life events took place and where worldview, values and attitudes have been shaped.
>
> (Taras, 1989, p. 62)

American Catholicism originally was mostly 'created' by Irish Catholics. The American Catholic Church was dominated by Irish laymen as well as Irish clergy. New migrants from other Catholic countries such as Italy or Poland were usually less religious and were quite often characterized as nominal Catholics. American migrants in the 19th and at the beginning of the 20th centuries, such as Slovaks, Lithuanians, Croatians, Slovenians and Poles, came from nations struggling to become states. According to Rodney Stark and Roger Finke, the nominal Catholicism of these migrants as they faced the American 'free market' at the beginning of the 20th century, was transformed into a vital religiosity.

> The basis of Catholic success is remarkably similar to that of the upstart Protestants – the Baptists and the Methodists. The Catholics aggressively marketed a relatively intense, otherworldly religious faith to a growing segment of the population. Besides offering familiar liturgy, symbols, and saints, the Catholic Church also emphasized personal renewal through devotional activities and in effect produced its own brand of revivalism.
>
> (Finke and Stark, 2005, pp. 114–115)

12 percent of parishes and 18 percent of the population used the Polish language (Finke and Stark, 2005, p. 128). Consequently Irish-American Catholicism, which had been rather exclusive and barely tolerant of other nations, was transformed into a competitive and vibrant religious group. Both ethnic groups, the Polish and the Irish, represented the same Catholic affiliation but meanwhile were well known for their mutual antipathy in America at the beginning of the 20th century. For instance, intense conflict between Polish parishes and Irish bishops were well known in Buffalo, Chicago and Scranton, Pennsylvania, and catalyzed the birth of the Polish National Catholic Church in America. Among Catholic migrants from Poland, the idea of Catholicity was vital. Most of them supported the idea of 'Polish Catholicism in a pluralistic church' rather than the 'catholic Polishness' which was represented by Franciszek Hodur who created a Polish National Church in America (Smith, 1978, p. 1184). In this way ethnicity, for all ethnic groups in the USA, was focused more on ethical rather than national aspects of life.

Despite internal conflicts within the Polish diaspora in America, at the beginning of the 20th century people were able to protect their cultural identity. In the second half of the 20th century Polish cultural identity came to represent cultural capital and heritage, which could be useful for social promotion in American society (Taras, 1989), for instance when the migrants started to wear clothes of a different style, or to use different household appliances. However many Catholic migrants were dissatisfied with the Catholic Church and converted to Protestantism. By 1918 there were some 25 thousand Italian converts in New York City alone (Handlin, 2002[1951], p. 122). Social groups who had already experienced overwhelming religious pluralism in their homelands dominated American immigration in the early 20th century. Both ethnic groups from Western Europe, such as the Scottish, Irish and Germans, represented many Protestant and Catholic denominations and also migrants from Central and Eastern Europe were accustomed to living in a pluralistic context, including not only Orthodox and Catholic denominations but also Jewish. 'In the Austrian province of Galicia, now southern Poland, Roman Catholic Poles, Greek Catholic or Orthodox Rusyns (or Ukrainians, as some of them came to prefer to be called), and Orthodox and Hasidic Jews lived together uneasily in the same towns and villages.' (Smith, 1978, p. 1164) In the new country of settlement, these identities and tensions were resolved in innovative ways.

Conclusions

This study of traditional religiosity suggests some very important conclusions. In traditional Polish society the socio-cultural and cultural systems were stable. Archer's formulation depicts this situation well: 'The coexistence of cultural and structural morphostasis together generated a high and lasting degree of everyday "contextual continuity" for the population in question: repetitive situations, stable expectations and durable relations' (Archer, 2007, p. 49). People did not transform their lives through their actions because culture unified the population and ideas were easily reproduced. Groups were subordinated to the entity of society and controlled in that way. Social hierarchy delivered unification and controlled cultural marginalities, such as deviant behaviour. The stability of cultural and structural contexts generated routine actions in daily life.

However, actions within traditional Polish society required reflexivity on the part of the individual. Even commitment to the practical order within the traditional culture, which would seem to imply non-discursive 'tacit knowledge' and 'embodied skills', in fact required reflexivity. In other words, the relationship of the individual to the practical order represented much more than the performance of routine actions. Commitment to the practical order included self-control and also reflexive reactions when unexpected circumstances occurred or when human mistakes were made. Reflexivity mediated between individuals and culture and acted as a simple communication mechanism, which linked an individual to significant others.

Tradition represented a binding social force because of the practices incorporated in the traditional socio-cultural system rather than the consistency of ideational elements of the cultural system. In traditional Polish society, the level of interdependence between cultural components was high. The study of Polish Catholicism confirms Archer's understanding of the 'myth of cultural integration' (Archer, 1988, pp. 1–24). The character of Polish traditional religiosity suggests that people in the past were not to be seen as being so strongly integrated with nature that even the identity of the individual was dismantled and a 'clear distinction between the mundane and the spiritual, the animate and the inanimate, the self and others or other things' (Archer, 1988, p. 10) was repudiated. The nature of traditional people should not be romanticized. The study of traditional Polish Catholicism suggests that traditional society should not been seen as characterized by uniformity of behaviour. Traditional Polish religiosity was not only dominated by routine, repetition and reproduction.

In other words, Polish believers were not 'inexorably trapped in a coherent cultural code which generates the behavioural uniformities observed' (Archer, 1988, p. 11). The integration of traditional Polish religiosity was rooted in the socio-cultural system rather than in any ideational consistency of their cultural system. The behavioural uniformity of traditional Polish religiosity was a result of their 'traditional way of life' rather than the uniformity of their cultural system. Again, traditional Polish society illustrates Archer's formulation well:

> Individuals could largely live inductively from past contexts to future ones because they were engaged in unchanging activities. But this was due to the stability of the structured context which promoted high Socio-Cultural integration since customary practices did continue to 'work'; rather than to their constrained enmeshment by an integrated belief system.
>
> (Archer, 1988, p. 12)

There is no doubt that in traditional society the social structure was integrated with religious institutions and the transcendental order was intertwined with the social, natural and also practical orders. The practical order was especially crucial in shaping religiosity. Religious rituals integrated human concerns with transcendence. Rituals shaped the relationship to transcendence, integrated human labour and directed natural human concerns towards religion. The life of Polish migrants in the United States highlighted the social role of religion. Polish Catholic parishes played an important role which was not only related to social but also to natural ones.

Such a vision of traditional society, as is commonly held, may imply the assumption that the individual in traditional culture was 'lost' in the social structure. In this chapter I have argued that to understand the individual in traditional society, especially where religiosity is concerned, it is necessary to include the category of human reflexivity. The understanding of traditional Polish religiosity requires much deeper insight. Based on the clarification of the concept of reflexivity presented in Chapter 2, I have demonstrated that traditional religiosity should not be reduced to the level of social structures which are separated from human subjectivity. From such a perspective, a person in the context of traditional religiosity experienced emotions and 'was equipped' with a personal relationship to transcendence. Religious concerns were interwoven with the search for safety and social support. Polish historical descriptions as well as the sociological analysis of traditional Polish culture provide us with many arguments for such a vision of 'folk religiosity'. Polish peasants shaped their traditional culture in a reflexive way. Rituals and religious experience included emotions. Human concerns were not shaped automatically, but rather, in a reflexive way. Such reflexively elaborated religious identity could be characterized as 'lived religion'. It encompassed not only the relationship to an abstractly understood state of transcendence but also to the transcendental, social and natural orders, in other words to individual and social identity. Catholicism even in traditional societies played an important social role which can also be studied from the perspective of social agency.

To respond to the metaphor mentioned in the opening paragraphs of this chapter, of European Christians as akin to smooth river stones, it is necessary to note that human subjectivity cannot be easily detached from its cultural and social context. In his statement, Cardinal Lamberto expressed an essentialist vision of human beings which strongly contrasts human nature with the social context. People living in traditional society were formed by its social structure and this social structure affected their nature more than is often assumed.

Notes

1. A peasant is a small landowner who tills the soil, grows crops, keeps animals, etc. and who could be said to belong to the lower social classes.
2. In 1595, the Church in the territory of modern-day Ukraine agreed under the Union of Brest to break relations with the Patriarchate of Constantinople and unite with the Catholic Church. Thus, the Greek Catholics are united with the Catholic Church but follow the Byzantine (Greek) liturgy.
3. The term 'Voivodeship' is based on the title of an administrative official. Originally a 'voievod' was a military commander, literally 'a leader of warriors'.
4. The partitions of Poland started in 1772 as a progressive process of territorial seizures and annexations. They were conducted by the Habsburg Monarchy of Austria (South Poland), the Kingdom of Prussia (West Poland), and the Russian Empire (East and Central Poland). The partitions ended in 1918.
5. In the teachings of the Roman Catholic Church, an indulgence is a way to reduce the amount of punishment one has to undergo after death for one's sins, by prayer, fasting or other forms of activity.
6. 'Desiatina' means 'tenth', in other words, a Tithe, or one-tenth of one's produce or earnings, paid as a contribution to the Church.
7. A city in the south of Poland, famous for the Holy Black Madonna (Virgin Mary) painting in the Jasna Gora Monastery
8. A special form of prayer, practised until now in the Catholic Church.
9. A prayer based on singing litanies to the Virgin Mary.
10. A Lent prayer based on singing songs concerning the Passion of Jesus Christ.

11. A title bestowed on the bishop of the oldest diocese in a country. Comes from the Latin 'primus' what means 'first'.
12. A small group of people who pray together.
13. A vicar in a parish is a priest assigned to the parish who collaborates with the parish priest.

References

Adamczuk, L., Marianski, J., Zdaniewicz, W. (1991). Zycie Religijne [Religious Life]. In: L. Adamczuk, W. Zdaniewicz eds., *Kosciol Katolicki W Polsce 1918-1990. Rocznik statystyczny* [Catholic Church in Poland 1918-1990. Statistical Yearbook]. Warszawa: Glowny Urzad Statystyczny i Zaklad Socjologii Religii SAC, pp. 174–196.

Ambroch, M., Czermak, G., Lisiak, E., Szydlowska, G. (2018). *100 Lat Polski W Liczbach. 1918-2018* [100 Years of Poland in numbers. 1918-2018]. Warszawa: Glowny Urzad Statystyczny.

Archer, M. S. (1988). *Culture and Agency. The Place of Culture in Social Theory.* Cambridge: Cambridge University Press.

Archer, M. S. (2007). *Making Our Way Through the World: Human Reflexivity.* Cambridge: Cambridge University Press. DOI: 10.1017/CBO9780511618932.

Bartminski, J. (2015). Tradycja Uspiona W Jezyku: Pytania O Zrodla Polskiej Tozsamosci Kulturowej [Tradition Dormant in Language: Questions About Sources Of Polish Cultural Identity]. In: J. Adamowski, M. Wojcicka eds., *Wartosci w jezyku i kulturze.* [Values in Language and Culture], Lublin: Wydawnictwo Uniwersytetu Marii Curie-Sklodowskiej, pp. 11–33.

Boudon, R. (1994). *Art of Self-Persuasion: the Social Explanation of False Beliefs.* Cambridge: Polity Press.

Bujak, F. (1903). *Zmiaca. Wies powiatu limanowskiego. Stosunki gospodarcze i spoleczne* [Zmiaca. A Village in the Limanowski District]. Krakow: G. Gebethner i Spolka.

Bujak, F. (1908). *Galicya. Tom I. Kraj. Ludnosc. Spoleczenstwo. Rolnictwo* [Galicyja: Volume I. Country, Population, Society, Agriculture]. Lwow-Warszawa: Ksiegarnia H. Altenberga, E. Wende i Spolka.

Bukraba-Rylska, I. (2008). Religijnosc Ludowa - Zjawisko I Zwiazane Z Nim Kontrowersje [Folk Religiosity – the Phenomenon and Its Controversies]. *Wies i rolnictwo*, 138, pp. 50–73.

Bystron, J. (1936). *Kultura Ludowa* [Folk Culture]. Warszawa: Nasza Ksiegarnia.

Chalasinski, J. (2013[1934]). Wsrod robotnikow polskich w Ameryce [Among Polish Workers in America]. In: G. Firlit-Fesnak, J. Godlewska-Szyrkowa, C. Zoledowski eds., *Migracje i migranci w pismach Ludwika Krzywickiego, Floriana Znanieckiego, Jozefa Chalasinskiego. Wybor tekstow* [Migration and Migrants in the Writings of Ludwik Krzywicki, Florian Znaniecka, Jozef Chalasinski. Selected Texts]. Warszawa: Instytut Polityki Spolecznej Uniwersytetu Warszawskiego, pp. 203–220.

Ciupak, E. (1965). *Kult Religijny I Jego Spoleczne Podloze: Studia Nad Katolicyzmem Polskim* [A Religious Cult and its Social Basis: a Study of Polish Catholicism]. Warszawa: Ludowa Spoldzielnia Wydawnicza.

Ciupak, E. (1968). *Katolicyzm Tradycyjny W Polsce* [Traditional Catholicism in Poland]. Warszawa: Centralny Osrodek Doskonalenia Kadr Laickich.

Ciupak, E. (1973). *Katolicyzm Ludowy W Polsce* [Folk Catholicism in Poland]. Warszawa: Wiedza Powszechna.

Constitution of the Second Republic of Poland. (1921). Dziennik Ustaw, 44(267).

Conway, M. (2008). *Catholic Politics in Europe, 1918-1945*. New York: Routledge.

Czarnowski, S. (1956). Kultura Religijna Wiejskiego Ludu Polskiego [The Religious Culture of Rural Polish Folk]. In: S. Czarnowski. *Studia Z Historii Kultury* [Studies in the History of Culture]. Vol. 1. Warszawa: Panstwowe Wydawnictwo Naukowe, pp. 88–121.

Datko, A. (2016). Polscy Swieci I Blogoslawieni [Polish Saints and the Blessed]. In: P. Ciecielag et al., ed., *1050 lat chrzescijanstwa w Polsce* [1050 Years of Christianity in Poland]. Warszawa: Glowny Urzad Statystyczny and Instytut Statystyki Kosciola Katolickiego SAC, pp. 133–158.

Durkheim, E. (1995[1912]). *The Elementary Forms of Religious Life*. New York: The Free Press (Simon & Schuster).

Dzwonkowski, r (1988). *Polska Opieka Religijna We Francji 1909-1939* [Polish Pastoral Care in France 1909-1939]. Poznan-Warszawa: Pallottinum, Zaklad Socjologii Religii.

Fiddler on the Roof. (1964). [musical] Broadway: Jerry Bock, Sheldon Harnick, Norman Jewison and Joseph Stein.

Finke, R., Stark, R. (2005). *The Churching of America, 1776-2005: Winners and Losers in Our Religious Economy*. New Brunswick, NJ: Rutgers University Press.

Firlit, E. (1990). Ekstensywne Funkcje Parafii [Extensive Parish Functions]. In: E. Firlit et al., ed., *Rola parafii rzymsko-katolickiej w organizacji zycia spolecznego na szczeblu lokalnym* [The Role of Roman-Catholic Parishes in Organizing Local Community Life]. Warszawa: Pallottinum, pp. 104–160.

Gombrowicz, W. (2012[1938]). *Ferdydurke*. Krakow: Wydawnictwo Literackie.

Gordon, M. (1964). *Assimilation in American Life: The Role of Race, Religion, and National Origins*. New York: Oxford University Press.

Greeley, A. (1971). *Why Can't They Be Like Us? America's White Ethnic Groups*. New York: E.P. Dutton.

Grygiel, S., Tischner, J. (1960). Szkic O Religijnosci Wsi Wspolczesnej [Essay On Modern Rural Religiosoity]. *Znak*, 150, pp. 1456–1473.

Guest, K. (2003). *God in Chinatown: Religion and Survival in New York's Evolving Immigrant Community*. New York: New York University Press.

Handlin, O. (2002[1951]). *The Uprooted: The Epic Story of the Great Migrations That Made the American People*. Philadelphia: University of Pennsylvania Press.

Kennedy, R. (1944). *Single or Triple Melting-Pot? Intermarriage Trends in New Haven, 1870-1940*. American Journal of Sociology, 49, pp. 331–339.

Kieniewicz, S. (1968). *Historia Polski 1795-1918* [Polish History 1795-1918]. Warszawa: Panstowe Wydawnictwo Naukowe.

Kosela, K. (1996). Wartosci Polakow W Latach 60. XX Wieku Z Perspektywy Polwiecza [The Values of Poles in the 1960s from the Perspective of the 20th Century]. In: E. Czaczkowska ed., *Milenium Chrztu Polski Prymasa Stefana Wyszynskiego. Perspektywa Teologiczno-Spoleczna* [The Millenium of the Baptism of Poland of the Primate Stefan Wyszynski. A Theological-Social Perspective]. Warszawa: Wydawnictwo Naukowe Uniwersytetu Kardynala Stefana Wyszynskiego, pp. 185–216.

Kosela, K. (2003). *Polak-Katolik. Splatana Tozsamosc* [Pole-Catholic: Confused Identity]. Warszawa: Instytut Filozofii I Soscjologii Polskiej Akademii Nauk.

Luczewski, M. (2007). *Popular Religion as Morality, Interpretation and Process.* *Ethnologia Polonica*, 28, pp. 5–21.

Majka, J. (1980). Uwarunkowania Katolicyzmu Polskiego [The Context of Polish Catholicism]. *Chrzescijanin w swiecie. Zeszyty ODiSS*, 94, pp. 27–44.

Marianski, J. (1983). Religijnosc Ludowa Na Wsi [Folk Religiosity in the Countryside]. In: W. Piwowarski ed., *Religijnosc Ludowa. Ciaglosc I Zmiana* [Folk Religiosity. Continuity and Change]. Wroclaw: Wydawnictwo Wroclawskiej Ksiegarni Archidiecezjalnej, pp. 241–280.

Marianski, J. (1991a). *Religijnosc W Procesie Przemian. Szkice Socjologiczne.* [Religiosity in the Process of Transition]. Warszawa: Instytut Wydawniczy Pax.

Marianski, J. (1991b). Katolicy W Strukturze Wyznaniowej Polski [Catholics in the Religious Structure of Poland]. In: L. Adamczuk, W. Zdaniewicz eds., *Kosciol Katolicki W Polsce 1918-1990. Rocznik Statystyczny* [Catholic Church in Poland 1918-1990. Statistical Yearbook]. Warszawa: Glowny Urzad Statystyczny – Zaklad Socjologii Religii SAC, pp. 37–56.

Milton, G. (1964). *Assimilation in American Life: The Role of Race, Religion, and National Origins.* New York: Oxford University Press.

Niedzwiedz, A. (2014). Od Kultury Ludowej Do Religii Przezywanej [From Folk Culture to Lived Religion]. In: B. Fatyga, R. Michalski eds., *Kultura Ludowa. Teorie, Praktyki, Polityki* [Folk Culture. Theories, Practices, Politics]. Warszawa: Instytut Stosowanych Nauk Spolecznych, pp. 327–338.

Pawelczynska, A. (1964). *W Powiatowym Miescie* [In a Local Town]. Warszawa: Osrodek Badania Opinii Publicznej.

Pawelczynska, A. (1969). *Studia Nad Czytelnictwem* [A Study on Reading]. Warszawa: Osrodek Badania Opinii Publicznej.

Pawelczynska, A. (1970). Postawy Ludnosci Wiejskiej Wobec Religii [Attitudes to Religion Among Rural Populations]. *Roczniki Socjologii Wsi. Studia i materialy*, 8. Wroclaw, pp. 71–93.

Piwowarski, W. (1968). Kontekst Spoleczenstwa Pluralistycznego a Problem Permanentnej Socjalizacji Religijnej [The Context of Pluralist Society and the Problem of Permanent Religious Socialization]. In: W. Piwowarski, W. Zdaniewicz eds., *Z badan nad religijnoscia polska. Studia i materialy* [From Research on Polish Religiosity. Studies and Materials]. Poznan-Warszawa: Pallottinum, pp. 73–82.

Piwowarski, W. (1968). The Image of the Priest in the Eyes of Parishioners in Three Rural Parishes. *Social Compass*, 38, pp. 235–249.

Piwowarski, W. (1981). Les orientations, les methodes et la problematique dans la sociologie de la religion en Pologne (1957-1977). In: W. Zdaniewicz ed., *Religiousness in the Polish Society Life. Chosen Problems.* Warszawa: Pallottinum, pp. 7–33.

Piwowarski, W. (1982). Continuity and Change of Ritual in Polish Folk Piety. *Social Compass*, 29(2–3), pp. 125–134.

Piwowarski, W. (1983). Wprowadzenie [Introduction]. In: W. Piwowarski ed., [Folk Religiosity. Continuity and Change]. Religijnosc Ludowa. Ciaglosc I Zmiana. Wroclaw: Wydawnictwo Wroclawskiej Ksiegarni Archidiecezjalnej, pp. 5–20.

Siekierski, S. (1995). *Kulturotworcze funkcje parafii katolickiej w spolecznosciach lokalnych w swietle pamietnikow.* [The Cultural Functions of Catholic Parishes in Local Communities According to Diaries]. Warszawa: Wydawnictwo Uniwersytetu Warszawskiego.

Smith, T. (1978). Religion and Ethnicity in America. *American Historical Review*, 83, pp. 1155–1185.

Stachura, P. (2004) The Poles in Scotland: 1940-1950. In: P. Stachura ed., *Poles in Britain: 1940-2000*. London: Frank Cass Publishers.

Statistics Poland (1939). *Maly Rocznik Statystyczny 1939* [Small Statistical Yearbook 1939]. Warszawa.

Stomma, L. (2002). *Antropologia kultury wsi polskiej XIX w. oraz wybrane eseje* [The Cultural Anthropology of the Polish Countryside in 19th Century and Some Essays]. Lodz: Piotr Dopierala.

Swiecicki, A. (1977). Situation De La Sociologie Des Religions En Pologne. In: *Acts of the 14th International Conference on Sociologie of Religion. Strasbourg 1977*. Lille: CISR, pp. 409–437.

Taras, P. (1989). *Polonia w Detroit. Problem kulturowej tozsamosci i spolecznego awansu. Socjologiczne studium spolecznosci etnicznej w USA* [Polonia in Detroit: The Problem of Cultural Identity and Social Promotion. A Sociological Study of an Ethnic Community in the USA]. Warszawa: Pallottinum and Zaklad Socjologii Religii SAC.

Taylor, C. (2007). *A Secular Age*. Cambridge: The Belknap Press of Harvard University Press. DOI: 10.1007/s10677-009-9212-4.

The Godfather. (1972). [film] Los Angeles: Francis Ford Coppola.

Thomas, W., Znaniecki, F. (1920). *The Polish Peasant in Europe and America: A Classic Work in Immigration History. Volume 5: Organization and Disorganization in America*. Boston: The Gorham Press.

Thomas, W., Znaniecki, F. (1927). *The Polish Peasant in Europe and America. Volume I: Primary-Group Organization*. New York: Alfred A. Knopf.

Tomicki, R. (1981). Religijnosc Ludowa [Folk Religiosity]. In: M. Biernacka, M. Frankowska and W. Paprocka. *Etnografia Polski. Przemiany Kultury Ludowej* [An Ethnography of Poland. Changes within Folk Culture]. Vol. II. Wroclaw: Zaklad Narodowy Imienia Ossolinskich - Wydawnictwo Polskiej Akademii Nauk, pp. 29–70.

Wat, A. (1990). *Moj Wiek. Pamietnik Mowiony* [My Century. Spoken Memories]. Warszawa: Czytelnik.

Wieruszewska-Adamczyk, M. (1978). *Przemiany Spolecznosci Wiejskiej. Zaborow Po 35 Latach* [The Transformation of Rural Communities: Zaborow 35 Years Later]. Warszawa: Instytut Rozwoju Wsi i Rolnictwa Polskiej Akademii Nauk.

Wierzbicki, Z. (1963). *ZMiaca W Pol Wieku* [Zmiaca: Half a Century Later]. Wroclaw – Warszawa – Krakow: Instytut Filozofii i Socjologii Polskiej Akademii Nauk.

Wierzbicki, Z. (1979). Tradycyjna Religijnosc Wiejska [Traditional Religiosity in Rural Areas]. *Roczniki Nauk Spolecznych KUL*, pp. 115–176.

Wilson, B. (1988). The Functions of Religion: a Reappraisal. *Religion*, 18, pp. 199–216.

Witos, W. (1978). *Moje Wspomnienia* [My Memories]. Warszawa: Ludowa Spoldzielnia Wydawnicza.

Witos, W. (1998). *Moje Wspomnienia*. Vol. I [My Memories]. Warszawa: Ludowa Spoldzielnia Wydawnicza.

Zarnowski, J. (1973). *Spoleczenstwo II Rzeczypospolitej. 1918-1939*. [Society in the 2nd Warszawa: Panstwowe Wydawnictwo Naukowe..

Zdaniewicz, W. (1978). *Kosciol Katolicki W Polsce 1987* [The Catholic Church in Poland 1987]. Poznan: Pallottinum.

Zybrzycki, G. (2015). Religion, Religious Tradition, and Nationalism: Jewish Revival in Poland and 'Religious Heritage' in Quebec. *Journal for the Scientific Study of Religion*, 51(3), pp. 442–455. DOI: 10.1111/j.1468-5906.2012.01666.x.

4   Modern Polish society
and religious identity

Photo 2 Priests during Youth Mass in Lednica in 2018. Photo: Author.

In terms of religious dynamics, Polish society at the turn of 21st century is often characterized as an exception (Joas, 2007). From the perspective of social transformation theory, the question is raised as to whether contemporary Poland is really a modern society. Some authors claim that the social processes which shaped the religious landscape in Poland since the 1980s are incomplete (Ascherson, 2011) and that the Polish transformation should therefore be labelled 'fake modernity' (Sztompka, 1991). As my primary focus is on religion, I do not wish to engage in the debate concerning the character of Polish modernization. However, from such a perspective it could be stated at the outset that after the period of Communism and civil mobilization in the 1980s, and after the democratic breakthrough, Poland embarked upon its new phase of modernization in 1989. This modernization was, of course, not a linear path but involved a very multifaceted political, economic, cultural and also religious process. Nowadays we understand much better than we did decades ago, that religious changes in Poland should not be described as deterministic or one-dimensional.

From the perspective of critical realism and especially Archer's perspective of morphogenesis, in the transition from Communism the Polish cultural system has been strongly and actively conditioned by collective agency. Catholicism played a crucial role in the morphogenesis of the society. Religious ideas and beliefs, as components accumulated within traditional Polish culture, causally influenced the socio-cultural level of the society. Moreover, individuals and groups exerted pivotal influence at the socio-cultural level. The transition from Communism into a more democratic system entailed the modification of the cultural system due to new interactions at the socio-cultural level. The growing agency of Catholicism within Polish society contributed to the general morphogenesis of the whole society. At this time religion was to some extent being introduced into political aspects of social life. After a period of post-war political marginalization, Catholicism began to play a public role, especially in the Solidarity era from 1980. The new political situation after 1989 resulted in the institutionalization of Catholicism.

In this chapter I will describe how religious identity became embedded in Polish society both at the level of the individual and from the perspective of institutions. I will present empirical data from the research conducted by myself and others on aspects of religious participation and belief, and daily life values and practices, and I will use this data to draw conclusions related to the above themes. It is of course not possible to include all aspects of the religious dynamics of modern Polish society. I will limit this study to some crucial elements from the perspective of morphogenesis. This focus on modern Polish Catholicism facilitates a better understanding of the religious background of Polish migrants, which will be examined in the next chapter and is the continuation of issues raised in the previous chapter, namely the relationship between the social, practical and natural orders and transcendence in Polish society. I am aware that the concept of modernity implies the time ahead of us so it is very difficult to grasp the 'now' in a sociological study. In this chapter my focus is on Polish Catholicism around the changeover from the 20th to the 21st century. My perspective for studying the transformation of modern Polish Catholicism goes beyond the dominant approach up till now, that is, seeing it as a one-dimensional secularization process. Instead I see it as a matter of social agency.

A cultural elaboration of Polish Catholicism

The demographic configuration of the nation is the result of social mobility during and after the Second World War. In 1939 after the signing of the secret Molotov-Ribbentrop pact, the Soviet Army invaded eastern Poland and German Soldiers invaded the west. Thus, Polish territory was divided between the Germans and the Soviets. During the War, Soviet and German secret services murdered or deported members of numerous Polish social groups to Siberia, Kazakhstan and Germany. In 1944 population transfers of Poles were initiated from the so-called *Kresy* [Borderlands], that is, the prewar eastern parts of Poland. In 1945 the Yalta Conference, known also as the Crimea Conference, agreed that Poland's borders should be changed. The President of the United States, Franklin Roosevelt, the Prime Minister of the United Kingdom, Winston Churchill, and the Premier of the Soviet Union, Joseph Stalin, decided to expel more than one million ethnic Poles from the *Kresy* to the western part of the new Polish territory. This was because, in 1943, during the Teheran Conference, these eastern Polish areas, which had been annexed by the Soviet Union, were formally incorporated into the Ukrainian, Lithuanian and Belarusian Republic of the Soviet Union. Subsequently between 1945 and 1946, according to some estimates, more than one million Poles left their local communities and moved to the western regions of Poland (Ciesielski, 1999). Later, from 1955 to 1959, a new process of deportation from *Kresy* was launched.

The recent history of Polish Catholicism is evidence that religious life should not be seen as static and resulting from institutional frameworks. As described in the previous chapter, the moral character of the national Polish community had become intertwined with religious values and religious identities. Despite being excluded from the public sphere, religion played a public role, a facet which has been revealed at critical moments of Polish history. As discussed above, in the Communist era, Catholicism in Poland continued to develop despite its weakened institutional and church infrastructure. The writings of Janusz Marianski show an awareness that any description of religious transformation in Poland in terms of a transition from traditional to intellectual, ethical or existential is strongly reductionist (1991, p. 318–320). For decades, two opposing forces shaped the situation of Catholicism in Poland – socialist activists and Catholic nationalists. The former emanated from the so-called 'secular intelligentsia' who were distanced from both the Communist state and Catholicism. Since 1956 many intellectuals began to criticize publicly not only religious institutions but also religious beliefs and ideas (Grabowska, 2008, p. 26). Yet such opposition between Catholicism and elements of the social elite had already been observed much earlier, by the end of the 19th century. Piotr Cywinski, in a very imaginative way, has described how the ideology of Catholic nationalists contrasted with that of socialist activists (Cywinski, 2010[1971]). However specific historical situations, especially occupation by foreign powers and the patriotic attitudes this provoked opened up new perspectives on reconciliation for both ideological camps. In parallel to the situation since 1956, some Polish cultural elites joined with the Catholic Church in the struggle against Communism. Such 'social union' gave power to the new mass mobilization of the 1980s (Gawin, 2013).

In the Communist era the role of religion in the public sphere in Poland was based upon opposing the version of official citizenship presented by the Communist authorities and was strongly linked to appeals for religious freedom. Despite the policy pursued by the Polish People's Republic in the 1950s, 1960s and 1970s, which aimed at excluding the Church from society, subsequently, together with the Solidarity movement and the inspirational grassroots transformations of the 1980s, the Catholic Church had become a symbol of freedom and an inspiration for systemic change. This greatly enhanced the historic link between Catholicism and national identity and renewed the symbolic role of the Church in shaping the national community. The Church, with its basic function of evangelization, stood in defence of democracy and human rights (Borowik, 2002), which meant the Catholic Church had a presence in the political sphere (Jasiukiewicz, 1993). Catholicism was allied with the struggle for freedom and national identity. The sense of being a Pole was related to some kind of national community rather than to a civil (political) institution. Catholicism was a source of symbolic power and a justification for the specific ethics of the Solidarity movement or even, it could be said, the spirituality of *Solidarnosc* (Krzeminski, 2013, pp. 136–140).

Polish Catholicism was strongly affected by the election of John Paul II who, with his dynamic pontificate, confirmed the social role of the Church in Poland. The Pope strongly influenced the Solidarity Movement, welcoming members of Polish trade unions to Rome in 1981. While visiting Poland, John Paul II met Lech Walesa in 1983 and 1987. Many other priests also exerted a strong influence on the Solidarity Movement. Such individuals as Rev. Jozef Tischner, Fr. Ludwik Wisniewski, Rev. Jan Zieja, Rev. Stanislaw Jankowski and Rev. Edward Frankowski shaped the course of social mobilization in Poland. In the 1980s, the Polish Episcopate demanded labour rights for Polish workers and actively encouraged the movement of *Solidarnosc* to represent the Polish nation. Moreover Catholicism was able to integrate some formal and informal organizations which advocated human rights and social freedom, such as *Komitet Obrony Robotnikow* [Workers' Defense Committee], *Ruch Mlodej Polski* [Young Poland Movement, *Ruch Obrony Praw Czlowieka i Obywatela* [Movement for the Defence of Human and Civil Rights], and *Konfederacja Polski Niepodleglej* [Confederation of Independent Poland] (Weigel, 2000, p. 505).

Polish Catholicism was rigorist rather than conservative. This means that religious dynamism within Polish society implied strict and authoritarian moral rules and norms rather than a conservative attitude towards the social order in terms of social stratification or authority. The distinguishing characteristics of Polish Catholicism were seen as a commitment to confession and an unequivocal attitude towards the sacraments. Religion in Poland was not an institutionalized burden: rather, it represented an inspiring and stimulating force (Majka, 1980, p. 39). Jozef Majka, when describing the religiosity of Polish society in the 1980s, claimed that some elements of secularization were traceable to the sphere of 'everyday life' (that is, the socio-cultural system) rather than to the domain of theological concepts shared by believers (the cultural system) (1980). In this way, it is important to distinguish the secularization of human behaviour and lifestyle from the secularization of the 'religious system'. When religious values, norms and forms are alienated from their transcendental elements, the religious system is in danger of becoming assimilated into secular systems (Majka, 1980, p. 33). Majka claimed that the cultural system of Polish Catholicism has preserved strong experiences of transcendence and was not easily subject to laicization (1980, p. 33). The impact of the secularization process occurring elsewhere in Europe was limited due to the fact that the Church also defended humanistic values, such as human dignity. In this way the Catholic Church in 1980s became the only 'native' institution for Poles (Szajkowski, 1983) and the voice of Polish society (Morawska, 1984). It combined faith with the pursuit of civil freedom, politics and culture. This demonstrates the strong integration of the institution of the Church with other social spheres.

Polish political transformation in the 1980s was initiated as a top-down process. Piwowarski claims that it was a 'top-down revolution' and argues that it hardly affected human attitudes. 'The concept of "popular democracy" implies the laicity of the state or even atheism. In Poland this model was faced with a "closed" and historically experienced Catholic society, which understood itself to be a "national state", fighting for independence and freedom.' (Piwowarski, 1983, p. 341) However, it is also worth noting that the religious revival in the 1980s corresponded with the decline in socialist ideology in public life and its identification with Marxist philosophy in people's minds (Marianski, 1991, p. 322).

The democratic breakthrough of 1989 opened up a new perspective for Catholicism in Poland. Thus, it could be said that the Catholic Church has been infiltrating the political system since 1989 with a high level of social capital, which manifested in its involvement in social transformation and grassroots activism. According to some Western experts, the Catholic Church in Poland emerged from the Communist era not only as the highest moral authority but also as the most powerful institution in the country (Eberts, 1998, p. 820). As a result of the Round Table Agreement in 1989 *Solidarnosc* became a legal political party. In the subsequent democratic elections anti-communist candidates attained the majority in parliament. Since the 1990s a new phase of Catholicism has been established. After the breakdown of Communism, the Catholic Church started on a long path of institutionalization. One of the most important contributions to political transformation in Poland was the introduction of new legislation relating to religious communities, including the Catholic Church. After the Cabinet of Tadeusz Mazowiecki decided on 2 August 1990 to include religion in the curriculum of public education, the Church made great efforts to prepare and organize religious teaching in schools, thus giving up almost entirely the practice of catechesis in parishes. Social insurance was introduced for clergyman and consecrated persons as a compensation for Church properties which had been confiscated by the Communist state. Abortion, after being totally legalized during the Communist period, was partially restricted again and religious education returned to public schools.

Some authors claim that the groundwork for the Polish version of civil religion was prepared at this time (Morawska, 1984), but such statements – often repeated by foreign observers – seem very superficial nowadays, from the perspective of 30 years later. Of course, the legal position of the Church was confirmed in the democratic reforms, which opposed the oppressive attitude of the former Communist state towards Catholicism. However, the Catholic Church has never been accepted as an 'official state religion'. As outlined in the Polish Constitution promulgated in 1997, the Polish state and religious organizations in Poland declare mutual 'respect for their autonomy and the mutual independence of each in its own sphere, as well as recognition for the principle of cooperation, for the individual and the common good'. What is more, 'Churches and other religious organizations shall have equal rights' (The Constitution of the Republic of Poland, art. 25). 'Released' after 1989 into the public space, Catholicism has not transformed into the Polish *civil religion* (Bellah, 1967) but has begun expanding its support in the form of organizational structures and institutions. During the first decades of the Polish transformation, some forms of anticlericalism and even political opposition to the public role of the Church were a relatively constant element of social life in Poland. Some anti-Catholic proposals such as the exclusion of religious education from public schools or the suppression of any form of public financial contribution to Church institutions were mentioned in socialist and post-Communist political party circles in Poland. The changing role of Catholicism in Poland also corresponds to the changing dynamics of trust in the institution of the Church. The highest degree of trust was observed before 1990 when the Catholic Church strongly supported the Solidarity movement and political mobilization. In the 1990s trust in the Church rapidly declined, which could be interpreted as resulting from its direct involvement in political and institutional conflicts in the country. At the turn of this century the attitude towards the Catholic Church was relatively stable until 2010,[1] when, after the emergence of new political conflict, the Church was often represented in the public sphere as an active participant in the political confrontations. Since that time trust in the Church has been steadily declining.

In 2008, the Polish Bishops' Conference published *Rules Governing the Formal Act of Defection From the Church*. According to this document 'the act of apostasy that has canonical consequences can only be performed by a person who is of age […] and has the legal capacity, in person, in a conscious and free way […], in writing, in the presence of the priest of the parish where he resides (permanently or temporarily), and two witnesses who are of age' (Conference of Polish Bishops, 2008, p. 5). In 2011, a strong campaign for religious apostasy in Poland was organized mainly by political forces and the anticlerical and antireligious party *Ruch Palikota* [Palikot's[2] Movement] gained about 10 percent of the vote in the parliamentary election of 2011. Happenings, demonstrations, as well as campaigns using social media, the Internet and public media were organized. In the 2019 European Union Parliamentary election, the political party *Wiosna* [Spring], which officially opposed the Catholic Church, was supported by more than six percent of voters. In 2018 and 2019 negative attitudes towards the Church were strengthened by sexual abuse scandals involving the clergy (Feliksiak, 2019a). These scandals shocked Polish society, especially in 2019 when the documentary film *Tylko nie mow nikomu* [Tell No One], about the abuse of minors by Catholic priests and the covering up of the perpetrators' actions by bishops, was posted on the Internet and watched by more than 20 million people.

Institutionalization

The Catholic Church in Poland at the turn of the century was character-ized by high levels of dynamic change which included also the process of institutionalization. After 1989 a progressive re-institutionalization of the Catholic Church in Poland can be observed. Despite this fact, Margaret Archer claims that 'in itself institutionalization is perfectly neutral with regard to morphostasis or morphogenesis' (Archer, 1988, p. 264) and the institutional aspect of religion in a society should be discerned from reli-giousness understood in terms of the socio-cultural system, without a study of its institutionalization, our understanding of changes within modern Polish Catholicism would be defective. As Elzbieta Firlit notes, the strong institutionalization of Polish Catholicism implies the need to investigate the adequacy of religious structures and 'religious communication' in post-1989 Poland (Firlit, 2014).

In Poland before 1989, there were 40 church denominations and religious associations officially registered by the state. Nowadays this number has increased to 178. The majority of them (97) were registered between the years 1990–1999. Since 2000, the incidence of newly registered confessions began to weaken. During the last 15 years no more than 33 new confessions have been registered (Gudaszewski, 2015, p. 93). According to the Polish census of 2011, which for the first time since the 1930s included a question on religious affiliation, the percentage of Catholics varied from 88.8 percent to 97.3 percent of the population. This high level of variance is a result of the non-response rate, as answering the question on religious affiliation was not obligatory in the census. The second largest religious group in Poland is the Greek Catholic Church. However the percentage of the Polish popu-lation who are affiliated with the Greek-Catholic Church does not exceed 0.44 percent. The third largest religious group is the Jehovah Witnesses, making up no more than 0.39 percent of the population. The percentage of people who do not belong to any religious group ranges from 2.41 per-cent to 2.64 percent depending upon the interpretation of the non-response rate (Gudaszewski, 2015, p. 93). The Pentecostal Church in Poland currently has about 23 000 members, divided into two communities, the Christian Pentecostal Community and the Evangelical Pentecostal Community (Ciecielag et al., 2016).

Without doubt, the Catholic Church is the most important religious institution in Poland. In the last three decades of the 21st century, more than 90 percent of new-born children have been baptized in the Catholic Church. In the second decade of the 21st century the level of Catholic affiliation in Poland clearly exceeds 90 percent and is relatively equal to the proportion of people who declare their belief in God. After 1989, the network of the Catholic Dioceses in Poland has been greatly expanded. Since 1972 there were 27 Diocesan units in Poland, including 24 Dioceses and 3 Apostolic Administrations[3] (in Bialystok, Drohiczyn and Lubaczow). In 1991, the Military Ordinariate[4] was restored in Poland. In 1992, nearly 20 new Dioceses were delineated. In 2004, 2 new Dioceses, Bydgoszcz and Swidnica, were created. As a result, since 2004, the administrative structure of the Catholic Church has been constituted by 44 entities: 41 Roman Dioceses, the Military Ordinariate of Poland, and 2 Dioceses of the Greek Catholic Rite. The increase in the number of Dioceses in Poland is also reflected in the number of bishops.

In the last three decades the organizational structure of the Catholic Church in Poland has been growing rapidly. The growth is even more striking in comparison with other countries (Zech et al., 2017) and is especially evident in the statistics on parishes and priests – both diocesan and religious.[5] For instance, the number of Catholic parishes in Poland shows a steady increase. In 1974 there were 7057 parishes. By 1985 the number of parishes had risen to 8302. At present (2017) the number of Catholic parishes is 10 378 (Figure 4.1). In recent years about 30 new parishes are formed in Poland every year but the growth-rate is now slowing down. At the turn

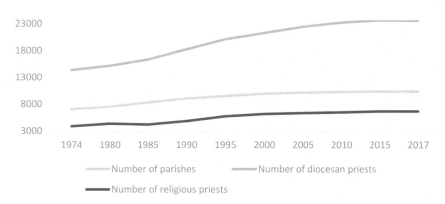

Figure 4.1 Number of Catholic parishes and priests from 1974 to 2017.

Source: Secretary of State of Holy See, 1974–7.

of this century, the number of diocesan and religious priests in Poland was steadily increasing. In 1980, at the beginning of the pontificate of John Paul II, there were 15 157 diocesan priests, and at the time of the Pope's death (2005), this figure had increased to 22 448, which means an increase of 48 percent. Between 1990 and 2010 the number of priests increased by 4978, i.e., by 27 percent. In terms of age, Polish priests are quite young. In 2010 more than half of them were under 50 years old, and 30 percent were under 40 (Zdaniewicz and Sadlon, 1).

In parallel with the slight decrease in the population in Poland in recent decades, the average number of parishioners in a Catholic parish in Poland is decreasing. In 1991, on average, there were 4031 people in one parish, decreasing to 3282 in 2011. Exactly 64 percent, a majority of all parishes, are located in rural areas, 15 percent represent so-called rural-city parishes which are most often located in cities, but encompass rural areas as well and 21 percent of parishes are located in cities. However, it is crucial to note that no more than 35 percent of the whole Polish Catholic population dwell in rural parishes compared with 39.8 percent of the total Polish rural population, the remaining 60.2 percent being urban dwellers (Sadlon, 2019a, pp. 358–359). This means that the character of parishes in the countryside compared with those in the cities is different in terms of the concentration of Catholics.

The process of institutionalization of Polish Catholicism during the last three decades refers especially to religious education. After the Second World War Catholic religious education was very limited, and took place only in the 'parish space'. The Church operated no more than eight schools and religious education was offered in (over ten thousand) 'catechetical points' organized within parishes and private homes. Only 300 catechetical points operated in public premises (Zurek, 1996, p. 7). After 1989, the number of Catholic schools in Poland grew steadily and since then the situation of religious education has changed rapidly. For instance, in the 2010s, 58 000 pupils attended 540 Catholic schools (Jaron, 2014, p. 232). In the 2010s 36 000 public schools offered religious education which accounted for 86 percent of all public schools in Poland and the number of 'teachers of religion', designated by the Catholic Church and employed in these public schools, amounted to 31 000. The majority (55 percent) were lay people, 34 percent were diocesan priests, 8 percent, nuns and 3 percent, religious priests. The data shows that the participation of Polish youth in religious education is widespread. Moreover, the dynamics of Polish Catholicism is confirmed by the dynamics of attendance at religious education in public schools in Poland. Since religious education began in public schools in 1990, declared participation in religious classes had been growing, from 81 percent in 1991 to 93 percent in 2010. However, since 2010 the proportion of students who declare their attendance at religious classes has been rapidly declining. In 2018 no more than 70 percent declared taking part in public religious education (Grabowska and Gwiazda, 2019, p. 162-165).

Since 1989 the Church has also shown an intense focus on developing charitable institutions. Compared to 1950, when the state authorities liquidated the National Caritas[6] Headquarters and the Church ran only 16 establishments – mainly social assistance homes such as orphanages - today we are observing the re-emergence of charitable institutions run by the Church. In the Dioceses the charity lies within the responsibility of the diocesan branch of Caritas, while male and female members of monastic Orders carry out their own charitable work. In 2014 there were over 800 charitable Church institutions in Poland, who conducted 5000 varieties of charitable work with 2.9 million beneficiaries (Sadlon, 2015b).

Social interactions

In his famous book *Public Religions in the Modern World* Jose Casanova reviews the historical role of Polish Catholicism in shaping the political situation in Poland, and highlights the possibility of the Catholic Church playing a social role even in pluralized and differentiated societies (1994, p. 92-113). However, as a key category for the characterization of religion in Poland, Jay Demerath adopts the term 'cultural religion'. He argues that the specific configuration of recent Polish history, especially in the 1980s resulted in strong bonds between politics, represented by the Solidarity Movement, and the Catholic Church. Catholicism became a criterion of national identity. 'To be Polish was to be Catholic; supporting the new Poland involved attending the old services' (Demerath, 2000, p. 128). For Demerath, such a form of religiosity denotes a manifestation of an eroded form of religion and 'the penultimate stage of religious secularization' (2000, p. 136-137).

The 'most religious' areas in Poland are the rural regions and the 'least religious' areas are the big cities. No other characteristics differentiate religious attitudes in Poland so strongly as age and location. When 'level of education' is correlated with 'religious attitudes', the distribution is quite even. But religious attitudes in Poland is strongly correlated with location. In other words, the Polish map of religiosity is highly differentiated. For some statistical indicators of religious practices, the gap between south Poland and northwest Poland exceeds 50 percentage points. For example, in the Diocese of Tarnow, one of the most religious areas in Poland, the *dominicantes*[7] indicator exceeded 70 percent of resident Catholics in 2017, while in the Diocese of Szczecin-Kamien it was estimated to be 22.7 percent (Sadlon, 2019b). In terms of religious practices, in some regions, especially in southeast Poland, more than 70 percent attend Holy Mass every Sunday. According to this indicator, the most 'religious' regions are in the east, such as Galicja (southeast) and Podlasie (northeast). Less religious are the western regions of Poland and the bigger cities. Thus we can see that religious practices in Poland vary greatly according to location.

Krzysztof Kosela strongly relates the social role of Catholicism with the resonance between religious and social affiliation. He even claims that 'It is not evident now, if traditional communities such as confessional, national, regional, professional, and sectional, will be able to accompany the process of modernization of Polish society', and that the 'confessional community is at risk in the face of growing pluralism' (Kosela, 2003, pp. 316–318). The diagnosis corresponds with the characterization of Polish Catholicism in the 'secular age' as proposed by Charles Taylor (2007). The so-called post-Durkheimian link between agential powers of Catholicism in shaping national identity could explain 'what is taking place in contemporary Ireland, or what is beginning to emerge in Poland' (Taylor, 2007, p. 491).

Many books have been written about the political influence of Polish Catholicism (Koczanowicz, Singer, Kellogg and Nysler, 2005; Zubrzycki, 2006 and Grzymala-Busse, 2015). While not repeating their conclusions here, I nevertheless want to highlight the fact that, since 1989, crucial changes have been observed in the relationship between the social and transcendental orders. According to Gergley Rosta's analysis the role of religion in determining people's political attitudes in Poland has been growing since 1990. The correlation between the religious attitudes of Poles and their right-wing political preferences had grown stronger by 2010, relative to data from 1990 and 1999. According to Rosta, political polarization based on religion has taken place in Poland, that is, the correlation between religion and political preferences is growing in Polish society (Rosta, 2014). The hypothesis of political and religious polarization, that is, the growing level of disagreement within Polish society (Sadlon, 2016a), is substantiated also by the increasing incidence of 'hate crimes' in Poland, which include crimes against religious freedom. For example, from 2012 to 2014, 908 acts of desecration of Catholic holy places (that is, churches, crosses, etc.) were recorded. During this period, priests in 12 percent of more than 10 000 Catholic parishes reported acts of discrimination (Sadlon, 2015a, p. 23).

However the relationship between social ties and religious attitudes is not limited to the context of national identity. The erosion of social cohesion has been mentioned as one of the most important factors in religious change in the second part of the 20th century, (Kubiak, 1972). In this domain Elzbieta Firlit notes the growing erosion of Polish Catholics' ties with their parish (2013a; 2013b). Therefore, Marianski's conclusion that the transformation of religiosity in Poland relates primarily to religious practices and to ties with the institution of the Church is most appropriate. Despite the fact that the majority of Poles still declare themselves to be attached to their local parish, at least to some extent, the general identification of individuals with a parish is declining. In 1991, 85 percent of Polish respondents identified themselves with a parish and by 2012 the figure was 75 percent (Firlit, 2013a, p. 135). Local social bonds related to the parish are much stronger in rural areas than in urban zones. In the countryside people often know parish priests personally and are more likely to be practically engaged in activities within their parishes (for example, participation in prayer groups) (Firlit, 2013a, p. 135). That is why differences between levels of religious practice and religious participation in parish-based Catholic organizations across the regions in Poland is often explained by their degree of urbanization (Lyson, 2014). In the biggest cities (having over 500 000 inhabitants), 83.5 percent of inhabitants declare their affiliation to the Roman Catholic Church, while in the rural areas, this figure is 96.3 percent (Ciecielag and Boryszewski, 2017, p. 115). The decline in religious affiliation is much deeper in big cities where, in 2018, non-believers represented 18 percent of the population compared to 7 percent in the general population (Grabowska, 2018, p. 172).

Strong differences can be observed between religious socialization in urban and rural areas. In the countryside religiosity is traditionally found among young people as well as adults. In small villages the youth are more influenced by religious institutions and their family environments than are youth in cities. Young people born in the countryside, supported in their religious socialization by their parents and the local community, perceive their religiosity once in the city above all through the prism of the rural environment. After leaving the village young people adopt new religious patterns and their original religiosity declines. Being a student in the city means detaching oneself from the original, inherited family religiosity. In the statistics pertaining to the life stage of student hood, there is no essential difference between the religiosity of young people coming from small villages or from cities. However, the disparity between religiosity as practised in the family context and personal commitment to religion during one's student days is even bigger among students coming from the village as compared with those from big cities. Children raised in cities during childhood experience their religiousness intensely, but the removal of support from the close kin environment (that is, the family) when they become students leads to the disappearance of this religiosity (Sadlon, 2020a).

Polish society at the beginning of the transformation was characterized by 'mechanical solidarity' but during the process, changes could be discerned in the direction of 'organic solidarity'. In order to describe the general religious situation in Poland, Wladyslaw Piwowarski (1996) implemented the concept of 'Church of choice' formulated by the German theologian Karl Rahner (1904-1984). This famous Jesuit defined the situation of Christianity in the modern world as a diaspora. He claimed that in pluralist societies faith is no more a matter of intergenerational heritage:

> Everyone must be conquered anew by a promotion campaign that appeals to his personal decision, to the autonomous individuality in a human being, not by a style of promotion where the human being is regarded to be no more than an element of the homogeneous masses, or as the

> product of a situation, of "public opinion" or of tradition. Christianity
> is turning from "the Christianity of fate" to "the Christianity of choice".
> (Rahner, 1959, p. 33)

In a similar way to Rahner, Wladyslaw Piwowarski contrasted the traditional Polish 'People's Church' to the 'Church of choice' (1996). The 'Christianity of choice' also implies a degree of selectivity in religious beliefs and moral rules. Piwowarski labelled this process as 'subjectivation' and claimed that religion in Poland had ceased to be transmitted within the general socio-cultural system (1986). In this context the role of consciousness and individual freedom in moral behaviour has increased. According to Piwowarski (1986), the evaluation of Polish religiosity would depend on the degree of integration of the family with Catholicism. Research on religiosity among youth has shown that religious socialization in Poland is a matter for the family, much more than school or other social milieus. Among parents, mothers are more religious than fathers, however the impact factor of both parents on children's religiosity is more or less equal. Negative attitudes towards religion among young people result from personal disaffection with religious institutions (Sadlon, 2020a).

Between movements and events

Up until the present day, the dynamics of Polish Catholicism have been affected by the historical events of the 1970s and 1980s (Grabowska, 2005). In the late 1970s religious experience in Poland found a new form in emerging new Catholic communities. After the Second Vatican Council (1962-1965), new types of religious organization were 'transplanted' into Poland from other Catholic countries such as Italy, Spain or France. Some new religious movements have also originated in Poland. The most significant of these is the *Light–Life Movement*, a Christian revival movement, founded by Franciszek Blachnicki. In its first stage the movement (also known as *Oasis*) focused on activity within parishes. The principal objective of the movement was to transform Catholic parish organizations into inclusive communities. Its activities included promoting temperance as well as pro-life and pro-family activities. These concerns imply moral and spiritual liberation from selfishness and sin (Sadlon, 2020b, p. 164-168). Miroslawa Grabowska interprets this religious change in terms of new social ties shaped by rituals and the growing sense of a religious community within Communist dominated Polish society (2005). At the end of the 1980s Mariański observed the need for new forms of expression in religious life (1991, p. 321).

Despite the fact that the above-mentioned religious movements were established many decades ago, the contemporary Catholic landscape in Poland cannot be understood without noting some signs of their continuity in the religious dynamics of the 21st century. In recent years grass-roots

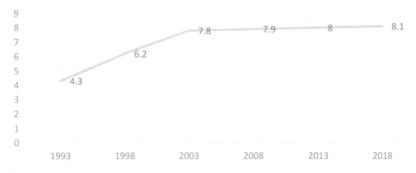

Figure 4.2 Percentage of Catholics participating in parish-based organizations (*participantes*) between 1993 and 2018.

Source: Sadlon and Organek, 2020, p. 33.

religious organizations are well represented in bottom-up religious activism in Poland. A growing number of Catholics are actively engaged in these parish organizations. Since the beginning of the 1990s, the number of these organizations has grown significantly. In 1998 there were 39 661 of them with 2.1 million people involved, and in 2018, there were over 65 500 parish organizations with over 2.6 million people involved. In 1993, only 4 percent of Polish Catholics were active in such organizations, but by 2013 this had doubled to 8 percent (Sadlon and Kazanecka, 2016). So-called *participantes* – that is, Catholics participating in parish organizations – has been growing since 1993 (Figure 4.2). These communities carry out various activities. Most of them are purely focused on prayer and spirituality.

In recent years the quantitative development of parish communities has been hampered. Despite some established in the Communist era, religious movements, such as the *Light-Life Movement*, are declining in number (Nosowska, 2012) and new Catholic revival movements are increasing. The most influential of these new movements seems to be the so-called *Schools of New Evangelization,* which are composed of Catholic societies, Diocesan teams, academic centres, parish schools and centres of the various religious orders. Between 2003 and 2016 the movement grew from about 50 centres with 5000 participants to 360 centres with 60 000 participants (Szlachetka, 2012). There are many mass events organized by this group such as evangelization festivals at the National Stadium in Warsaw, evangelization events in city streets and squares, as well as worship and prayers conducted in market halls. Nowadays, the activities of the New Evangelization Schools are much wider and transcend the boundaries of official Catholic structures to encompass grass-roots religious initiatives. However the contemporary impact of these Catholic movements is without doubt much more limited than in the 1970s and 1980s.

The manifestation of new forms of Catholic mobilization can also be traced in other religious events, for instance the so-called 'Lednica', which takes place near a historical centre of Polish Catholicism – Gniezno. Since the turn of the 21st century about 100 000 young people have been gathering annually for this event, a celebration of music, dance and theatre. Moreover, World Youth Day (WYD), which was held in Poland in 2016, could be seen as a manifestation of these new forms of religiosity. The results of a study which I carried out among participants of WYD in Poland (Mandes and Sadlon, 2018) clearly indicate that this is first and foremost an event of a religious nature. Young people designated 'faith' and 'religion' as their main motivations for participating in WYD. Additionally, for young Poles attending WYD was a way of demonstrating their faith in the public sphere. The celebratory aspect of WYD was based on the feeling of bonding with peers who have the same values and outlook on life and similarly, a relationship with the institution of the Catholic Church. Prayer was the fundamental element for them. Polish WYD participants and those coming from other countries regarded the event mainly in moral and spiritual terms; many were expecting to undergo a spiritual transformation. The Pope played a key role in WYD, being perceived primarily as a spiritual leader. Consequently, the participation of Polish youth in WYD was connected principally with their religiosity and Catholic identity. WYD was more like a contemporary form of pilgrimage rather than a pop festival. And in the same way that pilgrimage combines purely religious elements with secular culture, a feeling of community with joint prayer, a journey with spiritual transformation, WYD combines youth culture based on media and communication technology with Catholic religious rituals and celebrations.

My research showed that young people consciously experienced their faith as well as their personal and social identities at the event. Being deeply rooted in Polish culture and religiosity, they were able to separate its religious content from cultural and political issues. The Polish participants at WYD were proud of being Catholics and felt a strong connection with the Catholic Church. In addition, they were able to fit in with their peers from different countries who quite often embraced different values. The study showed that they had clearly defined standards of morality and consciously accepted the moral teachings of the Church. It also showed that the young could feel God's presence in their lives. At the same time, they could be empathic and sensitive to others and could build deep relationships with their family members, acquaintances and friends. The WYD study revealed young people's capability to create a community across borders and intercultural differences, to share the same religious experiences and jointly celebrate their faith despite all the differences (Mandes and Sadlon, 2018). However, the impact of World Youth Day among Polish youth was rather short-lived because it represented a distinctly religious event.

Changing personal concerns

It is surprising that most research on the transformation of post-1989 Poland focuses on economic and political issues because economics and politics never function independently of the norms, principles and values rooted in a society (Inglehart and Baker, 2000). Moreover, the driving forces of the Polish transformation, according to some, were more cultural than economic (Ekiert and Kubik, 2001); after 1989, Poland was strongly influenced by Western cultural patterns (Marianski, 2012).

The key values for Poles relate to their health and family. In 2015, 80 percent declared the family to be 'very important' in their life and 19 percent, 'important' (Sobestjanski and Bienkunska, 2017, p. 92). Similarly, in 2013, a clear majority (85 percent) claimed that 'everyone needs a family to be happy' (Boguszewski, 2013, p. 3). Similarly, Wojciech Swiatkiewicz observes the permanence of family values in Polish society but, at the same time, he notes the erosion of values related to social capital and the public sphere. He links this with the growing role of friendship, leisure time and personal interests, that is, with individual values (Swiatkiewicz, 2013).

This attitude towards the family is strongly correlated to religiosity, when compared with variables such as level of education and political preferences. People who practise religion regularly are more attached to the need to have sustained family bonds (Hipsz, 2013, p. 7). It is the religiously engaged who more frequently declare 'family', 'honesty', 'respect for people', and 'patriotism' to be very important values in their lives. For example, 90 percent of deeply religious people claim that 'family' is very important to them. In contrast, no more than 71 percent of non-religious persons declare 'family' to be a very important value. The same trend is observed in the case of such values as 'love', 'sense of stability' and 'sense of being useful'. 'Physical fitness' is equally respected by both religious and non-religious persons. 'Professional work', 'education', 'freedom of speech', 'entertainment', 'career' and 'hobbies' are more respected by non-religious persons who more often respect values relating directly to work and individual freedom (Ciecielag, 2017, p. 123–129). The majority of Poles also have a positive attitude towards religious marriage. A sign of religious vitality and attachment to the sacrament of marriage – apart from the most common interpretation of this phenomenon as a manifestation of unstable marriage bonds – is the interest among Poles in cancelling 'unsuccessful' religious marriages. The number of cases of the declaration of invalid marriages[8] was 1279 in 1989, and in 2010 this figure had more than doubled, to 3241.

Polish society is becoming more situationist in terms of moral behaviour. In 2005 about 31 percent of the Polish population claimed that everyone should have moral values and be obedient to moral norms. By 2016 this proportion had decreased by 10 percentage points (Figure 4.3).

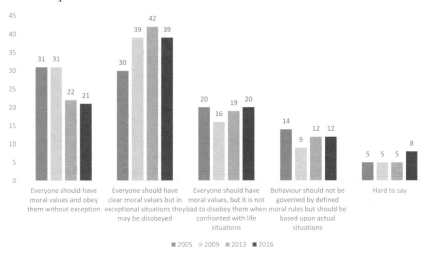

Figure 4.3 Changes in moral attitudes in Polish society from 2005 to 2016.

Source: Boguszewski, 2017a.

Polish society is also becoming more relativist in its relationship to moral norms. The attitude that everyone can subjectively decide what is good and what is bad has become more popular. In 2016, 69 percent of Polish inhabitants declared that defining what is good and what is bad depends on 'internal' (subjective) judgement, as presented in Figure 4.4 below.

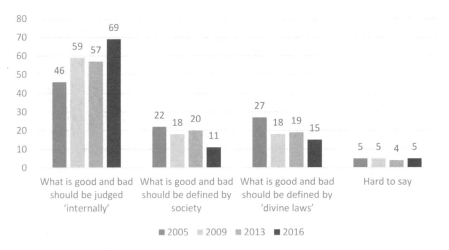

Figure 4.4 Basis of moral attitudes in Polish society from 2005 to 2016.

Source: Boguszewski, 2017a.

The proportion of people who declare that it is not essential to justify moral behaviour in a religious way because it is enough to use one's 'own conscience' has increased from 33 percent in 2009 to 48 percent in 2016 (Boguszewski, 2017a). The majority (78 percent) claim that moral norms are independent of religious values (Boguszewski, 2017a). In 2016 the majority (66 percent) of regularly practising persons agreed that the distinction between what is good and what is bad is based upon internal discernment.

According to statistical data, there exists a strong positive correlation between the general level of religiosity and moral attitudes. People who declare themselves to be more religious are more likely to declare negative attitudes towards abortion and sexual relationships outside religious marriage. Highly religious people who attend Holy Mass more often than once a week claim that divine law is essential in defining what is good and what is bad (Boguszewski, 2017a). Boguszewski (2017b) found that religiosity correlates with attachment to honesty and conscientiousness at work. However other scholars found that the level of religiosity is not correlated with attitudes towards professional work and work conditions. Similarly, there is no correlation between the acceptance of strong work ethos and religiosity. Religiosity does not even affect the incidence of participation in trade unions. What is more, religiosity does not interfere with engagement in political activity, or attitudes towards democracy. Only general political preferences (such as political party preferences) are related to the level of religiosity (Szawiel, 1996). Since 1989 the disapproval of abortion has been growing. Polish Catholics are increasingly inclined not to approve of abortion for any social or medical reason (Fratczak and Sikorska, 2009).

The post-1989 transformation of Polish society strongly affected people's everyday life in terms of lifestyle, how people spent their free time and attitudes towards family and social bonds. The positive assessment of changes in Poland after 1989 is dominated by an appreciation of the growing levels of freedom in the country, such as freedom of speech, the free market and easy social mobility (Badora, 2014). The Polish transformation is seen as a background to such elements as the growing role of values which emphasize the individual and self-realization, personal preferences, and freedom from traditional forces of authority (Fratczak and Sikorska, 2009, p. 78). These changes in the values of Poles at the turn of the century are accurately defined by Wojciech Swiatkiewicz as an 'axiological twist' (Swiatkiewicz, 2013, p. 191).

> The twistedness is born of wind and gales: synonyms for rapid and violent cultural transformation where winds blow in different, sometimes opposite directions, catalyzing new values and patterns of behaviour, fertilizing and revitalizing life, but also destroying and 'blowing away' traditional values and principles if they are poorly rooted in the soil of the indigenous culture.
>
> (Swiatkiewicz, 2013, p. 191)

Social transformation in Poland has also affected human health, quality of life and well-being. Generally speaking, since 1990, so-called subjective well-being has been steadily increasing. Since 2003, as a steady downward trend, fewer respondents indicated serious health problems such as strong headaches, heart palpitations, dyspnoea, etc. During the last two weeks of 2003, the respondents surveyed indicated they had experienced, on average, 0.88 of a symptom, that is less than one symptom, of a serious health problem. In 2015, this number was down to 0.61. Meanwhile satisfaction with health has been steadily increasing. In 2003, 66.1 percent of respondents were satisfied with their health and in 2015 this proportion was 75.4 percent (Czapinski, 2015, p. 231). Since 1993 the percentage of people who gave a positively evaluation of their life has also grown from 53.1 percent to 81.2 percent (in 2015). These results show that more Poles are declaring themselves to be happy in recent years than at the beginning of the1990s, despite the fact that indicators of happiness have been fluctuating. Moreover, the incidence of declared symptoms of depression has been steadily declining since the beginning of the 1990s.

Polish society tends to focus on health and social relationships rather than on money or religion as determinants of well-being (Feliksiak, 2017, p. 5). Furthermore Janusz Czapinski points out the strong contrast between the approach of some Poles to consider God, or to consider money, as the most crucial value in their lives (2015, p. 256). However, in line with some international trends (Pew Research Center, 2019), statistical research on the relationship between well-being and religiosity in Poland reveals a positive correlation. The level of religious commitment and life satisfaction is positive (Bienkunska and Piasecki, 2020). Religious people are more likely to be obese and less physically active than the non-religious. This is the case in Poland and in most countries surveyed in the Pew surveys. However in Poland religious people are more likely to abstain from smoking (also the case in most countries) (Pew Research Center, 2019; Sadlon, 2014b).

The dynamism of religious rituals

As outlined in the previous chapter, religious rituals played an important role in traditional religiosity. Religious dynamism in Poland is still stimulated by religious rituals which continue to be a vital element of religious life in Poland (Sroczynska, 2013; Mielicka-Pawlowska and Kochanowski, 2014). The transitions within Polish society have also shaped religious rituals. In the first decade of the 21st century, a small but systematic drop in the *dominicantes* rate has been observed from year to year. This means that fewer and fewer Poles are attending Sunday Mass regularly. In 2013 the *dominicantes* rate was 39.1 percent; this was the first time since 1980 it fell below 40 percent. The drop in the *dominicantes* rate applies to all regions in Poland and is a nationwide phenomenon.

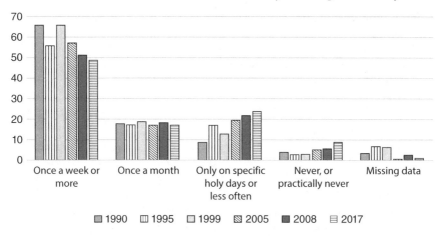

Figure 4.5 Declared frequency of religious practice in Poland (1990-2017).

Source: EVS, 2015 and 2017.

Poles' withdrawal from the customary religious practices on Sundays is also demonstrated in the studies based on the measurement of self-declared religiosity. Between 1990 and 2017, the proportion of people who declared themselves to be 'practising systematically' decreased from 65.6 to 48.8 percent (See Figure 4.5).

This percentage had been relatively stable from 1997 until the beginning of the 21st century. Since around 2005 the percentage of those declaring themselves to be 'practising regularly' has been declining and the percentage of 'practising irregularly' and 'non-practising' has been increasing. In 2020, 47 percent declared themselves to be 'practising regularly', 38 percent to be 'practising irregularly' and 15 percent, 'non-practising' (Bozewicz, 2020).

The decline in the personal practice of religion is associated with changes in the style of celebrating Sunday. As mentioned above, Poles are drifting away from their own parishes. Social relationships, spending time on leisure, among friends and in front of the TV are playing a more important role. These changes in the style of celebrating Sunday are confirmed by the dynamics of changes in Mass attendance times chosen by Poles. Although about 80 percent of Poles still go to church in the morning, the number of those who leave their participation in the Eucharist until the afternoon and evening is growing. In 2013, 15 percent of all people taking part in a Sunday Mass chose to attend one after 2.30 pm. Ten years earlier the percentage of such churchgoers was 13.5 percent (Sadlon et al., 2019, p. 29).

Polish Catholics tend to receive Holy Communion more often than before. In 1980, only 7.8 percent of Polish Catholics received Holy

Communion [*communicantes*] every Sunday, in 2018 this has increased to 17.3 percent. On the one hand, this trend may be interpreted as based on an increasingly liberal and subjective attitude toward the sacraments, as traditionally one could not take communion without having made confession. On the other hand, the practice of going to confession is quite common and the understanding of sin remains traditional but there are no precise data on the dynamics of the confession among Polish Catholics. In more religious regions, in terms of Mass attendance, the relative level of receiving Holy Communion [*communicantes*] is radically less frequent than in regions where people attend Mass less regularly. For example, in the Diocese of Tarnow, in South Poland, no more than 38 percent of Mass attendees receive Holy Communion. However, in the urban Diocese of Koszalin-Kolobrzeg, in Northwest Poland where the level of Mass attendees is one of the lowest in the country, about 46 percent of Mass attendees receive Holy Communion. The average proportion of receivers of Holy Communion among Mass attendees was 0.44 in 2017. Dioceses where the proportion of those receiving Holy Communion to those attending the Mass is higher than average are generally more urban. For example, in the Diocese of Katowice the proportion is 0.52, in the Diocese of Warszawa, 0.51, Warszawa-Praga 0.49, Gdansk 0.48 and Lodz 0.47. These are all major cities or urban conglomerates. It is also worth noting that a similar relationship is observed when one takes a gender perspective. In the more religious Dioceses, the proportion of men and women attending Mass is more balanced than in less religious regions of Poland. For example in the above-mentioned Diocese of Tarnow, women represent no more than 56 percent of all Mass attendees. However in the Diocese of Koszalin-Kolobrzeg women represent more that 63 percent of Mass attendees (Figure 4.6).

Christmas and Easter in Poland are especially associated with the family, tradition and religion. More than 90 percent of Poles declare themselves to be cultivating traditional family Christmas and Easter rituals such as Christmas supper, 'Oplatek'[9] or 'Swieconka'[10]. The analysis of the answers to the question 'What is your attitude towards Easter in Poland?' also provides interesting conclusions concerning the link between religious rituals and family life. From 1994 to 2018, the orientation towards transcendence (attending for the religious experience) during Easter has been declining in Poland. The focus on the family has increased while 'traditional' and 'transcendental' orientations toward Easter do not match these results (Figure 4.7). Moreover, for Polish families religious rituals and holidays are the most popular occasions for meeting and gathering (Feliksiak, 2019b). This means that religious rituals represent a context where religious concerns are related to social ties.

Participation in other Catholic religious rituals during the last few decades has been high but is declining also. In 2006 about 86 percent and in 2018, 85 percent of Poles declared themselves to be fasting on Good Friday.[11]

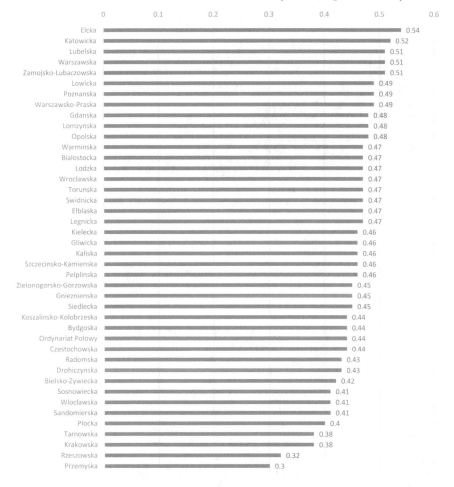

Figure 4.6 The proportion of *communicantes to dominicantes* in Roman Catholic dioceses in Poland in 2017.

Source: Sadlon, 2019b.

In 2006, 79 percent declared that they made confession at Easter; this figure was 67 percent in 2018. Participation in the ritual of 'Sprinkling the head with ashes' (Ash Wednesday), a Christian tradition strongly observed in Poland at the beginning of Lent, was confirmed by 71 percent in 2006 but ten years later this was 64 percent. Attending the Easter liturgy has also decreased slightly from 65 percent to 56 percent over that period of time (Glowacki, 2018).

Significantly, the erosion of some forms of religious ritual is accompanied by the development of new forms of devotion. In these, continuity with traditional Catholic rituals is clearly visible, especially in the case of devotion to

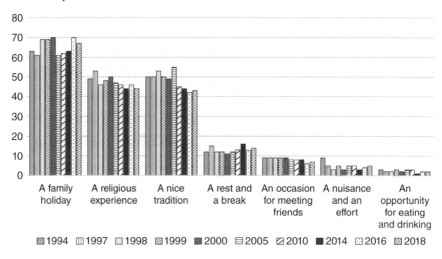

Figure 4.7 Attitudes towards Easter in Poland from 1994 to 2018 (in percent).

Source: Glowacki, 2018.

the Divine Mercy (Sister Faustina Kowalska), the saints, pilgrimages, benedictions, and also in the case of traditional Marian devotion. According to research conducted in 2016, in all Catholic parishes the Holy Rosary ritual[12] was celebrated. In every fourth parish (23.4 percent) the Rosary was prayed every day. The second most popular form of Marian devotion is the so-called 'May devotion to the Blessed Virgin Mary', which was celebrated every day during the month of May in 98 percent of Catholic parishes. Moreover, in every fourth parish (23.2 percent), on the 22th August, the faithful dedicated their lives to the Immaculate Heart of Mary (Sadlon, 2016b). During the last few decades the devotion to Our Lady of Fatima has become one of the most popular forms of Marian devotion in Poland. According to this research, most Catholic parishes in Poland (72 percent) have included special rituals and prayers to Our Lady of Fatima. This means that in the space of one generation a new form of Marian devotion has emerged, which has continued, but also transformed, existing forms of Marian devotion in Poland (Sadlon, 2016b).

Changing transcendental concerns

From the perspective of the socio-cultural system, Catholicism is without doubt the dominant religion in Poland. However, the phenomenon of religious decline in Poland during the political transformation era is a commonly accepted form of public knowledge, a general diagnosis or paradigm which also orients research in Poland within the discipline of the sociology of religion. Since the late 1980s some symptoms of 'spontaneous laicization' have been observed in Polish society. Janusz Marianski has characterized religious changes in Poland as 'crawling secularization' (Marianski, 2012).

Since 1997 the level of people defining themselves as 'believing' has not changed. Only slight changes are observed in the categories of 'deeply believing' and 'non-believer'. While the percentage of 'deeply believing' decreased from 12 percent in 2005 to 8 percent in 2020, the percentage of 'non-believing' increased from 4 percent in 2005 to 9 percent in 2020 (Bozewicz, 2020). The portion of the public identifying as Catholic dropped from 96 percent in 1991 to 87 percent in 2015 (Pew Research Center, 2017). Religion as a key value in people's lives is much less prevalent. In 2015 no more than 28 percent declared religious faith as 'very important', 34.1 percent as 'important' and 29.4 percent as 'rather important' or 'of little importance' (Sobestjanski and Bienkunska, 2017, p. 92). No more than 10 percent declare religious life as an essential part of everyday life (Feliksiak, 2017). Moreover, no more than 35 percent people claimed in 2015 that 'Poland today is a somewhat more religious country than it was in the 1970s and 1980s' (Pew Research Center, 2017). People's attitude towards institutional religiosity showed a reverse trend around the year 2005 which could be linked to the death of John Paul II (Boguszewski, 2015).

Declarations of religiosity among Polish citizens has decreased. People who declare themselves to be having the lowest levels of religiosity represent 9 percent of the population nowadays while the proportion of these who declare the highest religiosity has decreased from 75 percent in 1990 to 67 percent in 2017 (Figure 4.8).

Deep changes in religiosity are observed among the youngest generation in Polish society. Both the two oldest cohorts of the Polish population, which means people born before and after the Second World War, and people born in the 1970s or 1980s, declare relatively stable levels of religiosity.

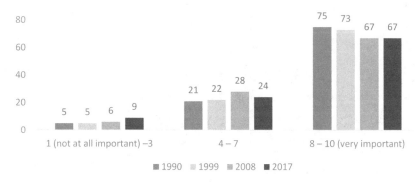

Figure 4.8 Declared importance of 'God in one's life' in Poland (1990-2017).

Source: EVS, 2015 and 2017.

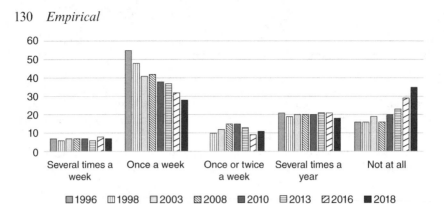

Figure 4.9 Declared frequency of religious practice of high school students (in percent).

Source: Grabowska and Gwiazda, 2019, p. 156.

Essential change is evident in the youngest generations, born after the middle 1990s (Grabowska and Gwiazda, 2018, p. 171–185). The youngest generations in Poland are characterized by significantly lower levels of religiosity. For instance, 35 percent of students at the end of high school, that is, aged 18 to 19 years, declared in 2018 that they did not practice religion at all (Figure 4.9) and 38 percent declared that they did not believe in God (Figure 4.10). Such a strong decline in the religiosity of Polish youth explains why Poland was estimated to be the foremost country in Europe in terms of exhibiting a religious generation gap. In a 2018 Pew Research Centre study which compared 45 countries, Poland ranked first in terms of the gap between the religiosity of younger persons (under 40) and older adults (aged 40 and

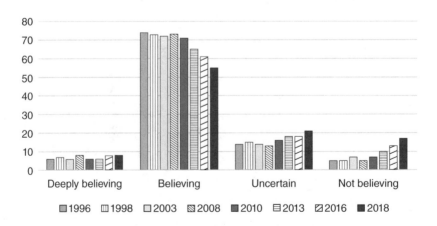

Figure 4.10 Declared religiosity of high school students (in percent).

Source: Grabowska and Gwiazda, 2019, p. 154.

above). In Poland considerably fewer young people than in the other countries declared religion to be 'very important in their lives', and attended religious services at least once a week. While the average gap in European countries between figures for people under 40 years versus people over 40 years of age is about 7 percentage points, in Poland 16 percent of adults under 40 and 40 percent of people over 40 (that is, a gap of 24 percentage points) say religion is very important to them. 26 percent of Polish adults under 40 say they attend religious services weekly, compared with 55 percent of their elders (a gap of 29 percentage points) (Pew Research Center, 2018). Since 1988 there has been a stable conviction among young generations that their religiosity is declining (Sadlon, 2020a). It is also important to note that while the percentage of young people who declare their detachment from religion is growing, the minority of youth who define themselves to be 'very religious' is stable in size.

From 2005 to 2014, the percentage of people declaring themselves to be believers who respect the Church's rules decreased from 66 percent to 39 percent. The percentage of people who claimed that they 'believe in their own way' increased from 32 percent in 2005 to 52 percent in 2015 (Boguszewski, 2017b). These changes in the religiosity of Polish men and women signify, above all, a moving away from the institution of the Church, or 'de-churching' (Juros, 1997). The result is a weakening of the role of the Church (institutionalized religion) and a distancing from the Church's view of faith, ritual and doctrinal rules as well as norms of moral behaviour, which means a lessening in the value of the Church's religious-symbolic forms of social integration (Marianski, 2010, pp. 101–102; Gabriel, 2008). Thus, in Poland we are dealing with bottom-up de-institutionalization and, associated with it, the individualization of religiosity (Figure 4.11). 'In the eyes of the individual, institutionalized religion loses the quality of absolute and objective validity which is guaranteed by ecclesiastical institutions; instead it is experienced in a subjective dimension.' (Marianski, 1997, p. 196) According to some researchers, since 2005 this process has been accelerating considerably (Marianski, 2014).

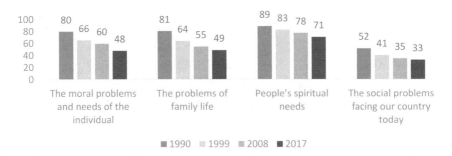

Figure 4.11 Declared relationship to the Church in Poland (1990-2017) (in percent).

Source: EVS, 2015 and 2017.

Surveys have shown that in Polish society there is still a deeply positive emotional attachment to the person of John Paul II. In 2018 about 96 percent of Poles declared that 'generally Poles remember John Paul II' and 71 percent that 'the majority of Poles know the teachings of John Paul II' (Boguszewski, 2018). Significantly, the attitude towards the Catholic Church itself is dominated by a 'spiritual' perspective. When asked to choose the key features of the Catholic Church from a list, with more than one choice possible, most Polish citizens identified the Church with people 'who search for God through prayer, Mass and the sacraments' (43 percent), 'who live according to the teachings of Jesus Christ' (33 percent) and 'who believe in the divinity of Jesus Christ' (32 percent). Less frequently chosen were categories which reflected either an institutional attitude towards the Church, which took hierarchy, tradition or priests as dominating aspects, or a communitarian attitude, which focused mainly on the Church as a religious community (Gierech and Dobrzanska, 2009, p. 104).

The role of institutionalized religion is not essential to my perspective of a person's religious identity. Quantitative research confirms that some aspects of spirituality, which cannot be associated with formally defined institutionalized Catholicism, are well represented in Polish society. Zbigniew Mikolejko is convinced that Polish society has inherited deep sources of religious syncretism (2007). Christian dogmatism should not be contrasted too readily with the traditional belief that there are spiritual powers at play in the natural world. In 2011 nearly 60 percent of Poles claimed that 'some people can predict the future' (Boguszewski, 2011). If we look at the data since 1997 this proportion has been in decline, as well as the belief in telepathy, Zodiac signs and 'unlucky dates'. On the other hand belief in 'bad spells' and 'communication with the dead' have become slightly more prevalent (Figure 4.12).

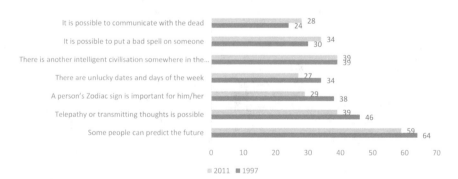

Figure 4.12 Faith in various beliefs (1997 and 2011) (in percent).

Source: Boguszewski, 2011.

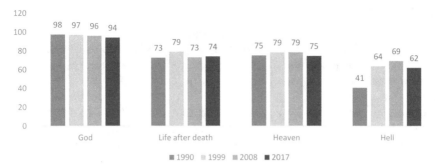

Figure 4.13 Declared belief in god, life after death, heaven and hell, in Poland (1990–2017) (in percent).

Source: EVS, 2015 and 2017.

This growing belief in 'the power of evil' corresponds with the commitment to the Christian belief in 'hell'. Although the general level of beliefs of an eschatological nature has been quite stable during the last thirty years, belief in hell increased in the first decade of the 20st century, as is presented below (Figure 4.13).

Conclusions

The recent history of Poland reveals the dynamic of strong socio-cultural interaction within Polish Catholicism. In comparison with the traditional culture of Polish Catholicism, the process of transformation (morphogenesis) of Polish society in recent decades has been especially strong. In the 1980s era of turbulent change Catholic beliefs and religious ideas exerted causal influence at the socio-cultural level of Polish society. Catholicism has been gaining dominance in shaping socio-cultural interactions. The relationship to the transcendental order formed within the Church in traditional society has been preserved and re-shaped within the newly emerging socio-cultural dynamics of post 1980s Polish society. The specific historical and cultural situation of Polish Catholicism developed, at the turn of the 21st century, some kind of 'communication' in relation to the transcendental order, which stimulated contextual continuity in the dynamics of religion in Poland.

Post-1989 political and structural changes in Poland, a new perspective on religious institutionalization emerged. This opened up the opportunity for the institutional influence of Catholic values and beliefs on Polish society, mediated especially by religious education. Catholicism has become, to some extent, a fundamental element of social structures in Poland and an active element at the socio-cultural level. After three decades of cultural elaboration, Polish society is still in the morphogenetic process

of transition between traditional and modern culture. This modernization consists in the tension between dominant traditional structures and
new forms of agency. The morphogenetic process, the transition from a
traditional to a modernist cultural system, is full of structural tensions
and 'contextual discontinuity'. Both traditionalists and modernists try to
legitimize their positions by producing ideational arguments and securing strategic positions. It seems however, that people's search for educational and occupational advancement or better life conditions is rather not
directly opposed to traditional social norms, such as family and stability.

The process of morphogenesis induces interactions between different
interest groups who identify themselves with reference to Catholicism.
Interest groups defend and promote their interests, signify the interests of
other groups and defend their positions, both by protecting the consistency of traditional Catholic culture, in the case of traditional groups, and
by promoting ideas antithetical to those of the supporters of the new cultural trends. During thirty years of social transformation in Poland new
life projects compete with the re-establishment of traditional cultural morphostasis and clash with the simple, uniform process of the reproduction of
traditional culture. From the perspective of the actors, their engagement in
either the traditionalist and or the modernist movements involves also their
relationship to Catholicism.

Despite the fact that strong changes can be observed in the relationship
between transcendental and social concerns, the elements of the traditional
form of Catholicism presented in the previous chapter do not belong only
to the past but are reconfigured and elaborated in the present. Traditional
Catholicism's transcendental concerns are still linked to social concerns and
are intertwined especially with family life and local communities, particularly in rural areas. However, people's identification of the Church's institutions with transcendence is declining. In other words, people's relationship
to transcendence is becoming more individual and de-institutionalized.
Nevertheless transcendental concerns are still dynamically and reflexively
elaborated within the socio-cultural system.

Notes

1. It is worth noting that in 2010, Polish politics were strongly affected by the
   airplane crash which killed the Polish President Lech Kaczynski, his wife, and
   96 public figures who were on board.
2. Janusz Palikot was a Polish activist, politician and businessman.
3. In the Catholic Church, an Apostolic Administration is designated by the
   Pope for a specific area. The area is not yet a diocese.
4. A Military Ordinariate is an ecclesiastical jurisdiction responsible for the pastoral care of Catholics serving in the armed forces.
5. Religious priests belong to religious orders as opposed to diocesan priests
   who belong to diocesan structures.
6. Caritas is a Catholic social service organization.

7. *Dominicantes* are those Catholics who attend Sunday Mass as opposed to *communicantes,* those who attend and receive communion. This statistical indicator represents a rather intuitive approach to measuring religious practices but includes methodological aspects which were originally formulated by some Polish sociologists of religion, especially those who are often cited in this book, Wladyslaw Piwowarski and Witold Zdaniewicz.
8. In the Catholic Church, the declaration of the nullity of a marriage is a judgment on the part of an ecclesiastical tribunal, determining that the marriage was contracted invalidly.
9. Oplatek – The tradition in which a Christmas wafer is baked from pure wheat flour and water, similar to the Communion wafer. During the celebratory Christmas Eve meal, the family gathers around the table, and each person breaks off a piece of the wafer while making a wish.
10. Swieconka is the blessing of the baskets containing the symbolic food of Easter, including eggs, bread and horseradish, on Easter Saturday, which the family eats together during the breaking of the Lenten fast, either later on Easter Saturday itself or on Easter Sunday.
11. Good Friday in the Catholic Church is a fast day, observed by having only one full meal and abstaining from eating meat.
12. The Holy Rosary ('the Rosary') is a form of prayer used in the Catholic Church. The prayer is arranged in sets of repeated prayers to Holy Mary.

References

Archer, M. S. (1988). *Culture and Agency. The Place of Culture in Social Theory.* Cambridge: Cambridge University Press.

Ascherson, N. (2011). *The Polish August.* London: Blumsbury Reader.

Badora, B. (2014). *Komunikat Z Badan: Czy Warto Było Zmieniac Ustroj? Ocena Zmian Ustrojowych Po 25 Latach* [The Reception of Political Change after 25 Years]. Warszawa: Centrum Badania Opinii Publicznej.

Bellah, R. (1967). Civil Religion in America. *Journal of the American Academy of Arts and Sciences*, 96, pp. 1–21.

Bienkunska, A., Piasecki, T. (2020). Religijnosc a Dobrobyt Subiektywny Na Podstawie Badania Spojnosci Spolecznej 2018 R. [Religiosity and Subjective Well-Being on the Basis of the Social Cohesion Survey 2018]. In: P. Ciecielag ed., *Wyznania Religijne W Polsce 2015-2018* [Religious Denominations in Poland 2015-2018]. Warszawa: Glowny Urzad Statystyczny, pp. 359–371.

Boguszewski, R. (2011). *Polacy Wobec Niektorych Pogladow Z Kregu New Age* [Poles and Their Opinions about the New Age]. Warszawa: Centrum Badania Opinii Publicznej.

Boguszewski, R. (2013). *Komunikat Z Badan: Rodzina – Jej Współczesne Znaczenie I Rozumienie*, BS/33 [The Family – Its Modern Meaning and Conception]. Warszawa: Centrum Badania Opinii Publicznej.

Boguszewski, R. (2015). *Zmiany W Zakresie Podstawowych Wskaznikow Religijnosci Polakow Po Smierci Jana Pawła II* [Changes in the Principal Religious Indicators of Poles after the Death of John Paul II]. Warszawa: Centrum Badania Opinii Publicznej.

Boguszewski, R. (2017a). *Komunikat Z Badan: Zasady Moralne a Religia* [Moral Values and Religion]. Warszawa: Centrum Badania Opinii Publicznej.

Boguszewski, R. (2017b). *Komunikat Z Badan: Etyka Pracownicza* [Employee ethics]. Warszawa: Centrum Badania Opinii Publicznej.

Boguszewski, R. (2018). *Pamiec O Janie Pawle II Ciagle Zywa* [Remembering John Paul II While He was Still Alive]. Warszawa: Centrum Badania Opinii Publicznej.

Borowik, I. (2002). The Roman Catholic Church in the Process of Democratic Transformation: the Case of Poland. *Social Compass*, 49, pp. 239–252.

Bozewicz, M. (2020). *Komunikat Z Badan: Religijnosc Polakow W Ostatnich 20 Latach* [The Religiosity of Poles in the Last 20 Years]. Warszawa: Centrum Badania Opinii Publicznej.

Casanova, J. (1994). *Public Religions in the Modern World*. Chicago and London: The University of Chicago Press.

Ciecielag, P., Boryszewski, P. (2017). Zaangazowanie Religijne [Religious Engagement]. In: A. Bienkunska, T. Piasecki eds., *Jakosc Zycia W Polsce W 2015 R. Wyniki Badania Spojnosci Spolecznej* [Quality of Life in Poland 2015. Results of a Social Cohesion Survey]. Warszawa: Glowny Urzad Statystyczny, pp. 113–142.

Ciecielag, P. et al. (2016). *Wyznania Religijne W Polsce 2012–2014* [Religious Denominations in Poland 2012-2014]. Warszawa: Glowny Urzad Statystyczny.

Ciesielski, S. (1999). *Przesiedlenie Ludnosci Polskiej Z Kresow Wschodnich Do Polski 1944-1947* [Resettlement from Kresy to Poland 1944-1947]. Warszawa: Neriton and Instytut Historii Polskiej Akademii Nauk.

Conference of Polish Bishops (2008). *Zasady postepowania w sprawie formalnego aktu wystapienia z Kosciola* [Rules Concerning Formal Withdrawal from the Church] [online] Available at: https://episkopat.pl/zasady-postepowania-w-sprawie-formalnego-aktu-wystapienia-z-kosciola [Accessed 13/06/2020].

Cywinski, P. (2010[1971]). *Rodowody Niepokornych* [Genealogy of the Unbowed]. Warszawa: Panstwowe Wydawnictwo Naukowe.

Czapinski, J. (2015). *Indywidualna Jakosc I Styl Zycia* [Individual Quality of Life and Lifestyle]. In: J. Czapinski, T. Panek eds., *Diagnoza Spoleczna 2015. Warunki I Jakosc Zycia Polakow* [Social Diagnosis 2015. The Life Conditions and Quality of Life of Poles]. Warszawa: Rada Monitoringu Społecznego, pp. 183–313.

Demerath, N. (2000). The Rise of "Cultural Religion" in European Christianity: Learning from Poland. Northern Ireland. and Sweden. *Social Compass*, 47(1), pp. 127–139.

Eberts, M. (1998). The Roman Catholic Church and Democracy in Poland. *Europe-Asia Studies*, 50, pp. 817–842. DOI: 10.2307/153894.

Ekiert, G., Kubik, J. (2001). *Rebellious Civil Society: Popular Protest and Democratic Consolidation in Poland. 1989-1993*. Ann Arbor: University of Michigan Press.

EVS (2015): European Values Study 1981-2008: Longitudinal Data File 1981–2008. GESIS. Data Archive. Cologne. DOI: 10.4232/1.12253.

EVS (2017): European Values Study 2017: Integrated Dataset 2017. GESIS Data Archive. Cologne. DOI: 10.4232/1.13511.

Feliksiak, M. (2017). *Komunikat Z Badan: Sens Zycia – Wczoraj I Dzis* [A Sense of Life – Yesterday and Today]. Warszawa: Centrum Badania Opinii Publicznej.

Feliksiak, M. (2019a). *Komunikat Z Badan 7/2019: Oceny Dzialalnosci Parlamentu, Prezydenta, PKW I Kosciola Rzymskokatolickiego* [Opinions on the Activity of Parliament, the Polish Voting Commission and the Roman Catholic Church. Warszawa: Centrum Badania Opinii Publicznej.

Feliksiak, M. (2019b). *Wiezi Rodzinne* [Family Ties]. Warszawa: Centrum Badania Opinii Publicznej.

Firlit, E. (2013a). Wspolnotowy Wymiar Religijnosci [The Communal Dimension of Religiosity]. In: L. Adamczuk, E. Firlit, W. Zdaniewicz eds., *Postawy Spoleczno-Religijne Polaków 1991-2012* [The Socio-Religious Attitudes of Poles]. Warszawa: Instytut Statystyki Kościoła Katolickiego, pp. 125–160.

Firlit, E. (2013b). Erozja wspolnotowego wymiaru religijnosci katolikow w Polsce [The Erosion of the Communal Dimension of Religiosity Among Catholics in Poland]. *The Religious Studies Review/Przeglad Religioznawczy*, 4, pp. 133–145.

Firlit, E. (2014). Die Modernisierung Der Strukturen Der Katholischen Kirche in Polen. In: M. Hainz et. al., ed., *Zwischen Saekularisierung Und Religioeser Vitalisierung. Religiositaet in Deutschland Und Polen Im Vergleich*. Wiesbaden: Springer, pp. 235–246.

Fratczak, E., Sikorska, I. (2009). *Changing Attitudes and Behaviour Concerning Contraception and Abortion in Poland*. Studia Demograficzne, 156, pp. 73–114.

Gabriel, K. (2008). Zwischen Entkirchlichung. Individualisierung Und Deprivatisierung: Institutionalisierte Religiositaet in Europa. In: B. Irlenborn, F.-J. Bormann eds., Religioese Ueberzeugungen Und Oeffentliche Vernunft. Zur Rolle Des Christentums in Der Pluralistischen Gesellschaft. Freiburg im Breisgau: Herder, pp. 45–60.

Gawin, D. (2013). *Wielki Zwrot. Ewolucja Lewicy I Odrodzenie Idei Spoleczenstwa Obywatelskiego 1956-1976* [Great Break. The Evolution of the Left and the Renaissance of the Idea of Civil Society 1956-1976]. Krakow: Znak.

Gierech, P., Dobrzanska, A. (2009). Polacy O Kosciele [Poles Speaking About the Church]. In: T. Zukowski ed., *Wartosci Polakow a Dziedzictwo Jana Pawla II* [Polish Values and the Heritage of John Paul II]. Warszawa: Centrum Mysli Jana Pawla II, pp. 87–121.

Glowacki, A. (2018). *Komunikat Z Badan: Wielkanoc 2018* [Easter 2018]. Warszawa: Centrum Badania Opinii Publicznej.

Grabowska, G., Gwiazda, M. (2019). *Mlodziez 2018* [Youth 2018]. Warszawa: Centrum Badania Opinii Publicznej.

Grabowska, M. (2005). Odnowa Wiary Jako Wydarzenie [Faith Renewal as an Event]. In: M. Grabowska, T. Szawiel eds., *Religijnosc Spoleczenstwa Polskiego Lat 80. Od Pytan Filozoficznych Do Problemow Empirycznych* [Religiosity in Polish Society in the 1980s. From Philosophical Questions to Empirical Problems]. Warszawa: Wydzial Filozofii i Socjologii Uniwersytetu Warszawskiego, pp. 239–258.

Grabowska, M. (2008). Ruchy odnowy religijnej przelomu lat siedemdziesiatych i osiemdziesiatych: spoleczne przyczyny i konsekwencje [Religious Renewal Movements in the 1970s and 1980s: Social Conditions and Results]. In: T. Szawiel ed., *Pokolenie JP2. Przeszlosc I Przyszlosc Zjawiska Religijnego* [The JP2 Generation. The Past and Future of a Religious Phenomenon]. Warszawa: Wydawnictwo Naukowe Scholar, pp. 22–49.

Grabowska, M. (2018). *Bog a Sprawa Polska. Poza Granicami Teorii Sekularyzacji* [God and the Case of Poland: Beyond a Theory of Secularization]. Warszawa: Wydawnictwo Naukowe Scholar.

Grabowska, M., Gwizada, M. (2019). *Mlodziez 2018* [Youth 2018]. Warszawa: Centrum Badania Opinii Spolecznej.

Grzymala-Busse, A. (2015). *Nations Under God: How Churches Use Moral Authority to Influence Policy*. New Jersey: Princeton University Press. DOI: 10.2307/j.ctv7h0sfx.

Gudaszewski, G. (2015). *Struktura Narodowo-Etniczna, Jezykowa I Wyznaniowa Ludnosci Polski. Narodowy Spis Powszechny Ludnosci I Mieszkan 2011* [National-Ethnic Structure, Language and the Confessional in the Polish Population. National Census 2011]. Warszawa: Glowny Urzad Statystyczny.

Hipsz, N. (2013). *Komunikat Z Badan: Spoleczne Oceny Alternatyw Zycia Malzenskiego* [Social Alternatives to Married Life]. Warszawa: Centrum Badania Opinii Publicznej.

Inglehar, R., Baker, R. (2000). Modernization. Cultural Change. and the Persistence of Traditional Values. *American Sociological Review*, 65, pp. 19–51.

Jaron, J. (2014). Szkolnictwo Katolickie I Nauka Religii [Catholic Schools and Religious Education]. In: P. Ciecielag, W. Sadlon, P. Lyson eds., *Kosciol Katolicki W Polsce 1991-2011. Rocznik Statystyczny* [Catholic Church in Poland 1991-2011. Statistical Yearbook]. Warszawa: Instytut Statystyki Kosciola Katolickiego and Glowny Urzad Statystyczny, pp. 231–234.

Jasiukiewicz, M. (1993). *Kosciol Katolicki W Polskim Zyciu Politycznym 1945-1989: Podstawowe Uwarunkowania* [The Catholic Church in Polish Public Life 1945-1989]. Wroclaw: Akademia Ekonomiczna.

Joas, H. (2007). Fuehrt Modernisierung Zur Saekulariesierung? In: P. Walter ed., *Gottesrede in Postsaekularer Kultur*. Freiburg im Bresgau: Herder Verlag, pp. 10–18.

Juros, H. (1997). *Kosciol. Kultura. Europa. Katolicka Nauka Spoleczna Wobec Wspolczesnosci* [Church. Culture. Europe. Catholic Social Teaching and Modernity]. Lublin-Warszawa: Fundacja ATK.

Koczanowicz, L., Singer, B., Kellogg, F., Nysler, L. (2005). *Democracy and Post-Totalitarian Experience*. Amsterdam and New York: Rodopi.

Kosela, K. (2003). *Polak-Katolik. Splatana Tozsamosc* [Pole-Catholic: Confused Identity]. Warszawa: Instytut Filozofii i Socjologii Polskiej Akademii Nauki.

Krzeminski, I. (2013). *Solidarnosc. Niespelniony Projekt Polskiej Demokracji* [Solidarity: An Unfinished Project of Polish Democracy]. Gdansk: Europejskie Centrum Solidarnosci.

Kubiak, H. (1972). *Religijnosc a Srodowisko Spoleczne. Studium Zmian Religijnosci Pod Wplywem Ruchow Migracyjnych Ze Wsi Do Miasta* [Religiosity and the Social Milieu. A Study of the Effects of Migration from Villages to Cities on Religious Change]. Krakow: Polska Akademia Nauk.

Lyson, P. (2014). Terytorialne Zroznicowanie Wybranych Wskaznikow Religijnosci [The Territorial Variable in Selected Indicators of Religiosity]. In: P. Ciecielag, W. Sadlon, P. Lyson eds., *Kosciol Katolicki W Polsce 1991-2011. Rocznik Statystyczny* [Catholic Church in Poland 1991-2011. Statistical Yearbook]. Warszawa: Glowny Urzad Statystyczny and Instytut Statystyki Kosciola Katolickiego, pp. 291–296.

Majka, J. (1980). Uwarunkowania Katolicyzmu Polskiego [The Context of Polish Catholicism]. *Chrzescijanin w swiecie. Zeszyty ODiSS*, 94, pp. 27–44.

Mandes, S., Sadlon, W. (2018). Religion in a Globalized Culture: Institutional Innovation and Innovation and Continuity of Catholicism – The Example Of World Youth Day. *Annual Review of Sociology of Religion*, 9, pp. 202–221. DOI: 10.1163/9789004380073_012.

Marianski, J. (1991). *Religijnosc W Procesie Przemian. Szkice Socjologiczne* [Religiosity in the Process of Transition]. Warszawa: Instytut Wydawniczy Pax.

Marianski, J. (1997). *Religia I Kosciol Miedzy Tradycja I Ponowoczesnoscia. Studium Socjologiczne* [Religion and Church between Tradition and Postmodernity: A Sociological Study]. Krakow: Nomos.

Marianski, J. (2010). *Religia W Spoleczenstwie Ponowoczesnym. Studium Socjologiczne* [Religion in Postmodern Society: A Sociological Study]. Warszawa: Oficyna Naukowa.

Marianski, J. (2012). Tendencje rozwojowe religijnosci katolickiej w Polsce [The Development of Catholic Religiosity in Poland]. In: E. Firlit, M. Hainz, M. Libiszowska-Zoltkowska, G. Pickel, D. Pollack eds., *Pomiedzy Sekularyzacja I Religijnym Ozywieniem. Podobienstwa I Roznice W Przemianach Religijnych W Polsce I W Niemczech* [Between Secularization and Religious Revival. Similarities and Differences in the Religious Transformation of Poland and Germany]. Krakow: Wydawnictwo WAM, pp. 31–48.

Marianski, J. (2014). *Praktyki Religijne W Polsce W Procesie Przemian. Studium Socjologiczne* [Religious Practices in Poland in Transition: A Sociological Study]. Sandomierz: Wydawnictwo Diecezjalne.

Mielicka-Pawlowska, H., Kochanowski, J. (2014). Religioeses Brauchtum Der Polen. In: E. Firlit, M. Hainz, M. Libiszowska-Zoltkowska, G. Pickel, D. Pollack eds., *Zwischen Saekularisierung Und Religioeser Vitalisierung. Religiositaet in Deutschland Und Polen Im Vergleich*. Wiesbaden: Springer, pp. 257–270.

Mikolejko, Z. (2007). New Age Po Polsku [The New Age According to Poles]. In: D. Hall ed., *New Age W Polsce. Lokalny Wymiar Globalnego Zjawiska* [New-Age in Poland. Local Dimensions of a Global Phenomenon]. Warszawa: Wydawnictwa Akademickie i Profesjonalne, pp. 9–17.

Morawska, E. (1984). Civil Religion Versus State Power in Poland. *Society*, 21, pp. 29–34. DOI: https://doi.org/10.1007/BF02695098

Nosowska, A. (2012). *Oazy Jako Zjawisko Spoleczne I Religijne. Rozwoj Ruchu I Jego Tozsamosc* [Oasis as a Social and Religious Phenomenon]. Warszawa: [Manuscript].

Pew Research Center (2019). *Religion's Relationship to Happiness. Civic Engagement and Health Around the World* [online] Available at: https://www.pewforum. org/2019/01/31/religions-relationship-to-happiness-civic-engagement-and-health-around-the-world [Accessed 17/06/2020].

Pew Research Center. (2017). *Religious Belief and National Belonging in Central and Eastern Europe. National and religious identities converge in a region once dominated by atheist regimes* [online] Available at: https://www.pewforum. org/2017/05/10/religious-belief-and-national-belonging-in-central-and-eastern-europe/ [Accessed 18/06/2020].

Pew Research Center. (2018). *The Age Gap in Religion Around the World* [online] Available at: https://www.pewforum.org/2018/06/13/the-age-gap-in-religion-around-the-world/ [Accessed 18/06/2020].

Piwowarski, W. (1983). Kosciol Ludowy a Duszpasterstwo [The Folk Church and Pastoral Activity]. In: W. Piwowarski ed., *Wprowadzenie, Religijnosc Ludowa. Ciaglosc I Zmiana.* [Folk Religiosity: Continuity and Change]. Wroclaw: Wydawnictwo Wroclawskiej Ksiegarni Archidiecezjalnej, pp. 333–367.

Piwowarski, W. (1986). Kontekst Spoleczenstwa Pluralistycznego a Problem Permanentnej Socjalizacji Religijnej [The Context of Pluralist Society and the Problem of Permanent Religious Socialization]. In: W. Piwowarski, W. Zdaniewicz eds., *Z Badan Nad Religijnoscia Polska. Studia I Materialy* [From Research on Polish Religiosity. Studies and Materials]. Poznan-Warszawa: Pallottinum, pp. 73–82.

Piwowarski, W. (1996). Od "Koscioła Ludu" Do "Kosciola Wyboru" [From "Folk Church" to "Church of Choice"]. In: I. Borowik, W. Zdaniewicz eds., *Od Kosciola Ludu Do Kosciola Wyboru. Religia I Przemiany Spoleczne W Polsce* [From the Church of Folk to the Church of Choice. Religion and Social Change in Poland]. Krakow: Zakład Wydawniczy Nomos, pp. 9–16.

Rahner, K. (1959). Der Christ in Der Modernen Welt. In: K. Rahner ed., *Sendung Und Gnade. Beitraege Zur Pastoraltheologie.* Innsbruck, Wien and Muenchen: Tyrolia-Verlag, pp. 13–50.

Rosta, G. (2014). Religiositaet Und Politische Praeferenzen - Polen Und Deutschland. In: M. Hainz et. al., eds., *Zwischen Saekularisierung Und Religioeser Vitalisierung. Religiositaet in Deutschland Und Polen Im Vergleich.* Wiesbaden: Springer, pp. 135–146.

Sadlon, W. (2014b). Bardziej ubogo. ale przyzwoiciej. Oddzialywanie religijnego kapitalu spolecznego w Polsce [Poorer but More Decent. The Impact of Religious Social Capital in Poland]. *Zeszyty Naukowe Katolickiego Uniwersytetu. Lubelskiego*, 57, pp. 11–29.

Sadlon, W. (2015a). *Annuarium Statisticum Ecclesiae in Polonia AD 2015* [online] Available at: http://www.iskk.pl/images/stories/Instytut/dokumenty/AnnuariumStatisticum2015.pdf [Accessed 16/06/2020].

Sadlon, W. (2015b). *Posluga charytatywna Kosciola katolickiego w Polsce. Raport z pierwszego ogolnopolskiego badania koscielnych instytucji oraz organizacji charytatywnych* [Charitable Activities of the Catholic Church in Poland. A Report from the Initial Research on Charitable Institutions and Organizations] [online] Available at: http://iskk.pl/images/stories/Instytut/dane/Dzialanosc_charytatywna_2015.pdf [Accessed 16/06/2020].

Sadlon, W. (2016a). Differentiation. Polarization and Religious Change in Poland. *The Religious Studies Review/Przeglad Religioznawczy*, 4(262), pp. 25–42.

Sadlon, W. (2016b). Kult Matki Bozej I Nabozenstwo Fatimskie W Parafiach Katolickich W Polsce. Raport Z Badania [Marian Devotion and Fatima Devotion in Catholic Parishes in Poland: A Research Report]. *Salvatoris Mater*, 18(1), pp. 454–479.

Sadlon, W. (2019a). *Cialosc I Zmiana Wiejskich Parafii Katolickich* [Continuity and Change Within Rural Catholic Parishes]. In: M. Halamska, M. Stany, J. Wilkin eds., *Ciaglosc I Zmiana. Sto Lat Rozwoju Polskiej Wsi* [Continuity and Change. One Hundred Years of Development of the Polish Countryside]. Tom 1. Warszawa: Instytut Rozwoju Wsi i Rolnictwa Polskiej Akademii Nauk, pp. 351–387.

Sadlon, W. (2019b). *Annuarium Statisticum Ecclesaie in Polonia AD 2019* [online] Available at: http://iskk.pl/images/stories/Instytut/dokumenty/Annuarium_Statisticum_2019.pdf [Accessed 18/06/2020].

Sadlon, W. (2020a). Students' Religiosity in Their Own Assessment. In: S. Zareba, M. Zarzecki eds., *Between Construction and Deconstruction of the Universes of Meaning. Research into the Religiosity of Academic Youth in the Years 1988-1998-2005-2017.* Berlin: Peter Lang, pp. 125–146. DOI: 10.3726/b16246.

Sadlon, W. (2020b). *Civil Cinderella. Religion and Civil Society in Poland.* In: R. Graf Strachwitz, ed., *Religious Communities and Civil Society in Europe.* Berlin: De Gruyter, pp. 149–182. DOI: https://doi.org/10.1515/9783110673081-009

Sadlon, W., Kazanecka, M. (2016). *Podmioty Wyznaniowe Prowadzace Dzialalnosc O Charakterze Pozytku Publicznego* [Religious Entities Conducting Public Benefit Activities]. In: M. Gos-Wojcicka ed., *Sektor non-Profit W 2014 R*. Warszawa: Glowny Urzad Statystyczny, pp. 148–161.

Sadlon, W., Nowotny, S., Lukaszewski, B., Organek, L. (2019) Czas Wolny W Zyciu Polakow A Swietowanie Niedzieli [Free Time in the Life of Poles and Celebrating Sunday] [online] Available at: http://iskk.pl/images/stories/Instytut/dokumenty/ Niedziela_raport_07.10_14.00.pdf [Accessed 20/02/2021]

Sadlon, W., Organek, L. (2020). *Annuarium Statisticum Ecclesaie in Polonia AD 2020* [online] Available at: http://iskk.pl/images/stories/Instytut/dokumenty/ Annuarium_Statisticum_2020_07.01.pdf [Accessed 12/09/2020].

Secretary of State of the Holy See (1974-2017). *Annurarium Statisticum Ecclesiae.* [1974-2017], Vatican: Libreria Editrice Vaticana.

Sobestjanski, K., Bienkunska, A. (2017). Wartosci i postawy wobec wybranych zachowan w przestrzeni spolecznej [Values and Attitudes Towards Some Public Behaviour]. In: A. Bienkunska, T. Piasecki eds., *Jakosc Zycia W Polsce W 2015 R. Wyniki Badania Spojnosci Spolecznej*. Warszawa: Glowny Urzad Statystyczny, pp. 91–112.

Sroczynska, M. (2013). *Rytualy W Mlodziezowym Swiecie. Studium Socjologiczne* [Rituals in the World of Youth. A Sociological Study]. Krakow: Wydawnictwo FALL.

Swiatkiewicz, W. (2013). Miedzy rodzina a zyciem publicznym – ciaglosc i zmiana orientacji na wartosci [Between Family and Public Life – Continuity and Change in Value Orientation]. In: L. Adamczuk, E. Firlit, W. Zdaniewicz eds., *Postawy Spoleczno-Religijne Polakow 1991-2012* [The Socio-Religious Attitudes of Poles]. Warszawa: Instytut Statystyki Kosciola Katolickiego, pp. 185–206.

Szajkowski, B. (1983). *Next to God... Poland, Politics and Religion in Contemporary Poland*. New York: St. Martin's Press.

Szawiel, T. (1996). Postawy i orientacje spoleczne polskich katolikow w trzy lata po rozpoczeciu reform politycznych i ekonomicznych [Attitudes and Social Orientations of Polish Catholics Three Years after the Start of Political and Economic Reforms]. In: I. Borowik, W. Zdaniewicz eds., *Od Kosciola Ludu Do Kosciola Wyboru. Religia I Przemiany Spoleczne W Polsce*. Krakow: Zaklad Wydawniczy Nomos, pp. 49–95.

Szlachetka, W. (2012). *Fenomen Szkol Nowej Ewangelizacji* [The Phenomenon of New Evangelisation Schools]. Krakow: Nomos.

Sztompka, P. (1991). The Intangibles and Imponderables of the Transition to Democracy. *Studies in Comparative Communism*, 3, pp. 295–312.

Taylor, C. (2007). *A Secular Age*. Cambridge: The Belknap Press of Harvard University Press.

The Constitution of the Republic of Poland of 2nd April, 1997. *Dziennik Ustaw*, 78(483).

Weigel, G. (2000). *Swiadek Nadziei. Biografia Papieza Jana Pawla II* [Witness of Hope. The Biography of Pope John Paul II]. Krakow: Znak.

Zdaniewicz, W., Sadlon, W. eds.2011). *Spis Duchowienstwa Diecezjalnego Oraz Czlonkow Instytutow Zycia Konsekrowanego I Stowarzyszen Zycia Apostolskiego* [Census of Diocesan and Religious Priests]. Zabki: Instytut Statystyki Kosciola Katolickiego.

Zech, C. et al. (2017). *Catholic Parishes of the 21st Century*, New York: Oxford University Press.

Zubrzycki, G. (2006). *The Crosses of Auschwitz. Nationalism and Religion in Post-Communist Poland*. Chicago and London: Chicago University Press.

Zurek, J. (1996). *Polityka Oswiatowa Panstwa Wobec Kosciola Katolickiego W Polsce W Latach 1961-1976* [State Educational Policy Towards the Catholic Church in Poland 1961-1976] [Manuscript]. Warszawa.

5   Migration and the shaping of religious identity

Photo 3 Polish Catholics during a Sunday Mass in Dublin. Photo: Author.

At the conference of the Irish Sociological Association in Galway in 2019, I concluded my presentation on Polish migrants in Ireland with the statement that Polish migrants generally have a positive attitude towards Irish Catholicism because they are convinced that it is not as normative and oppressive as Polish Catholicism. In the discussion which followed, one sociologist in the audience spontaneously exclaimed: 'What is it about Catholicism in Poland that makes people regard our Irish Catholicism as so friendly and human?' In my opinion this question reveals the challenges Polish Catholicism confronts in a new cultural context. The traditional link between culture and religion is confronted with new cultural constellations.

Following the ideas formulated by Gabriel Le Bras, Andrew Greeley described the religious attitudes of migrants. Referring to the myth of the 'magical station', (Greeley, 1971, p. 38) he claimed that the migration of peasants results in a radical decline in their religious attitudes. According to this myth, there was a railway station in Paris that had 'magical powers', so much so that any French immigrant from Bretagne who passed through that station seemingly never set foot in a church again. It is true that migration strongly affects people's attitudes, including those related to religion and the religious life. However, this is not a mechanical process. The metaphorical railway station did not shape migrants in some automatic fashion. Changes related to religious attitudes include the dimension of human reflexivity and the elaboration of human concerns, especially in relation to transcendence. This magic spirit of the station has the face of social forces.

Polish migrants to the Republic of Ireland were born and educated in Poland. Almost all such Poles in Ireland today arrived after 2004, when Poland joined the European Union. Moreover, there are no two countries in Europe as similar in terms of religion and the traditional link between national and religious identity as Ireland and Poland, with both countries being traditionally Catholic. The first generation of Polish migrants share the configuration of religious concerns shaped within the Polish cultural system. But migration opens a new cultural context for migrants, and they are faced with new cultural ideas and concerns that are reflexively elaborated.

This study of religious transformation among Polish migrants necessarily follows my detailed presentation of religious aspects of the cultural and socio-cultural system in Poland in previous chapters. To some extent, I assume that religious changes affecting the first generation of Polish migrants reflect the religious transformation taking place within Polish society itself. In this chapter, I describe the religious changes which are related to migration, building upon the experience of Polish migrants to Ireland. This exercise creates the opportunity for a more specific understanding of the transformation of religion within Polish society and the dynamism of Polish Catholicism. I will firstly review previous research related to the religious aspects of migration. Then I will focus on the findings from my study of Polish migrants to Ireland which I conducted in 2018 and 2019.[1] This research included a survey that was based on an innovative Respondent-Driven Sampling method.[2] This survey was supplemented with three focus groups conducted in 2018 and 2019, composed of Polish migrants resident in Dublin and Cork. Additionally, one focus group was organized with religiously engaged Polish migrants in Dublin in 2019, and in-depth interviews were conducted with 15 such Polish migrants. Finally, a survey was conducted among practising Catholics in one of Dublin's Polish pastoral centres.[3]

This chapter has a different character from the previous ones. It is less systemic and general at a macro level, being focused on the analysis of original empirical data, and thus aims to present some new perspectives of religious life related to migration. However, in this chapter I also aim to shed new light on the morphogenesis of Polish Catholicism by looking at it in a diaspora context. I believe that the conclusions of the research presented here provide some very important knowledge about the morphogenesis of Polish Catholicism today. And so, my study of Polish Catholicism overseas necessarily includes some reference to the Irish religious context, which is described in this chapter as well.

The dynamism of Polish migration to the Republic of Ireland

Migration today is more frequent and more popular than in recent centuries. The total number of international migrants living around the world has grown substantially over the past 50 years, climbing from about 80 million people (or 2.6 percent of the world's population) in 1960 to about 214 million (or roughly 3.1 percent of the world's population) in 2010 (Pew Research Center, 2012, p. 7). When migrants are defined as 'those staying for at least one year in a country other than the one in which they were born', Poland, with 2.9 million emigrants (Pew Research Center, 2012, p. 29), ranks seventh in the world as an exporter of its population.

The group of people born outside Poland whose ancestors left their home country is called 'Polonia'.[4] According to official data, 18–20 million Poles and people of Polish origin live outside Poland, with one-third of them having been born in Poland. When the number of Poles living outside Poland is examined 'in terms of the ratio of their number to the home country's population, Polish expatriates rank sixth in the world'. The biggest Polish community is located in the United States, where 9.66 million people are declared to be of Polish descent. Close to one million Poles live in Canada, 1.5 million in Brazil, 120 000 in Argentina, 170 000 in Australia and 30 000 in South Africa. The Polish minority in Western Europe is estimated at 4.2 million: 1.5 million in Germany, 800 000 in both France and Great Britain, 200 000 in the Netherlands, 150 000 in Italy, 110 000 in both Sweden and Norway, 100 000 in Belgium, 85 000 in both Austria and Spain, 60 000 in Denmark, 11 000 in Iceland, 10 000 in Greece. Close to a million people of Polish extraction live in the post-Soviet area (Ministerstwo Spraw Zagranicznych, 2015).

The democratic transition opened the borders for all Polish citizens and motivated them to search for better living conditions in Western countries and the United States. Before Poland's accession to the European Union the amount of emigration from Poland was estimated to be not more than 770 000 people (Orlowski and Zienkowski, 1998). However, a new wave of emigration was initiated by the accession and subsequent liberalization of the labour market. In 2004, when Polish citizens were officially allowed to work in many western countries more than two million Poles left the country. According to the Polish census, in 2011 1.5 million Polish citizens stayed abroad for at least one year and 2.1 million for at least three months. In 2007, most Polish migrants resided in Great Britain (625 000), Germany (470 000), Ireland (120 000), and the Netherlands (95 000) (Slany and Solga, 2014, pp. 10–15). At the end of 2016, the Polish Central Statistical Office reported that 2 515 000 Polish citizens stayed for more than three months outside Poland, with most of them staying in Europe, more specifically in the European Union, (2 214 000 and 2 096 000, respectively). About 80 percent of Polish emigrants stay outside Poland for more than 12 months (Glowny Urzad Statystyczny, 2017). According to Poland's Institute for Catholic Church Statistics, 2.6 million Polish citizens were resident overseas in 2014 (Sadlon, 2016, p. 8).

Migration has had a strong demographic impact on Polish society. Polish citizens have migrated especially from the eastern and northern regions of Poland and from Opolszczyzna[5] (Sleszynski, Banski, Degorski and Komornicki, 2017). From a demographic perspective, Poland has, since 2004, experienced a strong depopulation process; about 70 percent of its territory now shows evidence of this. Though emigration has reduced unemployment, it has also had negative effects on the economy. After 2004, the stream of Polish migrants was overrepresented by younger and the more well-educated sections of the population coming from urban areas. According to the Polish census of 2011, nearly two-thirds (65.9 percent) of all Polish migrants came from urban areas, with slightly more than half (51.1 percent) of Polish migrants being women. A significant majority (72.8 percent) emigrated for the purpose of finding better work opportunities (Slany and Solga, 2014, p. 16).

Polish immigration to Ireland started in the 19th century when a Polish immigrant took part in the creation of the biggest university in Ireland, University College Dublin. When the English convert to Roman Catholicism, influential thinker and future Catholic cardinal, John Henry Newman, attempted to create the Catholic University of Ireland in Dublin in the 1850s, there were no more than eleven students enrolled, including a Polish count whose name is not known. Later Polish-Irish relationships were strengthened when a famous Irish politician and revolutionary nationalist, Constance Markievicz née Gore-Booth, married the Polish nobleman Casimir Markievicz. Constance Markievicz was actively involved in the political life of the future Republic of Ireland. She took part in the nationalist uprising of 1916 and was the first woman elected to the British House of Commons; she was also the first woman in the world to hold a cabinet position. Today, there is a small park in the western part of Dublin named after her.

However, modern Polish – Irish relations can be traced back to 1979 when Polish Catholics living in Ireland initiated the Irish Polish Society. The creation of this association is linked to the pastoral visit of the Polish Pope, John Paul II, to Ireland. The Society actively supported democratic changes in Poland during the period of communist rule. In 1991, the Irish Polish Society established official contacts with the Polish Embassy in Dublin. However, more vibrant Polish-Irish relations were initiated when Poland entered the European Union and the Irish labour market was opened to foreign citizens. According to the Irish census of 2016, there were 122 515 people with Polish ancestry resident in Ireland. Given that the population of the Republic of Ireland was only 4.762 million in 2016, Poles constituted a relatively important social group within Irish society (3 percent). Moreover, the composition of this Polish group is predominantly young, with almost all (89 percent) being under 44 years of age in 2016, and with most having been in Ireland for 12 years or less (Central Statistical Office, 2016). The Response Driven Sampling Survey of 2018 delivered very similar results to the Irish census data. According to my survey of 2018, the average (arithmetical) age of respondents was 40.7 years, with females representing 49 percent of Polish migrants and males, 51 percent.

Those Poles who have migrated to Ireland are integrated within the society there; its cultural system exhibits many similarities with that of Poland. Both countries are relatively monolithic in terms of religion, with both countries exhibiting a link between national identity and Catholicism. However, Christianity was introduced into Ireland about five centuries earlier than in Poland. In 431, Pope Celestine I sent Bishop Palladius to minister to the Christians who already existed in Ireland. Saint Patrick arrived on the island the following year. Already by the 6th century the new faith of Christianity was so strong that the Irish monk Saint Columba was sent to Britain where he spread Irish customs, including the Christian faith. By the 9th century, Christianity had become dominant in Irish culture, with Christianity in Ireland being characterized by some practices that distinguished it from other parts of Christian Europe, as Irish Christians venerated the Pope and stayed unified with Rome. By the time Poland began to become Christian, Ireland was already in its so-called Gaelic period, with a dominant, well-developed Christian culture. The tension between national and religious identity in Ireland began after the English Reformation, when Henry VIII broke ties with Rome in 1534. Nevertheless, at that time, the Pope still had suzerainty over Ireland. But, in 1536, Henri VIII of England brought Ireland under English control and was proclaimed King of Ireland by the Irish Parliament in 1541.

Irish national independence was inaugurated in the 19th century with some similarities between the Irish struggle for independence and Polish uprisings. In Ireland, the symbolic figure of this national movement was Daniel O'Connell, who was a Catholic, and was illegally elected to the British Parliament. Future conflicts between Unionists and supporters of the Home Rule bill resulted in the exclusion of six of the nine counties of the northern province of Ulster, thereby creating Northern Ireland. In 1916, the Easter Rising was carried out by the Irish Citizen Army. After the election of 1918, the pro-independence party Sinn Fein proclaimed an Irish Republic with own parliament and government. And, in 1937, a new Irish constitution was ratified, with Catholic social teaching shaping important parts of the constitution.

Although the tension between the political regime and religious identity started much later in Poland, there are some similarities between the dominance of Protestant Prussia and Orthodox Russia in some parts of Poland and the English political influence on Catholic Ireland. However, one major difference between Polish and Irish history emerged after the Second World War, when Poland fell under Communist control. By the time Poland started its political and economic transformation in the 1990s, Ireland had already experienced significant economic development, with the country being known as the Celtic Tiger. From 1995 to 1999 the average annual GDP growth in Ireland was about 9 percent. And, in 1999, Ireland joined the Eurozone. By 2000, the Irish GDP per capita was estimated to be the 6th highest in the world. However, in 2008, Ireland was shocked by a financial crisis from which they are still recovering.

The Irish population is predominantly Catholic. However, adherence to the faith had varied over time. At the beginning of the 19th century, prior to the Great Famine, Catholicism in Ireland was rather nominal. Mass attendance in the 1830s was around 40 percent (Larkin, 1997, p. 8). However, during the middle of the 19th century, Irish Catholicism experienced a growth that finds no parallels in Polish Catholicism, as, after the Great Famine of 1845–1851, Catholicism in Ireland experienced the so-called 'Devotional Revolution'. The famine depopulated the poorest groups in Irish society who were also less religious. And, following the famine, a gradual growth of income among Irish Catholics contributed to building programs of various Catholic institutions, such as schools, monasteries and hospitals. In fact, during the second half of the 19th century, the Catholic Church in Ireland was strong enough to 'export' priests, particularly to the United States. And, by the beginning of the 20th century, nearly 90 percent of the Irish attended Mass weekly (Hirschman, 2004, p. 1219).

Today, both Ireland and Poland are among those societies in Europe with the highest share of Catholics in their populations. But, despite the fact that the two countries have many historical similarities, the contemporary situation of Polish and Irish Catholicism reveals many differences. Since the turn of the Millennium, both countries show some decline in religious attitudes, but that decline is much deeper in Ireland. Already by 2009, the Catholic Church in Ireland was shaken by the depth of the Catholic sex-abuse cases, with even Pope Benedict XVI recognizing the failures of the Church authorities in Ireland. Thus, during the post-Communist period when the Catholic Church in Poland has been developing its institutions, Catholic institutions in Ireland have been declining. The sex-abuse cases in the Catholic Church contributed to a decrease in the number of Irish people who declared themselves to be affiliated with the Church. According to the Irish census of 2011, 84.7 percent of their citizens declared themselves to be Roman Catholics, but in the 2016 census, only 78.8 percent did so. The number of people claiming 'no religious affiliation' grew over the same period of time, with 5.6 percent claiming no religion in 2011, 9.6 percent in 2016, and among those

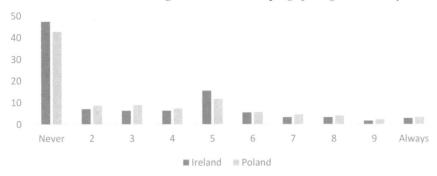

Figure 5.1 The attitude towards abortion in Ireland and in Poland in 2008.

Source: EVS, 2015.

in the census with Irish nationality the numbers rose from 4.4 percent to 8.5 percent (Central Statistical Office, 2016).

But, according to the European Social Survey, the share of Catholic affiliation in Ireland is actually much lower than what is revealed in the national census data. (European Social Survey, 2016). According to this survey, 91 percent of Polish people declared some religious affiliation, whereas the corresponding figure among the Irish was 74 percent. Likewise, the level of Mass attendance is lower in Ireland than in Poland. Again, according to the European Social Survey of 2016, whereas 49 percent of all Poles claimed attending religious services at least once a week, only 38 percent did so in Ireland. While 12 percent of the Irish population declared themselves to be 'not religious at all', the corresponding figure for Poland is 4 percent, and while 5 percent of the Irish declare themselves to be 'very religious', in Poland 12 percent do so (European Social Survey, 2016). During the period when Polish migration to Ireland began, Polish attitudes toward abortion, as seen in Figure 5.1, were somewhat more liberal than Irish attitudes towards abortion.

The decline in affiliation with the Catholic Church among those with a Polish nationality in Ireland has also been somewhat similar in nature, falling from 90 percent in 2011 to 85.9 percent in 2016. To a certain extent, this drop in the level of affiliation with the Catholic Church has been associated with a growth among those who claim affiliation with other religious bodies. Among Poles in Ireland, between 2011 and 2016, there has been a slight growth (1.5 percent) in those claiming affiliation with other Churches, such as the Church of Ireland, the Church of England, the Anglican Church and the Episcopal Church. The figure for those with Polish nationality resident in Ireland who declared 'no religious affiliation' has risen from 1.7 percent to 2.9 percent over the same period (Central Statistical Office, 2016). However, Polish migrants to Ireland are generally less religious than Polish citizens

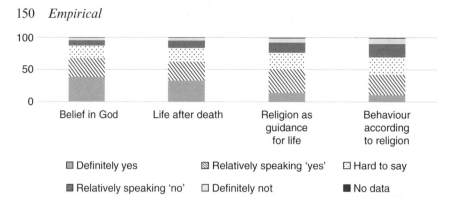

Figure 5.2 Religious beliefs and religious concerns of Polish migrants to Ireland in 2018.

Source: own research.

who stay in their homeland. As can be seen in Figure 5.2, our Random Driven Sample Survey conducted in 2018 reveals that 68 percent of Polish migrants to Ireland declared 'a belief in God', 65 percent 'a belief in life after death', with 51 percent claiming that 'religion delivers some kind of guidance in their life' and 43 percent stating that they 'try to behave according to religious rules'.

When the institutional relationships between Polish and Irish Catholicism in Ireland are examined, one finds that there are no independent Polish pastoral structures. Polish pastoral ministry is organized within Irish Catholic dioceses, and Polish pastoral centers are organized within Irish parishes.[6] There are about 30 Polish priests in Ireland, and Polish priests are delegated by the Polish Bishops to deliver ministry among Polish migrants. Irish Catholic organizations do not actively engage in service for Polish migrants, and the strategy of some Polish priests is to encourage Polish Catholics to participate in Irish parishes. However, not all Polish priests agree with this strategy. For example, in some centers, the First Communion celebration is organized in Polish. And, in Dublin there continues to be, even in 2019, nine Masses every Sunday celebrated in Polish as happens in Poland, whereas in Irish parishes there are traditionally only one or two Masses on a Sunday. Nevertheless, Polish priests face many organizational problems, as the Polish Catholic ministry's operations are strongly affected by the social mobility of Polish migrants. Not only do Polish migrants move from one part of the city to another, but they may also move abroad in search of income. That is why the relationship between Polish migrants and Polish priests, who may have migrated also, is very unstable and unbalanced.

Migration and reflexivity

In international statistics, migration is defined as a stable change of residence from one country to another. However, migration should be distinguished from tourism, which is why migration is often defined as something that lasts óne year or more. Migrants must manage to live in a society which is different from the one from which they emigrated, and interact with people belonging to different cultural systems. Thus 'transnational migrants' are able to build a set of networks beyond their home nation. The cultural effects of migration are often described in terms of cultural diffusion, whereas the impact of migration on traditional cultures has been characterized in diverse ways.

The study of Polish migrants represents a methodological opportunity for studying religious change from the perspective of the 'mobility turn' (Schiller and Salazar, 2013), which relates to the modern increase in migratory movements that are mediated by reflexivity that occurs between social structure and agency. From this perspective, migration in modern culture is more frequent, more individualistic and more reflexive, because social relationships in this context are themselves more fluid. Migrants search for stability and meaning (Hirschman, 2004, p. 1219), and migration exposes migrants to new ideas and provides an opportunity for live in new configurations of relationships for the individual and to the existing social structure. That is why, as notes Anna White, studying migrants may help the analyst to decipher social trends that are not observable from the perspective of 'methodological nationalism' (White, 2018). The social and cultural differences between one's current place of residence and those of one's place of origin inclines migrants to search for safety, whether psychological or physical in nature, in their new place of residence (Saar, 2018).

Izabela Grabowska examines the relationship between social and spatial migration among Poles, and she highlights reflexivity as a crucial factor shaping their accounts of migration (Grabowska, 2016). She studied Polish migration from the perspective of 'social remittances,' and she noticed that changes in norms, values and attitudes were among the most commonly noted consequences of migration occurring in the 19th, 20th and 21st centuries. Though the decision to migrate may be based on economical calculations between the costs and benefits of migration, decisions to migrate are not based on economic considerations only. They also entail decisions involving 'hard to measure' elements related to social relationships, such as leaving one's extended family and friends. Thus, for some Poles in the UK, research has shown that the decision to migrate from Poland was not solely an economical decision (Grabowska and Engbersen, 2016). Hence, what is transferred in the process of migration should not be reduced to the circulation of money between the place of origin and the destination. The Polish migrant, with norms and values acquired within a Catholic, and local Polish, cultural context confronts a new cultural environment at the destination. Migration thereby opens up new perspectives, and it affects human reflexivity by setting people within a new social and natural environment with potentially different norms, values and desired performance competencies from one's country of origin.

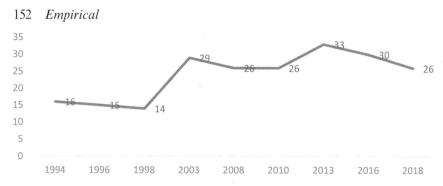

Figure 5.3 'If you had problems in finding a proper job, after finishing your studies would you go abroad?' Percent of respondents at high school (mostly 18–19 years of age).

Source: Grabowska and Gwiazda, 2019, p. 94.

Polish migrants frequently experience anxiety and fear in their new place of residence. They may feel lost in the new culture. Over time, these emotions change to either feelings of satisfaction and self-fulfillment or to feelings of solitude and frustration. Decisions to migrate involve a search for better and fairer job opportunities, as young people sometimes find opportunities to work are limited in Poland. Frequently, 'Mobility is perceived as the enterprise of youth and an alternative to a traditional, sedentary existence [...] (as) current migrants perceive the Polish workplace as a site of struggle and competition with a patriarchal and backward facing work culture' (Botterill, 2012, p. 154). And, as shown in Figure 5.3, the willingness of young Poles to migrate to find a job has increased over the past two decades, although during the last five years there has been a decline in the percentage of young people declaring the desire to go abroad to look for a job.

Polish culture is often perceived as harbouring a system of antagonistic and redundant values. Polish migrants experience a tension between individual aspirations and moral expectations related to their family. Krystyna Slany and Brigida Solga suggest that migration has contributed to a higher rate of divorce among Poles (2014, p. 24). Social mobility promotes circumstances that 'require people to deliberate upon how they can and should live amidst such change' (Mellor and Schilling, 2014, p. 280). Justyna Bell and Markieta Domecka have studied reflexive and emotional aspects of Polish migration to Belfast in North Ireland, focusing on the relationship between the subjectivity of migrants and their settlement context. They argue that migration can be potentially transformative, but only when it is accompanied by structural enablement and agential powers of reflexivity (Bell and Domecka, 2017). Migration brings transformative potential which can be used as reflexive elaboration of 'the past, present and future, including the reflection on their gender roles, their significant places and the movement between them' (Bell and Domecka, 2017, p. 2).

Migration consists not only in changing one's inhabited space. Apart from some exceptions, whether to migrate or not is a decision which takes into account the advantages and disadvantages of leaving one's homeland. After emigration human beings are also faced with a different cultural system which presents them with new cultural ideas, beliefs, rituals, norms and other elements of the new culture. The unfamiliar life context stimulates reflexively for elaborating new *modus vivendi* of personal concerns. In these new social conditions Polish immigrants are faced with fresh problems which must be resolved with deliberation. Generally speaking, Polish migrants express negative emotions towards the social situation in Poland. For them, Polish society is strongly normative and even oppressive. From their perspective, Polish Catholicism is viewed as being strict and lacking spontaneity. Such negative emotions emerge largely because they contend that living in Poland does not enable them to enjoy a comfortable and stable life. Moreover, distrust is prevalent in Poland. Some migrants claim that mistrust was a function of life under Communism which continues to have a negative impact on Polish society. Contact with Polish institutions prompts largely negative emotions. And, from this perspective, Catholic institutions also frequently hold negative connotations for Polish migrants. Living in Poland is characterized by Polish migrants as being full of stress and hurry, whereas living In Ireland is viewed to be much more comfortable, calm, and relaxed. When asked about Irish social bonds, Polish migrants claim that human relationships in Ireland are more spontaneous and natural. As described by a man (45) living in Cork:

> In Poland, I did not behave like this, as I do here, for example. There, I was running all the time: work, home, work, home, work, home. There I had a child, a wife, and so on, but somehow, I did not have time to be with them. I went abroad. Here I have much more time to talk, stop for a moment. There, in my work, and my own private life, I did not have such time. I did not have it with my colleagues at work and it turned me off. Here I like it more, because in Poland I did not have time for anything.

As a result, living in Ireland evokes very different types of emotions. Generally speaking, Polish migrants share very positive attitudes towards Ireland and Irish culture. Positive attitudes are not only simply directed toward the Irish people but toward Irish social structures as well. From their perspective, Irish citizens are friendly and very nice which derives largely from the migrants' experiences related to safety and well-being. Not only do Polish migrants feel safe in Ireland, but migrating Poles also feel that they have been supported by Irish institutions, especially the Irish welfare state.

> However, when it comes to such experiences, why I am here, I am delighted with how the state cares about families. At least, for me as a

single mother, I came here in 2005, so my children were not yet adult. I got all the help, even though I worked, of course, but the earnings were not enough to keep my two children here, the third was already adult, so I always got this help and I think that education is much better here than in Poland.

(Woman, Cork, 39)

Some authors claim that religion plays an important role in the migration process, especially in the 'decision to migrate, to endure the perils of the voyage and to build transnational community structures' (Hagan and Ebaugh, 2003, p. 1159). For example, Sylwia Urbanska has argued that religious concerns can impact migration decisions. She contends that religion can, in some cases, affect the decision to migrate (for instance, in the case of members of religious minorities), but that religion has also shaped the gender roles and attitudes of migrants. She admits, however, that religion is likely to have had a stronger influence on migration decisions in the past than it does today (Urbanska, 2016, p. 52). Research on modern migration reveals that religion plays a rather secondary role in such decisions. However, after people have migrated, the religious attitudes of immigrants are sustained in part through migrants staying in touch with their native religious communities. Sylwia Urbanska also points out the paradoxical nature of migration studies, contending that some authors who study migration tend to ignore religion in their research despite the fact that conducting fieldwork within religious organizations is one of the most convenient contexts for reaching migrants (2016, p. 53).

My study of Polish migrants in Ireland reveals that religion played a relatively unimportant role in their migratory decisions, as only a small percentage of Polish migrants (14 percent) claimed that religion had any impact on their decision to migrate. Religion constitutes no more than a background factor in the decision to migrate, as practical concerns largely shape such decisions. This is why the religious concerns noted about migration related to very pragmatic considerations such as the decision to baptize one's child or to marry in the Church. After immigrating to Ireland, Polish migrants largely retain their religious faith. One third of Polish migrants (33.3 percent) report that their level of religious attitudes has not changed since leaving Poland. However, a larger percentage reports that their faith has declined in strength (18.1 percent) as opposed to becoming stronger (7.1 percent). However, when examined by other measures, it becomes clear that migration to Ireland is accompanied by some religious decline. When asked about religious practices first in Poland and then in Ireland, it becomes obvious that migrants attend Mass less often, pray less frequently, and declare themselves to be less religious in Ireland than when they lived in Poland. 17 percent of Polish migrants reported attending Holy Mass regularly 'on Sundays or more often' in Poland, whereas only 8 percent report doing so since living in Ireland. A similar decline in religious behaviour

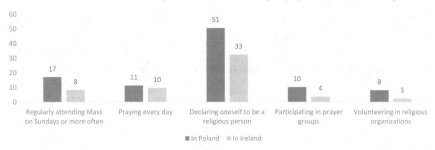

Figure 5.4 Declared religious attitudes before and after migration to Ireland in 2018.

Source: own research.

was evident in the practices of engaging in personal prayer, participating in prayer groups, and volunteering for religious groups. As a result, while a majority of Polish migrants to Ireland (51 percent) declared that they could be characterized as 'a religious person' when they lived in Poland, no more than 33 percent claim the same since living in Ireland (See Figure 5.4).

Significantly, such expressions as perceiving oneself as being less religious in Ireland than in Poland are not based on some perceived higher level of religiosity associated with the Irish people. In fact, only 3 percent of Polish migrants claim that the Irish are more religious than Poles, with 29 percent claiming that Poles are more religious than the Irish and another 30 percent indicating that they are equally religious. Nor do Polish migrants perceive Irish Catholicism to have more value than Polish Catholicism. In fact, while only 3 percent contend that Irish Catholicism is 'more precious to me' than Polish Catholicism, 24 percent claim that Polish Catholicism has more personal value than Irish Catholicism, with another 28 percent indicating that they are of equal value.

Living in another culture may prompt migrants to talk about their religion or the religion of the country to which they have emigrated. And, our 2018 survey of Polish migrants reveals that many Polish migrants do talk about religion. About one-third of Polish migrants claim to talk about religion with other people, but most often they talk about religion within their family, either with their children (27 percent) or with their spouse (23 percent).

The search for well-being

Post-accession Polish migration is often characterized as 'labour migration' (Kaczmarczyk, 2018). Migration from Poland has been largely motivated by economic factors, as the desire for 'money and jobs' encourages people to leave Poland and to move abroad (Slany and Solga, 2014, p. 15). A similar conclusion is reached by Frelak and Grot (2013, p. 600) – recent

Polish migration is oriented toward securing jobs and earning money. For the study of religious change, it is important to recognize that migrating due to labour is related to a special facet of human concerns. Migration related to the search for a better paying job and the struggle to live under better economic conditions not only relates to present concerns but also to future considerations. Despite the fact that migration is most often an individual and autonomous decision, recent migration has been increasingly characterized by settlement motivations. In 2011 about 16 percent of Polish emigrants declared emigration was due to family bonds (Slany and Solga, 2014, p. 15). Labour migrants can be distinguished from 'lifestyle migrants', with the latter being more motivated by the search for a better life and 'potential self' (Benson and Osbaldiston, 2014; Benson and O'Reilly, 2009). However, neither the labour nor lifestyle motivation should be understood as being independent of the search for well-being. Studying migration from the perspective of those seeking well-being directs one's attention not only to personal concerns but also to the role of social organization and institutions, including religious ones. Religious institutions provide resources to migrants (Hirschman, 2008), not just spiritual aspects of life. Instead, religious institutions also organize assistance for migrants, foster their new social networks, and even provide jobs or housing opportunities (Cadge and Ecklund, 2007, p. 362).

Many Polish migrants chose to escape Poland largely due to well-being aspirations, as their decisions to leave are primarily related to earning money and having a good job. As shown in Figure 5.5, Poles who migrated to Ireland were generally in search of better, more comfortable, stable, peaceful living conditions.

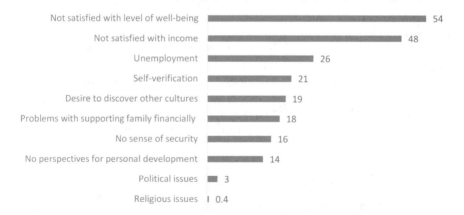

Figure 5.5 Reasons for leaving Poland according to Polish migrants in Ireland in 2018 (in percent).

Source: own research.

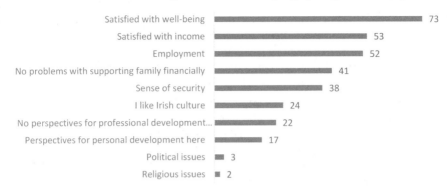

Figure 5.6 Reasons for remaining in Ireland according to Polish migrants in 2018 (in percent).

Source: own research.

More than half the Polish migrants claim to have left their homeland in search of greater well-being, and they stay for the same reasons (see Figure 5.6). Polish migrants report that living in Irish society is more comfortable and not so stressful. Having a job ensures adequate economic stability and living conditions.

Only in recent years has financial risk arisen due to the rising cost of securing flats as rental accommodation. Polish migrants also claim that, in their subjective perception, the level of well-being is much higher in Ireland than in Poland, and they see Irish culture as being more focused on the individual. Hence the educational system places more stress on individual achievements and is student-centred; moreover, there is more social trust in Ireland than in Poland. A comment by a Polish migrant from Cork reflects well these concerns related to well-being:

> From the general impressions that I have here, it is much easier here, it is easier to live and my impression of the Irish as a nation, in general, is that they are extremely nice, that it is a nice nation'
>
> (Woman, 45)

Migrants face many challenges, such as unemployment, illness or social marginalization. And, difficult experiences such as these may motivate individuals to search for theological meaning or religious explanations for traumatic situations. For some, migration can foster greater religious commitment. As Katarzyna Gmaj explains, for religious Polish migrants in Norway, belonging to the Polish Catholic community represents a way of 'taming space'. This 'taming' consists of religious rituals that are regular and repetitive and that are the same as those in Poland. Engaging in such rituals enables Polish migrants to feel safe and sheltered (Gmaj, 2018,

p. 176). From this perspective, one's relation to transcendence emerges when Polish migrants confront the existential tensions that are associated with migration. Given that relating to God and strengthening one's bonds with God, as a safeguard related to the transcendental order and the force that directs individual life, is a relatively common experience among migrants, 'it is justified to assume that religion represents an aspect of identity which is gaining importance among some migrants' (Krotofil, 2013, p. 195).

However, any religious change that is experienced in a reflexive way by some Polish migrants should not be interpreted as the transition to some institutionalized or 'Church' religiosity. Michal Garapich argues that the 'Polish Catholic Church' organizations in the UK were more interested in 'maintaining dominant positions and their symbolic power than offering advocacy, support networks or a common platform of inter-generational communication' (2008, p. 744). He suggests that, when compared to market forces, Catholic organizations have played a rather small role in the inclusion of Polish immigrants in the UK. And, he contends that 'traditional Polish ethnic associations and institutions, especially the Polish Catholic Church, have been rather slow in reacting to and assisting the newcomers' (Garapich, 2008, p. 744). As Polish priests recall, Polish migrants to Ireland searched for social support in Polish 'parishes' when the Polish migration wave began after 2004. However, once Polish migrants became well integrated into Irish society, Polish 'parishes' did not continue to deliver important social support for Polish migrants.

Facing new cultural contexts

Some authors contend that migration changes traditional family roles (White, 2011), whereas others stress that migration does not put an end to traditional norms and structures (Ryan, 2010). Stephen Warner points out that migrant negotiate not only social or practical concerns but also their religious identity (1998). This is so because migration affects human attitudes both in the direction of reinforcing some rules and norms and also in the direction of weakening others. According to some authors, recent Polish migration results from not only structural factors, such as unemployment, but also from the process of individualization in the formation of life biographies (Slany and Solga, 2014, p. 5).

To help understand the new relationship between national identity and religion among Polish migrants, Agata Gorny and Dorota Osipovic differentiate between types of migrants: *Odyssean refugees* and *Rubicon refugees*. According to them, the post-war wave of Polish refugees represents the first type of refugees who, being forced to escape from their country, were intensely oriented towards Poland. Odyssean refugees remain psychologically engaged with the society they have left. As such, these Polish refugees strongly identify with their Polish compatriots and celebrate their national and social identity in connection with their homeland. Odyssean refugees are also concerned about the next generation of those remaining in their native land. Accordingly, the two authors claim that that post-war Polish migrants in Great Britain exhibit a 'double orientation' with regard to England and Poland by enjoying the quality of life in Britain while still being symbolically and practically engaged in the ideological and political situation in Poland (Gorny and Osipovic, 2006, p. 31–35). Although using somewhat different terminology, Anna White makes a similar argument by claiming that post-World War II migration should be viewed more in terms of 'diaspora' in that it is characterized by a strong collective ethos, 'passionate commitment to remaining Polish' and a sense of exile from the homeland. In the post-World War II wave of Polish migration, the identity of Polish migrants was largely formed in relationship to the political situation in their native country; as such migrants had a staunch anti-communist orientation. Their formation of strong Polish organizations represented a form of political involvement, while developing the feeling of being apart or even excluded from their homeland (White, 2018, p. 186).

In the post-accession era of Polish migration, the second type, Rubicon refugees, strongly differs from the diaspora model of migration. First, the political situation in Poland is now very different, as Poland has become a member of the European Union and other international and democratic organizations. While post-World War II Polish migration was primarily related to political considerations, post-accession migration is largely based on non-political factors. And after 2004 many Poles have migrated for economic reasons, while some others have done so for social and cultural reasons. According to Katherine Botterill, some migrants may search for autonomy and freedom from some of the moral restrictions that prevail in Poland. In particular, some who are divorced and cannot stay in a religious marriage may find it easier to be accepted abroad than in their home communities. Likewise, migration for some Poles may be a way of escaping from family control or domestic violence (Botterill, 2012).

Migration today is radically different from what it was, only two or three decades ago. Poles who migrate today are far better able to stay in touch with their homeland, thanks to easier transport and to more effective communication infrastructures. Hence post-accession migrant Poles can stay in touch with their families and friends back in their homeland much more easily than post-World War II migrants. Given the changes related to ease of border crossings, speedier transportation and new communication technologies, new transnational social patterns have emerged which also make the post-accession migration experience qualitatively different from post-World War II migration. For example, raising, socializing and caring for children have taken on a 'trans-national character'. Sarah Bojarczuk and Peter Mühlau describe the phenomenon of 'floating grandmothers', as some grandmothers are able to travel to other countries to take care of their grandchildren, often without a basic knowledge of the foreign language of that country (Bojarczuk and Muhlau, 2018). Similarly, through various virtual and online mechanisms, some migrants take care of their parents who remain in Poland, and Polish migrants are also involved in the transnational care of their children who remain with their grandmothers in Poland. They do so via Skype or phone, taking part in doing homework together, having access to teachers' evaluations of their children, or even doing online shopping. Family members may come to visit migrants living abroad, and migrants may also return to visit their families in Poland, particularly during Christmas, Easter and other holidays (Maksymowicz, 2013). Migrants may also help to support members of their families back in Poland by providing emotional support or by helping practically with various forms of technology (for example, through the use of phone or internet connections) and by providing financial support (Slany and Solga, 2014, pp. 62–63).

Botterill claims that 'the rules and expectations of the Church are perceived to create barriers to formal worship' among those oriented towards individual well-being (Botterill, 2012, p. 203). In her research conducted among Polish migrants in Great Britain, she demonstrates that some of the justifications offered for detachment from the Catholic Church during the emigration process are similar to those shared by Catholics who stay in Poland; these include not only criticisms related to institutional aspects of Catholicism but disapproval of certain theological elements as well (Botterill, 2012, p. 202). And, as Joanna Krotofil claims, migration may well liberate migrants from religious norms they once held (2013, p. 204). Anna White notes that 'Poles abroad today are often believed, and sometimes seem to be, more liberal, less religious and more individualistic than Poles in Poland' (2018, p. 187). Therefore, they are sometimes seen to be 'less Polish' by those Poles who hold a normative view of Polish identity as being distinctively Catholic, adding that migration offers more choice of lifestyles. Polish migrants to Scotland have encountered clear social expectations based on the assumption that all Poles are pious Catholics. As a result, Some Polish migrants were surprised to learn that many Scottish people expected them to go to Church every Sunday (Botterill, 2012, p. 202), even though Polish post-accession migrants are not as attached to the Catholic Church as were the post-war Polish migrants. Recent migrants were socialized within a different religious culture from that experienced by earlier migrants. As a result, strong tensions can, at times, be observed between 'old' and 'new' Polish migrants within Polish parishes (Trzebiatowska, 2010). Moreover, the post-accession migration is mainly composed of the younger generation of Poles who, as a group, already tend to be less religious than the older generations (Frelak and Grot, 2013, p. 60).

On the other hand, it is not clear that migration necessarily leads to a decline in Polish national identity. Polish migrants in the United Kingdom could be characterized, according to Seweryn Kapinos, by the interconnection between their national and religious identity, as well as by the emotional attachment they express toward their national traditions (Kapinos,

2018, p. 138). He argues that the social situation of Polish migrants in Britain has encouraged the strengthening of their Polish national identity (Kapinos, 2018, p. 140). For many churchgoing Poles, 'Catholicism is a symbolic extension of their national identity' (Trzebiatowska, 2010, p. 1059). This merging of religious and national identity can create certain difficulties for Poles who migrate. Recent Polish migrants to Britain can serve as a good example of how difficult it can be to overcome such 'religion-national mythologies' that link certain religious expectations with particular national identities (Trzebiatowska, 2010, p. 1069). For Polish Catholics, especially those involved in the charismatic movement discussed below, national belonging plays no role in their identity, as the strong national identity, which characterized Polish migrants in the past, has now been replaced by an identity shaped with direct reference to transcendence (Krotofil, 2013, p. 230).

The Catholic Church is transnational in character and in theory; the religious beliefs of Catholics should be the same regardless of their national context. Likewise, the organizational structure of the church should be similar regardless of national context. However, cultural differences may emerge among different ethnic or national groups of Catholics residing within the same geographical context. Polish Catholic migrants share with British Catholics a minority status within Great Britain. Yet, various scholars (for example, Grzymala-Moszczynska and Marta Trzebiatowska) have noted that there are sharp cultural and religious differences between Polish and British Catholics in Great Britain (Grzymala-Moszczynska, Hay and Krotofil, 2011, p. 1066–1067; Trzebiatowska, 2010). Polish Catholic migrants to the UK discern deep differences between themselves and British Catholics in their relationship to transcendence (Trzebiatowska, 2010, p. 1066–1067). Nevertheless, the study of the role of religion among Polish migrants needs to be more attentive to the local religious context to which they migrate, as migrants can contribute to local Catholic communities in different ways, depending on the particular context. For example, in countries where the Catholic Church is a minority faith within a highly pluralized society (e.g., Norway), Polish Catholics may be welcomed to help supplement local parishes (Erdal, 2017). However, when Catholicism represents the dominant religion in the society to which one migrates, Polish migrants may consider religion to be an element that serves to integrate them with others within their new society (Galent, Goddeeris and Niedzwiedzki, 2009).

The ability to speak the language of the country to which one has migrated can be considered an important marker of the extent to which the migrant has become integrated within the new country of residence. Based on our survey, Polish migrants in Ireland report that they possess relatively good and improving, language skills. When these Poles migrated to Ireland, only 16 percent claimed that they could speak English well. But, now, 70 percent claim that they are able to do so. Despite living in an

English-speaking country, many Polish migrants to Ireland prefer to worship using the Polish language, either exclusively or by including English language services occasionally. Close to 20 percent of our respondents indicated that they preferred to worship using *only* the Polish language (18.5 percent) – more than twice as many as those who indicated that they preferred to worship using only the English language (8.1 percent). Most Polish migrants, however, indicated that they preferred worshipping using a mixture of the two languages, with a somewhat higher percentage preferring the use of Polish primarily and English only occasionally (27.5 percent) than those preferring English primarily and Polish only occasionally (17.9 percent).

However, while Polish migrants to Ireland may express a preference for worshipping in the Polish language, they are far less likely to indicate that they feel attached to the Polish pastoral services provided within Ireland. Only 23 percent of the Polish migrants reported such an attachment. Nor do such migrants express attachment to the local Irish pastoral ministry; only 12 percent did so. Clearly, many Polish migrants do not feel attached to any Catholic pastoral services, whether they are Polish or Irish. For those Polish Catholics who participated in the Sunday Mass in a Polish 'parish' in Dublin, being a Pole was important to them, with Polish Catholicism viewed as being 'more precious to me' than Irish Catholicism. Almost all such worshippers (97 percent) declared that being a Pole is important for them. And to the extent that these migrant Poles perceived differences between Polish and Irish Catholicism, they were far more likely to report that they viewed Polish Catholicism as being 'more precious' than Irish Catholicism (23.5 percent) than the reverse (2.7 percent).

Polish migrants express the same level of attachment to their host country as they do to their homeland. Based on our 2018 survey, slightly more than two-thirds (71 percent) of our Polish migrant sample claimed that they are attached to Ireland and to Poland. Polish migrants to Ireland often have spouses or partners living with them; 77 percent of our respondents had a Polish spouse/partner with them in Ireland, with two-thirds reporting that they also had children living with them in Ireland. A relatively small percentage reported that either one or both of their parents also lived in Ireland (9 percent), with nearly twice as many Polish migrants (17 percent) reporting that they had a sibling living in Ireland as well. Polish migrants to Ireland report most frequently (72 percent) that they have parents living back in Poland, while small percentages report that they have a wife/husband (4 percent) or a partner (2 percent) back in Poland. Polish migrants are more likely to be separated from their children (13 percent) than from their spouses/partners (6 percent), suggesting that some Polish migrants either have adult children living back in Poland or that some migrants are divorced, having children but no spouse living back in Poland. In addition to having family members living with them in Ireland, many Polish migrants report that they have also made many Irish friends while living in Ireland;

35.6 percent of our Polish migrant respondents reported having 'many Irish friends', although a larger percentage (51.2 percent) reported that they still had 'many Polish friends'.

Many Polish migrants view the socio-cultural system in Poland to be strongly normative and more community-oriented, whereas they view the Irish socio-cultural system to be less normative and restrictive and more individualistic in nature. Accordingly, many migrants report that their relationship to transcendence in Ireland is more joyful and pleasant. As a Polish woman from Dublin explained, the Irish culture is more human-centred than in Poland, where one's relationship to transcendence is strongly affected by social pressure.

> I remember when I was eight months pregnant in Poland and went to church without tights, it was very hot. I was with my aunt, who is an older woman, not particularly elderly, but she's been living in Poland for many years, and she is a doctor. Here I am in the eighth month of pregnancy, and I'm sweating, and she said to me, "N, you do not have tights on and you come to church?" I replied, "Yes auntie, it would be very uncomfortable for me." She advised me, "No, wait, we have to go back, wait, where is the nearest open kiosk? But what is wrong with you? How can you come without tights?"
>
> (Women, Cork, 39)

Finally it is also worth noting that cultural diffusion also occurs when migrants return to live in the villages they formerly left. Return migration seem to affect Polish Catholicism nowadays in a similar way as in the past. Krystyna Duda-Dziewierz has shown that, in South Poland, reverse migration affects the village's way of life upon the return of the migrant. Following the return to their village, households were run in a more professional and systematic way. In addition, the social role of the parish was reduced (Duda-Dziewierz, 1938), as migrants who return to Polish village life enjoyed greater freedom, with the social pressure motivating them to attend Mass or pray having been reduced.

Performing religious rituals

Scott Myers found that migrants in general are less religious in comparison to people who do not migrate. Yet, European immigrants to the United States are more religious than Europeans in general (Myers, 2000). Thus, the level of religious attitudes of migrants is shaped not only by the religious context of their homeland but also by the context in the country to which they are emigrating (Connor, 2009). For example, Christian Smith, in his study on American evangelicalism, examined the effects on church attendance of regional migration within the United States and found that the religious attitudes of migrants correlated with the level of religious commitment in the region to which they had migrated. When people move to a region with a high level of religious practice, religious identity tends to increase, but when they move to an area where the level of religiosity is lower, religious identity decreases (Smith, Sikkink and Bailey, 1998). On the other hand, other quantitative studies suggest that migration generally results in the decline of religious attendance (Wuthnow and Kevin, 1979).

Moreover migration is associated not only with various levels but also with different patterns of religious attitudes. For example, immigrants to the United States who exhibit high levels of church attendance, but are worshipping in their native language, are less well integrated into American society. Wendy Cadge and Elaine Howard Ecklund found that the level of religious attendance can be negatively correlated with integration into American society, as 'native' parishes, congregations or other religious centres can serve as 'buffers' against American society (2006). A similar situation is evident in Norway regarding Polish 'native' parishes. Catholic Masses are celebrated in the Polish language in nearly all Catholic parishes in the country; there are about 44 such places. These Polish parish structures generate feelings of social trust and confidence, with Polish communities growing up around them. As a result, belonging to a Polish parish in Norway represents a manifestation of Polish identity in the new space, with these Polish communities playing not only religious, but also social roles (for instance, when such communities help other Polish migrants in searching for a new job or for accommodation) (Gmaj, 2018, p. 177).

Given these patterns, one would expect Polish migrants to exhibit religious practices more in conformity with the country to which they have emigrated. Hence, given that regular church attendance in Ireland is less than that evident in Poland, one would expect Polish migrants in Ireland to exhibit lower rates of religious participation than that of their homeland. However, what is less clear is the extent to which attendance at Holy Mass is shaped by the presence of Polish priests and services being conducted in the Polish language. For example, Seweryn Kapinos has studied the religious practices of Polish migrants in the area of Hertfordshire, and he found that 29 percent reported engaging regularly (at least once a month) in religious practices, with another 28 percent declaring that they only did so several times a year (Kapinos, 2018, p. 138). However, Kapinos believes that this relatively low level of religious practice evident among Polish migrants in Hertfordshire was limited by the absence of Polish priests and Polish parishes, as almost 40 percent of the Polish migrants declared that they would attend Holy Mass more often if there were a 'Polish' parish with Polish priests in their neighbourhood (2018, p. 138-139).

Generally speaking, Polish migrants to Ireland are not well integrated into the life of the local Irish community (Dzieglewski, 2011). Part of this lack of integration into local society may be a function of the fact that many Polish migrants decide to travel back to Poland in order to participate in religious ceremonies there. These journeys with a religious focus occur particularly for such occasions as a christening, First Communion, weddings and funerals (Ignatowicz, 2011). However, these decisions to return for such religious occasions depend, in part, on the importance given by the returning migrant to his or her religious practices or religious tradition. Yet, these decisions to return may frequently become detached from their initial religious pretext, just as 'religious holidays' are, and so, according to Anna Wojtynska, they are 'gradually turning into family celebrations and part of leisure time' (2011, p. 118).

Our 2018 survey of Polish migrants reveals a more complex picture concerning the extent to which Polish migrants are integrated into local Irish life (see Figure 5.7). On the one hand, many Polish migrants continue to

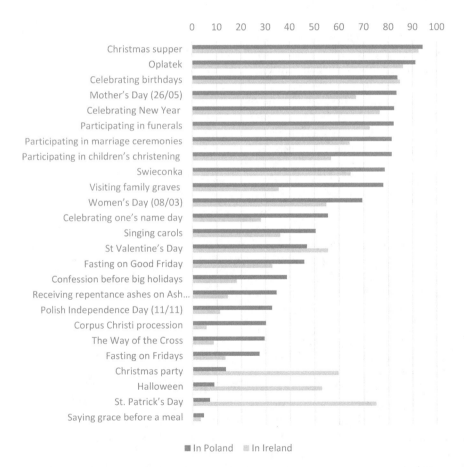

Figure 5.7 The practice of Polish traditions in Ireland by Polish migrants in 2018 (in percent).

Source: own research.

participate in a number of Polish rituals. For example, according to our survey of Polish migrants, about 90 percent report that they continue the tradition of Christmas supper and that of 'Oplatek'. Other rituals, such as celebrating one's birthday or the coming of the New Year, are relatively universal across cultures, and the extent to which Polish migrants celebrate such occasions remains at a similar level to that of Poland once in Ireland. Other Polish customs continue to be practised, but not as the same level as that which was evident in Poland (for example, 'Swieconka' and Good Saturday). The same is true with certain other practices, but lower levels of participation in these events could well be explained by the spatial distance from one's family and friends who remain in Poland (for example, celebrating Mother's Day, participation in funerals, the christening of children, marriages and visiting family graves).

On the other hand, our sample of Polish migrants report participating in new rituals related to the country in which they are living; 75 percent of Polish migrants surveyed reported that they celebrated St. Patrick's Day. Likewise, many Polish migrants reported that they had participated in a Christmas party or celebrated Halloween in Ireland with greater frequency than they had in Poland. On the other hand, various other religious rituals (such as, fasting, going to confession, participating in an Ash wednesday service or a Corpus Christi procession) are much less popular among the Polish migrants in Ireland than in Poland.

Many religious practices are related to the family and they foster bonds among family members. That is why many Polish migrants who miss the Polish rituals are searching for rituals that will help to unite their families. Among our migrant sample, more than half (57 percent) reported that they participated in religious rituals related to religious socialization. Among those choosing to participate in these rituals, nearly one-half (49 percent) chose to prepare their children for their First Communion within an Irish parish, while only 8 percent decided to organize the First Communion within some Polish 'parish' either in Ireland or Poland. However, when christening a child, Poland remains the most popular place to do so. Nearly 40 percent declared that they had christened their child in Poland, while another 24 percent had done so within a Polish 'parish' in Ireland. Only 24 percent reported that they had had their child christened in an Irish parish.

While similar religious rituals in the Catholic Church are celebrated in both Poland and Ireland, Polish migrants distinguish between the style of Polish and Irish Catholic rituals. For many migrants, Irish religious rituals are viewed to be more transparent and spontaneous, more joyful and less normative in nature. On the other hand, our Polish migrant sample frequently recall that taking part in Catholic rituals in Poland was more stressful in nature, producing feelings of pressure and anxiety, whereas participation in these rituals in Ireland are reported as a friendly, enjoyable and pleasant experience. As a Polish woman recalls:

The child had First Communion in Ireland and, for example, I remember it very well, I did not feel burdened as a parent. Contrary to my memories, my own communion, which was something very stressful to M., As I talk with cousins from Poland, I realize that too much has not been changed.

(Woman, Cork, 40)

Despite this, it is worth noting that among Polish migrants who attend Sunday Mass, 93 percent indicated that their faith helped them to overcome daily problems, And, Polish migrants also viewed certain other religious rituals as exhibiting greater transcendence when done within a Polish rather than an Irish context. For example, as expressed by a Polish man in Dublin:

Their marriages are an absolute tragedy. They do not even give a piece of cake. I would like to have everything elegant and perfect, so, nicely set tables and so on. And at their weddings it is only until six o'clock, whereas we have dinner and then we have a few glasses served, and then even serve the cake on napkins. They make a place to dance and people sit against the wall and I think it's awful.

(Man, Dublin, 35)

Emerging social engagement

Migration changes the relationship between an individual and the social structure within which they are located. And, migration can shape perceptions related to human agency. Research has shown that women experience greater emancipation as the result of the migratory experience, as Polish migrants who return from the United Kingdom are less supportive of traditional gender roles (Fuszara, 2005). And, religiosity may well foster agency among women migrants (Urbanska, 2016, p. 60), as their religious faith may help them overcome feelings of loneliness and helplessness as a result of separation from their children and the stress as they face performing multiple roles, such as household manager and caretaker of elderly parents (Slany and Solga, 2014). Moreover, studies have revealed the growing importance of individual autonomy and more rational and purpose-driven actions among Polish migrants in the first half of the 20th century. 'Rationality about spending and budgeting; belief in life success; and changing attitudes towards the Catholic Church leading to changes in religious practices whereby individual effort and achievement were recognized and praised.' (Grabowska and Engbergsen, 2016, p. 104) Likewise, Polish migrants who return to live in Poland frequently develop a more critical relationship with the Catholic Church, a more rational worldview, and more entrepreneurial attitudes.

However Polish migrants do not represent a homogenous social group. Some researchers have shown that the motivation for migrating among highly skilled migrants is oriented more towards self-development whereas the motivation among low-skilled migrants relates more to structural (that is, economic) reasons (Slany and Solga, 2014, p. 5). When one compares religiously engaged Polish migrants in Ireland with other Poles in Ireland, major differences are observed in their relationship to Irish culture and Irish Catholicism. The majority of Polish Catholics typically appreciate Irish Catholicism and Irish culture, and they assume that Catholic parishes in Ireland deliver what they need. Furthermore, they claim that there are fewer obstacles and exigencies to receiving the sacraments in Irish parishes compared to parishes in Poland. These generally positive attitudes toward Irish Catholicism are also evident with regard to their attitudes toward Irish culture, as they perceive Irish culture to be much more open and friendly than Polish culture.

In contrast, Polish migrants who are 'religiously active' are far more reserved in their attitudes towards Irish Catholicism. They do not like the way Irish priests celebrate the sacraments and are critical of the ways in which transcendence is realized within Irish Catholicism, including its liturgy and its practice of confession. In addition, they lament the diminishing role of Catholicism within Irish society and claim that Irish Catholicism is becoming too liberal. Some of them express disappointment with the moral rules advanced by Irish priests, as in this short statement:

> You must be aware of it. I, as I say, the friend I once mentioned, went for confession to a priest. He is living in a non-sacramental relationship and he confessed it, and the priest said, "love her, love her" and from what I know, he got absolution.
>
> (Man, Dublin, 50)

Religiously committed Polish Catholics in Ireland also criticize the way Irishmen practise prayer. According to them, there is not enough silence and veneration practised within Irish churches.

> I terribly dislike it, it is a very difficult matter, when, after the Mass or before, there is no focus, when someone prays in the church, most often the Irish behave like they are at a market, exactly like that. It does not have enough seriousness for someone who just wants to pray. This is one small example, but there are many such things.
>
> (Woman, Dublin, 45)

Our research showed that deeply religious Polish migrants are also concerned with the humanistic values of Irish culture, as they have strong normative inclinations that pinpoint highly important differences between Polish and Irish culture. They perceive Irish culture to be lacking a sense of the transcendental, something they oppose and try to challenge. Concerning Irish social and political life, religiously committed Polish migrants advocate a strong pro-life agenda. Many religiously-committed Polish migrants are fearful that the educational system in Ireland may not only weaken their children's allegiance to their religious tradition but that it may also weaken the moral and ethical attitudes of the younger generation. They observe a crisis in Irish education. They complain that children do not obey any rules and do not respect authority. As a result, religiously committed Polish migrants sometimes define themselves as 'counter-popular' and readily define their role in terms of duty. As a woman from Dublin (42) stated:

> I have a sense of mission that gives me the strength to live here. My mission is to give testimony.

What is more, among the religiously committed Polish migrants, (representing no more than 8 percent of the Polish migrants), their awareness of holding views contrary to mainstream public opinion is dominant. This perception results from the fact that Polish migrants who actively participate in the life of Polish 'parishes' in Ireland discern strong cultural differences between Polish and Irish Catholicism in that they perceive a strong secularization within Irish culture. For some of them, migration has constituted an opportunity for religious engagement or even conversion. The basis for this greater religious engagement was reported to be the desire for greater holiness, the search for meaning, and/or the desire for community. Thus, the way to greater religious engagement can be mediated by emotional crisis and the loss of extended family relationships. For some Polish migrants, emigration and separation from 'traditional' Catholicism stimulated reflexivity and shaped religious concerns.

> In Poland, I never interrogated my faith, I considered myself religious, practising, believing, but I never questioned it. After arriving here, after some time, it turned out that I just do not have a sense of community. A huge, excruciating feeling of loneliness and fear overcame me, and I started to cope as best as I could with the life and surrounding environment, problems, language, through intense work and as I can say most briefly, in a nutshell, who, if not you? [...] For me, the family was previously a community. I did not even know it, but I was in this community, I was strong because I was led by the faith of my ancestors who were with me. There was my mother, they were my parents, they were everything. I behaved automatically.
>
> (Woman, Dublin, 40)

Some migrants may well search for some 'deeper meaning' related to their migration experience (Krotofil, 2013, p. 230). Living through the process of migration, particularly when accompanied by feelings of loneliness, can be a means by which perspectives related to transcendence are transformed. For some, participation in a charismatic movement can foster a new perspective related to one's participation in the religious community as well as to one's agency within it, by reshaping the traditional distinction between controlling and being controlled by religious rules. As opposed to some 'Sunday' or 'Church' form of religiosity where transcendence is experience solely within the context of collective participation in religious services in the church, participation in a charismatic movement promotes a personal relationship with God, with experiences of transcendence that deliver feelings of peace and internal harmony (Krotofil, 2013, pp. 219–222). Although participation within a charismatic movement may, to some extent, be identified with the process of religious individualization, such 'charismatic individualization' should not be seen as a process of distancing oneself from religious institutions and some form of alienation from a normative religious order. Rather, within such religious movements, the nature of belonging to, and participating within, institutional religion is redefined and reshaped, as belonging to the traditional Church is now seen as based in the sharing of common religious experiences and a shared relationship to transcendence. As a result, the role of traditional rituals in integrating the social and transcendent orders is diminished, whereas rituals within the charismatic movement which focus on worship evoking strong emotions and fostering the personal experience of spiritual renewal, thus redefine the traditional borders between priests and laymen (Krotofil, 2013, p. 230 and 218).

Conclusions

Migration places human beings within a new structural and cultural context that requires a new relationship with orders of reality. Thus, with regard to Polish migrants to Ireland, the ideas and values they acquired in Poland are confronted with new cultural ideas and values. As a result, a new relationship between the individual and the social structure emerges through the process of migration. As Polish migrants confront the new social environment of Irish culture, their traditional Catholic values and practices undergo a process of adaptation and religious decline. On the margins, this process may also generate a smaller group of 'counter-popular' Catholics who may seek to change Irish society to more fully embody the traditional Catholic values and practices evident in the country from which they emigrated. Finally, taking the perspective of traditional society, it must be stated that although migration is destructive of 'contextual continuity', it also re-establishes new continuities which go beyond traditional Polish religious forms.

The Polish migrant's decision to immigrate to Ireland is largely shaped by perceived new opportunities. And upon arrival in Ireland, Polish migrants are engaged in a search for well-being and their efforts to adapt to Irish society. Despite some exceptions described above, this adaptation reconfigures also their involvement with transcendence, such that a new mode of integration between transcendental concerns and the new social environment emerges. The example of Polish migrants demonstrates that they become more interested in material issues related to objective well-being, rather than to internal or religious values. Ways of thinking that were previously dominated by values are now subordinated to instrumental goals. As the example of these 'counter-popular' Catholics shows, if Polish migrants desire to maintain continuity with their former lives in Poland, they may be able to construct 'contextual continuity' for themselves, but to do so requires that they be consciously committed and determined to prioritize the logic of continuity over that of opportunity.

However, religious change among Polish migrants could not be explained without reference to a process of reflexivity that was already shaped before the migrant's decision to leave the country. Poles emigrate after deliberating upon the opportunities and limits, circumstances and life chances involved, and in order to make decisions for their own well-being. Polish citizens are thereby compelled to evaluate for themselves those resources to which they will have access and the future costs associated with their decisions. Traditional collective migration agencies no longer support this evaluation with routinized guidelines, and, consequently, decisions have become more individualistic in nature. Polish citizens and Polish Catholics are thus provided with opportunities to break with tradition, that is, with their social origins and socialization in Poland. They have the scope to reformulate their 'ultimate concerns' and to redefine their commitments. New opportunities imply conceiving life as a project which can be shaped and accomplished. Life projects should not be understood as the achievement of instrumental goals but rather as itineraries which are sustained and advanced through discernment and self-monitoring. Migration is associated with the *decline of routine action*, the transformation from a 'given identity' into a 'task identity', which is achieved and actively performed. In comparison with traditional society, collective forms of participation are declining, and Polish Catholics are forced to develop their own life projects with direct reference to the global system. Migration deconstructs traditional religiosity, especially as found within local communities in Poland. Migration highlights the process of structural change, including aspects related to religious institutions.

Reflexivity is a requirement for Polish migrants to operate successfully within the globalized society and establish a *modus vivendi*. Polish migrants establish well-conceived projects, which should not be understood as simply the result of some momentary deliberation, because their life projects are shaped through personal commitment and accompanied by a sustained process of reflexive discernment and self-monitoring. Growing reflexivity is linked to increases in social individualism because Polish migrants are forced to elaborate their own 'self-culture' and their own 'life way'. Migration stimulates reflexivity which results in greater detachment from traditional Polish culture and Catholicism. The history of Polish migration shows that new technologies, especially the Internet, have fostered novel forms of social interaction. Traditional ideas are no longer controlled by institutions, as now technology also distributes them within the cultural system. The social order changes so rapidly that 'new continuities' cannot be re-established. Migration affects Poles in that this process of social penetration and change is accompanied by the lack of development of new mediating institutions within society.

Practical concerns related to labour emerge concurrently with religious ones. Religious institutions may play an important role in the lives of Polish migrants, but they remain largely separated from the practical concerns related to well-being. According to Polish migrants, their personal aspirations stand opposed to the social norms embodied within traditional Polish society. Polish Catholics in Ireland may 'use' religious institutions, but they do not feel part of them. Subjectively, they are distanced and alienated from them. Polish Catholicism is identified with the restraining nature of the Polish socio-cultural system, and by religious norms which are linked to a social order that is perceived to be restrictive and confining. Migration liberates Polish migrants from these traditional structures and cultural norms. Although migrants cultivate basic religious rituals individually and share commitment to religious practices with their children, their engagement in such religious rituals is sporadic and limited to the family network; thereby failing to integrate their daily lives with transcendence.

Notes

1. The research was conducted thanks to the National Science Centre, grant no. 2017/25/B/HS1/02985: 'Religion versus Migration: the Determinants of Religiosity of Polish Immigrants in Ireland (2018-2019)' (Project Director: Marcin Lisak).
2. Implemented Random Driven Sampling (Salganik, 2006; Salganik and Heckathorn, 2004) combines a sampling and estimation technique which allows researchers to make asymptotically unbiased estimates. Initial recruits were located in Dublin, Galway, Cork and Cavan. The referral chain then expanded up to the methodologically significant level of 5. The final number of respondents was 520. Demographic variables as sample means were calibrated with Irish census data concerning Polish migrants.
3. Respondents included all attendants of Sunday Masses on 5th May 2019 (N=280).
4. In some sources 'Polonia' refers both to emigrants and people born outside Poland (Lagodzinski, 2013).
5. Opolszczyzna lies in southwestern Poland.
6. That is why, in this chapter I mention pastoral centers offering ministry in Polish as 'parishes' only in a metaphorical way.

References

Bell, J., Domecka, M. (2017): The Transformative Potential of Migration: Polish migrants' Everyday Life Experiences in Belfast, Northern Ireland. *Gender, Place & Culture*, 25(6), pp. 866–881. DOI: 10.1080/0966369X.2017.1372379.

Benson, M., O'Reilly, K. (2009). Migration and the Search for a Better Way of Life: A Critical Exploration of Lifestyle Migration. *The Sociological Review*, 57(4), pp. 608–625.

Benson, M., Osbaldiston, N. eds.2014). *Understanding Lifestyle Migration. Theoretical Approaches to Migration and the Quest for a Better Way of Life.* Houdsmill, Basingstoke: Palgrave Macmillan.

Bojarczuk, S., Muhlau, P. (2018). Mobilising Social Network Support for Childcare: The Case of Polish Migrant Mothers in Dublin. *Social Networks*, 53, pp. 101–110.

Botterill, K. (2012). *Polish Mobilities and the Re-making of Self, Family and Community.* A thesis submitted for the degree of Doctor of Philosophy in the School of Geography, Politics and Sociology at Newcastle University [online] Available at: https://dspace.ncl.ac.uk/jspui/bitstream/10443/1647/1/Botterill%20 12%20%2812%20mth%29.pdf [Accessed 22/06/2020].

Cadge, W., Ecklund, E. (2006). Religious Service Attendance Among Immigrants: Evidence From the New Immigrant Survey–Pilot. *American Behavioral Scientist*, 49, pp. 1574–1595.

Cadge, W., Ecklund, E. (2007). Immigration and Religion. *Annual Review of Sociology*, 33, pp. 359–379.

Central Statistical Office (2016). *Census 2016 Reports* [online] Available at: https://www.cso.ie/en/census/census2016reports [Accessed 19/06/2020].

Connor, P. (2009). International Migration and Religious Participation: The Mediating Impact of Individual and Contextual Factors. *Sociological Forum*, 24, pp. 779–803.

Duda-Dziewierz, K. (1938). *Wies Małopolska a Emigracja Amerykanska: Studium Wsi Babica Powiatu Rzeszowskiego* [The Village in Lesser Poland and American Emigration: A Study of Babica Village in Rzeszów District]. Poznan and Warszawa: Polski Instytut Socjologiczny.

Dzieglewski, M. (2011). Bariery na drodze integracji polskich emigrantów poakcesyjnych w Irlandii [Barriers to Integration of Polish Post-Accession Migrants in Ireland]. *Studia Migracyjne - Przegląd Polonijny* [Migration Studies – Review Of Polish Diaspora], 2(140), pp. 131–148.

Erdal, M. (2017). 'When Poland Became the Main Country of Birth Among Catholics in Norway': Polish Migrants' Everyday Narratives and Church Responses to a Demographic Re-Constitution. In: D. Pasura, M. Erdal eds., *Migration, Transnationalism and Catholicism. Global Perspectives.* London: Palgrave Macmillan, pp. 259–290. DOI: 10.1057/978-1-137-58347-5

European Social Survey (2016). *Round 8 Data. Data file edition 2.1.* NSD - Norwegian Centre for Research Data, Norway – Data Archive and distributor of ESS data for ESS ERIC. DOI: 10.2133/NSD-ESS8-2016.

EVS (2015). *European Values Study 1981-2008: Longitudinal Data File 1981–2008.* GESIS. Data Archive. Cologne. DOI: 10.4232/1.12253.

Frelak, J., Grot, K. (2013). Uczestnictwo Polakow w zyciu spolecznym i politycznym w Wielkiej Brytanii – wymiar historyczny i społeczny [The Participation of Poles in Social and Political Life in Great Britain – Historical and Social Dimensions]. In: J. Kucharczyk ed., *Nic O Nas Bez Nas. Partycypacja Obywatelska Polaków W Wielkiej Brytanii.* Warszawa: Instytut Spraw Publicznych, pp. 43–79.

Fuszara, M. (2005). Between Feminism and the Catholic Church: The Women's Movement in Poland. *Czech Sociological Review*, 6(41), pp. 1057–1075.

Galent, M., Goddeeris, I., Niedzwiedzki, D. (2009). *Migration and Europeanisation.* Krakow: Zaklad Wydawniczy Nomos.

Garapich, M. (2008). The Migration Industry and Civil Society: Polish Immigrants in the United Kingdom Before and After EU Enlargement. *Journal of Ethnic and Migration Studies*, 34(5), pp. 735–752.

Glowny Urzad Statystyczny [Polish Statistics] (2017). *Informacja o rozmiarach i kierunkach czasowej emigracji z Polski w latach 2004 – 2016* [Information on the Size and Direction of Temporary Emigration from Poland 2004-2016] [online] Available at: https://stat.gov.pl/download/gfx/portalinformacyjny/pl/defaultaktualnosci/5471/2/9/1/informacja_o_rozmiarach_i_kierunkach_czasowej_emigracji_z_polski_w_latach_2004-2015.pdf [Accessed 19/06/2020].

Gmaj, K. (2018). 'Oswajanie' Norwegii – wzory osiedlencze polskich migrantow w Norwegii [Domesticating Norway – Settlement Patterns of Polish Migrants in Norway]. *Studia Migracyjne – Przegląd Polonijny* [Migration Studies – Review Of Polish Diaspora], 1(167), pp. 163–188.

Gorny, A., Osipovic, D. (2006). *Return Migration of Second Generation British Poles.* Warszawa: Osrodek Badan nad Migracjami, Uniwersytet Warszawski, pp. 31–35.

Grabowska, G., Gwiazda, M. (2019). *Mlodziez 2018* [Youth 2018]. Warszawa: Centrum Badania Opinii Publicznej.

Grabowska, I. (2016). *Movers and Stayers: Social Mobility, Migration and Skills.* Franfkurt am Main: Peter Lang.

Grabowska, I., Engbersen, G. (2016). Social Remittances and the Impact of Temporary Migration on an EU Sending Country: The Case of Poland. *Central and Eastern European Migration Review*, 5, pp. 99–117.

Greeley, A. (1971). *Why Can'T They Be Like Us? America'S White Ethnic Groups.* New York: E.P. Dutton.

Grzymala-Moszczynska, H., Hay, D., Krotofil, J. (2011). Between Universalism and Ethnic Particularism: Polish Migrants to the United Kingdom. Perspective from the Psychology of Religion. *Studia Migracyjne – Przegląd Polonijny* [Migration Studies – Review of Polish Diaspora], 1(139), pp. 223–236.

Hagan, J., Ebaugh, H. (2003). Calling Upon the Sacred: Migrants' Use of Religion in the Migration Process. *International Migration Review*, 37, pp. 1145–1162.

Hirschman, C. (2004). The Role of Religion in the Origins and Adaptation of Immigrant Groups in the United States. *International Migration Review*, 38, pp. 1206–1233.

Hirschman, C. (2008). The Role of Religion in The Origin and Adaptation of Immigrants' Groups in The United States. In: A. Portes and J. DeWind, ed., *Rethinking Migration: New Theoretical and Empirical Perspectives*, New York, Oxford: Berghahn Books.

Ignatowicz, A. (2011). Travelling Home: Personal Mobility and 'New' Polish Migrants in England. *Studia Migracyjne – Przegląd Polonijny* [Migration Studies – Review of the Polish Diaspora], 1(139), pp. 33–47.

Kaczmarczyk, P. (2018). Post-Accession Migration and the Polish Labour Market. Expected and Unexpected Effects. In: A. White, I. Grabowska, P. Kaczmarczyk, K. Slany eds., *The Impact of Polish Migration on Poland. EU Mobility and Social Change.* London: UCL Press, pp. 90–107. DOI: https://doi.org/10.14324/111.9781787350687.

Kapinos, S. (2018). (Nie)dylematy tozsamosciowe Polakow w Wielkiej Brytanii na przykladzie badan w hrabstwie Hertfordshire [Identity Non-Dilemmas of Poles in Great Britain: A Case study of Hertfordshire]. *Studia Migracyjne – Przegląd Polonijny* [Migration Studies – Review of the Polish Diaspora], 1(167), pp. 117–143.

Krotofil, J. (2013). *Religia w procesie ksztaltowania tozsamosci wsrod polskich migrantow w Wielkiej Brytanii* [Religion in the Process of Shaping Identity among Polish Migrants in Great Britain]. Krakow: Zaklad Wydawniczy Nomos.

Lagodzinski, S. (2013). Reemigracja I Powrot. Zarys Zalozen Teoretycznych Stosowanych Do Analizy Wywiadow Z Poakcesyjnymi Emigrantami Powrotnymi Oraz Powracajacymi Ze Wschodu [Re-Emigration and Return. An Outline of Theoretical Assumptions Used for the Analysis of Interviews With Post-Accession Emigrants Returning and Then Re-Emigrating from the East]. In: S. Lagodzinski, R. Lange, S. Maksymowicz, R. Wyszynski, K. Leszczynski eds., *Kierunek +48. Powroty do domu. Raport podsumowujący wyniki badań w ramach pilotażowego programu wsparcia migrantów powrotnych.* [Direction +48. Coming back home. Report on pilot research concerning the program dedicated to return migrants].Warszawa: Stowarzyszenie Wspolnota Polska, pp. 5–27.

Larkin, E. (1997). *The Historical Dimensions of Irish Catholicism.* Washington D.C: Catholic University of America Press.

Maksymowicz, L. (2013). Zogniskowane wywiady grupowe w wojewodztwie mazowieckim, dolnoslaskim i podkarpackim [Focus Group Interviews in Mazowieckie, Dolnoslaskie and Podkarpackie Voivodeships]. In: S. Lodzinski, R. Lange, S. Maksymowicz, R. Wyszynski, K. Leszczynski eds., *Kierunek +48. Powroty do domu. Raport podsumowujący wyniki badan w ramach pilotazowego programu wsparcia migrantow powrotnych* [Direction +48. Coming back home. Report on pilot research concerning the program dedicated to return migrants]. Warszawa: Stowarzyszenie Wspolnota Polska, pp. 57–170.

Mellor, P., Shilling, C. (2014). Re-Conceptualising the Religious Habitus: Reflexivity and Embodied Subjectivity in Global Modernity. *Culture and Religion*, 15(3), pp. 275–297. DOI: 10.1080/14755610.2014.942328.

Ministerstwo Spraw Zagranicznych [Polish Foreign Ministry] (2015). Rządowy program wspolpracy z Polonia i Polakami za granica w latach 2015-2020 [Govermental Program for Cooperation with Polonia and Poles Abroad 2015-2020] [online] Available at: https://www.gov.pl/web/dyplomacja/rzadowy-program-wspolprac-z-polonia-i-polakami-za-granica-w-latach-2015-2020 [Accessed 19/06/2020].

Myers, S. (2000). The Impact of Religious Involvement on Migration. *Social Forces*, 79, pp. 755–783.

Orlowski, W., Zienkowski, L. (1998). Skala Potencjalnej Emigracji Z Polski Po Przystapieniu Do Unii Europejskiej: proba Prognozy [The Scope of Potential Migration from Poland after EU-Accession: Prognosis]. *Biuletyn Komitetu Przestrzennego Zzagospodarowania Kraju PAN*, 184, pp. 55–67.

Pew Research Centre (2012). *Faith on the move. The Religious Affiliation of International Migrants* [online] Available at: https://www.pewforum.org/2012/03/08/religious-migration-exec [Accessed 19/06/2020].

Ryan, L. (2010). Transnational Relations: Family Migration Among Recent Polish Migrants in London. *International Migration*, 49(2), pp. 80–103.

Saar, M. (2018). Using Reflexivity to Explain Variations in Migration Among the Highly-Skilled, Identities: Global Studies in Culture and Power. *Identities*, 26(6), pp. 688–705.

Sadlon, W. (2016). *Annuarium Statisticum Ecclesiae in Polonia AD 2016* [online] Available at: http://iskk.pl/images/stories/Instytut/dokumenty/AnnuariumStatisticum2016.pdf [Accessed 19/06/2020].

Salganik, M., Heckathorn, D. (2004). Sampling Estimation in Hidden Populations Using Respondent Driven Sampling. *Sociological Methodology*, 34(1), pp. 193–240. DOI: https://doi.org/10.1111/j.0081-1750.2004.00152.x

Salganik, M. (2006). Variance Estimation, Design Effects, and Sample Size Calculations for Respondent-Driven Sampling. *Journal of Urban Health: Bulletin of the New York Academy of Medicine*, 83(7), pp. 98–112. DOI: 10.1007/s11524-006-9106-x

Schiller, N., Salazar, N. (2013). Regimes of Mobility Across the Globe. *Journal of Ethnic and Migration Studies*, 39(2), pp. 183–200. DOI: 10.1080/1369183X.2013.723253

Slany, K., Solga, B. (2014). *Spoleczne Skutki Poakcesyjnych Migracji Ludnosci Polski* [Social Effects of Post-Accession Migration from Poland]. Warszawa: Komitet Badan nad Migracjami Polskiej Akademii Nauk.

Sleszynski, P., Banski, J., Degorski, M., Komornicki, T. (2017). *Delimitacja obszarow strategicznej interwencji panstwa: obszarow wzrostu i obszarow problemowych* [Delimitation of Strategic Areas of State Intervention: Growth and Problematic Areas]. Warszawa: Instytut Geografii i Przestrzennego Zagospodarowania PAN.

Smith, C., Sikkink, D., Bailey, J. (1998). Devotion in Dixie and Beyond: A Test of the 'Shibley Thesis' on the Effects of Regional Origin and Migration on Individual Religiosity. *Journal for the Scientific Study of Religion*, 37, pp. 494–506.

Trzebiatowska, M. (2010). The Advent of the 'EasyJet Priest': Dilemmas of Polish Catholic Integration in the UK. *Sociology*, 44(6), pp. 1055–1072.

Urbanska, S. (2016). Czego nie dowiemy się o globalnej rewolucji plci bez badania religii w zyciu migrantow [What We Will Not Know about the Global Gender Revolution Without Research on Religion in a Migrant's Life]. *Studia Humanistyczne AGH*, 15(3), pp. 51–67.

Warner, R. (1998). Religion and Migration in the United States. *Social Compass*, 45, pp. 123–134.

White, A. (2011). *Polish Families and Migration in Poland Since EU Accession*. Bristol: Policy Press.

White, A. (2018). How Are Countries Affected by Migration? In: A. White, I. Grabowska, P. Kaczmarczyk, K. Slany eds., *The Impact of Polish Migration on Poland. EU Mobility and Social Change*. London: UCL Press, pp. 1–9. DOI: https://doi.org/10.14324/111.9781787350687.

White, A. (2018). *Polish Society Abroad*. In: A. White, I. Grabowska, P. Kaczmarczyk, K. Slany eds., *The Impact of Polish Migration on Poland. EU Mobility and Social Change*. London: UCL Press, pp. 186–212. DOI: https://doi.org/10.14324/111.9781787350687.

Wojtynska, A. (2011). Traditions in Dialogue: Celebration Patterns Among Polish Migrants in Iceland. *Studia Humanistyczne AGH*, 2, pp. 115–127.

Wuthnow, R., Kevin, C. (1979). The Effects of Residential Migration on Church Attendance in the United States. In: R. Wuthnow ed., *The Religious Dimension: New Directions in Quantitative Research*. New York: Academic Press, pp. 257–276.

Epilogue

Some readers read a book, especially an academic one, by starting with the conclusion. After a long study of the research problem, very often the last paragraphs contain the most important statements which summarize the whole opus. To follow these characteristics of an epilogue I will present here my principal observations concerning the transformation of religion and religious life in the transition from traditional to contemporary society.

This book is a case study of Polish Catholicism with all its social specificities and historical peculiarities. The overall proposition of the book is that religious phenomena are, to some extent, a 'mystery' of human subjectivity in terms of their relationship to transcendence and the other orders of reality, which is shaped in socio-cultural interactions. In saying this I neither intend to demonstrate sociological ignorance nor to argue that religion cannot be studied scientifically. On the contrary, I wish to convey the message that to describe and analyze the dynamics of religion requires hard work and sophisticated theoretical tools. Understanding the relationship between religion and human subjectivity in a social context is a very demanding task because our perspective can easily be limited by the research approach chosen.

Critical realist ontology makes it possible to grasp the concepts of religion and religiosity with more dynamism, that is, in terms of their relationship with the dynamics of social life, which cannot be understood without reference to human reflexivity. In this way critical realism opens up new perspectives for the study of religiousness. This new ontology provides ample perspectives for studying religious attitudes, not only in their institutional aspect but also in relation to more deinstitutionalized forms of religion. It even overcomes many classical distinctions in the sociology of religion, such as between spirituality and religion, or between religious experience and religious institutions.

The critical realist perspective has provided me with theoretical tools to describe the dynamism of religion in Polish society in a way that seems to be quite new in sociology but nevertheless is fully consistent with a very classical understanding of religion. This social ontology elaborated by Margaret Archer 'personalizes', to some extent, the sociology of religion and the study of Polish Catholicism. Religiosity represents much more than abstract norms and so-called moral templates. The understanding of religion needs a broader perspective than institutional models, and it is important to take into account the distinction between a religious cultural system and a religious socio-cultural system. That is why, when religiosity is described within sociological studies, attention to human reflexivity is essential. Furthermore, religiosity represents much more than human cognitive capacities, which affect human attitudes or behaviour in a causal way. I have argued that no religiosity is able to exist if believers are not 'equipped with' reflexivity. Even in traditional societies normative order was not able to cover all the contingencies which a human being could potentially face in his or her life. Social norms and social order are not sufficiently potent to transform human beings into unreflexive automatons.

In a critical realist perspective, the dynamism of religion in Poland is grasped in a more relational and dynamic way, not only from the perspective of structure and general trends on the one hand, but also from subjective perspectives and individual experience on the other. The individual's relationship to transcendence is shaped by the social structures and intertwined with the culture in which he or she lives. Religion represents a very fragile fabric of social life grounded in the social configuration of structure, culture and agency. Religious change is a matter of the shifting character of the relationship of the individual to the structural and cultural context. Hence researching religious change should include a focus on the relationship between structure, culture and agency. The relationship of the individual to transcendence is the crucial element in studying religious change from the perspective of critical realism. Religious values and norms are able to shape human behaviour and action but also religion is embedded in culture and is shaped by social structures.

The relationship between the individual and religion, between religiosity and social institutions, is mediated by reflexivity. Human beings relate to transcendence not in a mechanical way but on the basis of human reflexivity. This is why my comprehension of their relationship to transcendence includes an understanding of human reflexivity and the nature of human relationships in all their complementarities. And it is also the reason why this study of Polish Catholicism includes structural, cultural and agential aspects and examines the interplay between them over time. It has therefore required a focus on human subjectivity and reflexivity which is not 'conflated' with social structures (Archer, 1995). In my study of Polish Catholicism, I have purposefully avoided reference to the concept of 'secularization' as I consider this to be an overly broad and ambiguous term. Instead I have aimed to present a sociological or even ontological background to religious change, which is very often characterized as 'secularization'. My intention has been to show that religious change is not deterministic.

Morphogenesis in the context of religion is mediated by the interrelationship between structure, culture and agents themselves. In traditional society religious institutions retained the unification of culture and structure and individuals were embedded in the stable cultural context of their community. But as I argue in this book, traditional social structures and traditional cultures were not only shaping specific traditional forms of religiosity but were also mediated by agency. Traditional society provided a context which related human beings to transcendence in all orders of reality, including not only the community (the social order) but also the natural and practical orders. In traditional Polish society the transcendental order was *partout* [everywhere]; it was interwoven with everything else. In the past, the individual's relationship to transcendence was unchallenged and unproblematic, because it was structurally conditioned. In traditional society the relationship between national and religious identity was especially strong and the practical order, as represented by religious rituals, dominated religiosity. Rituals functioned to consolidate religiosity with other aspects of society. Transcendental concerns were elaborated especially in religious rituals and indeed, just by being present in the life of the local community. This is still easily discernible, especially in the domain of Polish family life. In traditional society religious socialization was supported and stimulated by social structures. Such characteristics of traditional religiosity may suggest that in the past religion was dominated by structural aspects and in fact did not stimulate human reflexivity. The category of reflexivity, as proposed by Margaret Archer, when implemented in the study of Polish traditional religiosity, highlights the fact that religion in the past was not mechanical but related also to human subjectivity. Structural aspects of traditional society shaped the individual's relationship to transcendence, which was reflexively elaborated and emerged as religious concerns (which very often represented ultimate concerns). In this way religiosity was an institutional aspect of social life in which, performatively, subjects reinforced their choice of social identity.

Studying Polish Catholicism from the perspective of critical realism I have been able to examine traditional religiosity, or better, 'folk religiosity', in a way which is new for the sociology of religion. I have demonstrated that traditional religiosity should not be seen as lacking reflexivity in a simplistic way. On the contrary, in order to understand 'folk religiosity' with its strong structural dimensions of social and religious life, it is crucial to comprehending the individual's relationship to transcendence, which is formed by human reflexivity. When human beings, who can be characterized as belonging to traditional, especially local, communities, participate in traditional rituals, when they identify with a social group and face natural concerns, they form religious concerns which transcend other aspects of reality. In this way their relationship to transcendence can be seen as emerging in the sphere of folk religiosity. I am using here the present tense to describe this logic of the transcendental order within the traditional order not only because some examples of 'folk religiosity' are still alive in Poland but generally because such structurally conditioned processes of reflexively which give rise to religious concerns, relate to the ontological nature of human and social life. If specific conditions are adequate, an analogous process can also be observed in modern social groups, especially the family, the neighbourhood and communities, which have an impact on religious socialization in general. I have tried to present the argument that religion, even in traditional local communities, is related to social agency. In fact, the political and historical situation of Poland has supported Catholicism as a 'lived religion'.

The next step in the book was to study the modern face of Polish Catholicism especially since the 1980s when religious actors took an active role in group interactions resulting in structural and cultural elaboration. My focus here was principally on social interactions at the institutional level and the role of Catholic institutions. I have tried to show that the Catholic Church contributed to the social agency of the Polish people and moreover that the relationship of individuals to transcendence was strongly shaped by the historical context and such concerns as freedom and well-being. The growing role of Catholic institutions as an outcome of the political agency of the Catholic Church has resulted in a kind of normative pressure, which was experienced by various elements of Polish society. The institutionalization of Catholicism which is emerging in the 21st century could be understood as the result of this social agency related to transcendence among members of the Catholic Church. Three decades after the turbulent socio-cultural elaboration of Polish society, Catholicism has come to represent an aspect of the social structure and the cultural system rather than an agential force. This is especially evident in the crisis of religious socialization.

This book presents the argument that religious change in Poland can only be understood by acknowledging the agential aspect of Polish Catholicism. The rupture between Polish traditional society and migrant diasporic society is outlined as the particular situation of Polish Catholicism, which, at the end of the 20th century, played an important social role in the sense that Polish Catholicism was characterized by strong social agency. The role of the specific configuration between social structure, culture and agency in shaping Polish Catholicism is highlighted by the discontinuity in the religious life of Polish migrants to Ireland. In fact, Polish migration to Ireland reveals the dynamics of religion in Poland as a complex phenomenon characterized by the relationship between national and religious identity and strong social mobilization, especially in the 1980s. The special situation of Catholicism in Poland in recent decades could be labelled as 'transitional' or 'agential'.

Despite the fact that Polish migrants to Ireland were socialized within the Polish social system, their religious identity was shaped to a certain extent in the late phase of the Polish transformation when the traditional religious forms and agential forces of Polish Catholicism were in decline. And it is important to note that religious change in the diaspora after migration is also shaped by the new structural and cultural context which conditions the religious identity of the Polish migrants in a new way. Polish migration to Ireland is a case study which demonstrates how religion, in this instance shaped by a Polish setting, changes in the new context. Polish migrants, particularly young people, have a very critical attitude towards traditional religious institutions. Recent Polish migration is much more oriented towards the search for better life conditions. Despite the fact that religious rituals in Polish society, even after migration, still play an important role in family life, the practical order is dominated by the search for well-being, which is strongly detached from religious concerns. The empirical data show that Polish migrants to Ireland perceive Polish culture to be associated especially with strong norms and obligations; they are adapting well to Irish society and they find Irish culture attractive. In other words, for them religious concerns are less integrated with social concerns. New modes of integration emerge between the practical and natural orders and transcendental concerns. New migrants are not particularly susceptible to the cultural context in their new place of residence. Thanks to advances in communication technology, social support and growing language skills, newly arrived migrants can easily shape their biographies in more individual ways. Thus, migration is also seen as a way of shaping life biographies and attaining a more comfortable life. That is why Polish culture especially, with its rigid norms and lived values, becomes a potentially limiting factor for personal development, especially in a situation where the higher religious attitudes of Polish society are identified with lower well-being and quality of life.

Religious change consists in the fact that 'late modernity' deconstructs the social context which has delivered special circumstances for the building and shaping of the religious imagination and emotions. In 'late modernity' human biographies become more project-like and the logic of opportunity dominates. The role of Catholicism in the fabric of Polish society is a good example of such a process. In 'late modernity' Catholicism is an option, and human projects related to the natural order and natural concerns are much more individualized and can be attained without necessitating a strong attachment to the social order as in the past. Well-being does not require support from a social group but is much more attainable by the individual.

However, 'late modernity' should not necessarily be identified with migration. Migration was also characteristic of Polish society in the past. But it was the specific form of migration which has also revealed the character of traditional society. Although migration in the past liberated human beings from their traditional and original cultural roots, in fact it placed migrants in a context where traditional culture was even more dominant in terms of the important role it played. Migrants especially in the 19th and in the first half of the 20th century needed their ethnic communities to survive in a daily life context. Interchange between ethnic groups and support from social institutions in the destination country were very limited. It could be said that the role of Polish Catholicism as a resource for agential power was strengthened by the migratory configuration which incorporated elements of foreign culture and unrelated social structures.

The question arises concerning to what extent religious actors in modern society will be able to relate the experience of changing natural concerns with transcendence. To express this in general terms, the contemporary emergence of religious concerns relates more to subjectivity and subjective powers than in the past. Migration strengthens this process of change in the direction of reflexivity to liberate human beings from the traditional cultural system. In a wider perspective my study of Polish Catholicism is methodologically based upon the historicity of emergence. What I mean by this is that the emergent properties of the structure are not reducible to the emergent properties of the agents also, in a temporal sense. The book explains the interplay of structure and agency as a 'causal mechanism' of the emerging new configuration of religious identity in 'late modernity', by distinguishing three cyclic phases in the morphogenesis of Polish Catholicism.

The traditional configuration of structure, agency and culture represents the first phase of the morphogenetic cycle.[1] As I have shown, traditional Polish Catholicism was dominant in the past but, in a limited way, was conditioning religion in Polish society until the beginning of the 21st century. In the 1980s, the strong transformation of Polish Catholicism began.[2] The emerging new configuration between structure, culture and agency contributed to the transformation of religion in Polish society especially during the 1990s and 2000s. In that time, Polish Catholicism was both conditioned by its traditional social arrangement and shaped by the emerging new configuration of agency, culture and structure. Religious identity and the general relationship to transcendence played an important role in this phase because of the inherent elements of social agency in Polish Catholicism. This resulted in sustaining the Catholic forms of religion during this phase. However, the structural and cultural elaboration taking place in Polish society, especially in the 1990s and 2000s, introduced a new set of cultural and structural conditions. Based on empirical research, this book argues that the results of this elaboration of Polish Catholicism become especially evident around 2005. Around that time, after strong social interaction and structural elaboration related to Polish Catholicism, a new socio-religious configuration emerged.[3] Despite the fact that religion seemed to play a crucial role in the public space after 2005 (especially after the political unrest initiated in 2010), the structural and cultural conditioning of Catholicism is, instead, a consequence of past actions which came into play in the previous phase. Moreover migration, as a specific example of the situation of Polish Catholicism in 'late modernity', initiates a new morphogenetic cycle. The outcomes of this morphogenetic cycle are hard to predict because of the intervention of contingency factors and cross-cutting generative mechanisms such as the new global and European cultural movements. But what is certain is that the agential forces of Polish Catholicism, both in Poland and among Polish migrants, came to be configured in a different way from previously.

The results of my study on different phases of Polish Catholicism correspond well with Archer's empirical formulation of the internal conversation indicator based on in-depth interviews. In her 'reflexive trilogy' (Archer, 2003; 2007 and 2012) Archer empirically investigates the concept of internal conversation and distinguishes general *'modes of reflexivity'*, which delineate how reflexivity guides the choice of occupations that people seek to follow in their lives, and shapes patterns of social mobility in different social contexts. From such a perspective, religious identity within traditional Polish culture could be classified as a context for the first mode, *'communicative reflexivity'*. This is because the religious socialization of persons in traditional Catholicism was carried out in relatively stable social structures. A stable environment, which weakened the boundary between the public and private spheres and created similarities between family, school and local community members, shaped specific reflexivity, which refers to the social relations established in achieving a *modus vivendi* and specifying life projects. People living in stable contexts share similar experiences and have opportunities for frequent interactions. A stable social context shapes 'communicative reflexivity' which represents the 'agential property that reinforces social stability' (Archer, 2007, p. 148). In 'communicative reflexivity', transcendental concerns are personalized and mediate personal relations. When 'communicative reflexivity' is dominant, people practise religion because of personal relationships with other believers. Often their religious behaviour is influenced by parents, friends or other people.

'Autonomous reflexivity' is based on 'contextual discontinuity', for instance when Polish Catholicism was turbulently elaborated by new structural and cultural conditioning. Polish Catholics characterized by this mode of reflexivity have become more autonomous and have tended to reduce ties with their natal religious environment. In life projects they privilege the practical order and are intensely engaged in achieving performative skills. 'Autonomous reflexivity' results in upward social mobility. People characterized by this mode of reflexivity pay more attention to getting ahead in their careers and competing with others in life achievements (Archer, 2007, p. 14).

Migration generates a mixture of 'autonomous' and 'meta-reflexivity'. *'Meta-reflexivity'* is so named because people characterized by this mode are committed to values, they elaborate upon influential ultimate concerns ('dreams'), which influence other concerns and cause tension between concerns and context. Personal concerns are not congruent with concern for the social environment, as was the case in traditional Polish Catholicism. 'Meta-reflexivity' is dominated by 'contextual incongruity' because Polish migrants are not integrated with the normative context of the environment. 'Such subjects increasingly render themselves incapable of sharing this "concern" within their natal context. Effectively, they are unknowingly working at disqualifying themselves from the possibility of communicative reflexivity'. (Archer, 2007, p. 155) This results in 'socio-occupational volatility'. Migrants do not devote themselves to achieving social success, but rather, are focused on personal interests and concerns which do not correspond to the expectations of the environment.

I would like to finish my book with an intuitive insight that the future of religion should be explored not in structural terms but through an inquiry into the moral and subjective power of religion. To express this in a different way, religion persists if it is able to engender an experience of 'anamnesis', in other words, to renew its role, which is to apprehend human beings in a state of transcendence. From the perspective of Polish Catholicism, globalization represents a great challenge. According to the optimistic vision of Archer, in the era of globalization 'meta-reflexivity' increases, 'providing a growing fund of highly visible value-commitments that subjects adopt as their personal concerns' (Archer, 2007, p. 324).

The examination of Polish Catholicism with the use of critical realism and the morphogenetic approach formulated by Margaret Archer also allows me to highlight how crucial is the transcendental order in the understanding of agency. I am however fully aware that this was just the first trial to be conducted with such an approach. In the sociology of religion, we need further theoretical endeavor to grasp more fully the nature of the transcendental order and the mechanisms of its relationship to human reflexivity and other orders of reality. My study has highlighted that the transcendental order should not be grasped as parallel to other orders of reality but rather as a 'meta-order' of human reality, or as a 'trans-order', which penetrates the natural, the performative and especially the social order, and in doing so delivers points of focus which shape concerns related to these other orders of reality. The transcendental order should not be excluded from the sociological description of human reality. On the contrary, if sociology does not want to limit itself to a shallow, static vision of human beings, it must broaden itself to include the notion of transcendence in its research field. As I have demonstrated in this book, transcendence neither automatically implies a focus on the traditional religious realm nor on the theological way of thinking. Critical realism delivers new 'tools' for the sociological study of religion in societies where faith cannot be implicitly assumed, but rather, studied as a central aspect of religion. In this way critical realism opens up a new platform for dialogue with philosophy and theology which will only serve to make sociology more dynamic and vibrant.

The critical realist, morphogenetic approach is an adequate approach for studying religious identity as it embodies a commitment to the whole person which allows us to grasp religion in a more dynamic way. This shares many characteristics with Weber's notion of 'vocation'. Such an approach to religion which puts the human person at the centre could also be labelled 'personalistic'. Here, the complex nature of religious experience is not reduced to cognitive reality but is a relational phenomenon. In a critical realist perspective religious identity emerges from reflexively elaborated religious experience, shapes human self-worth and the social configuration, and, what is also important, it 'embraces' the natural order, which includes both the biological nature of human beings and their natural environment. Further exploration of Archerian social ontology within the sociology of religion is especially challenging in the domain concerning the link between the biological nature of human beings and transcendence. In this context also critical realism opens up new perspectives for studies within the sociology of religion. For instance, traditional concepts of 'sublimation' or even the more recent investigations on 'transhumanism' would be enhanced by a realistic approach to transcendence. In this way it creates the potential for a new dialogue between the sociology of religion and the cognitive sciences.

The biggest challenge for the development of critical realism within the sociology of religion is to study the nature of the transcendental order which has been strikingly neglected in present sociological studies. In my opinion, further studies of agency from the perspective of the sociology of religion will inject new dynamism into the discipline. I hope that this book also provides a solid rebuttal to the argument that statistical methods are suitable only for positivist or functionalist social ontology. Realist theoretical concepts fit well with empirical or even statistical inquiry. In sociology we are becoming more and more aware that statistics and quantitative methods are not in opposition to qualitative research. We need however a new impulse for theoretical and methodological studies which will implement critical realist ontologies in quantitative research especially in the sociology of religion. As my study has demonstrated, the path towards new conceptualizations within the sociology of religion will still require much effort.

Social structure and culture condition religion either by supporting believers' reflexive elaboration of their relationship to transcendence or by weakening this relationship. This means that social structure and culture are by degrees more or less 'religious' through the lens of agency. Institutions and organizations gain religious character through the reflexively elaborated individual's relationship to transcendence. That is why, from the perspective of religious change, the most crucial dynamic is the relationship between agency and the emerging configuration of social structure and culture. This emphasis on agency from the critical realist approach of Margaret Archer which I have employed in this study sheds some light on the future of Catholicism and religious identity, in the world and also in Polish society. The future of religion depends upon agency and is a matter of agency. In other words, if religion were to be apprehended as having a more human component and, in this sense, be characterized by reflexively elaborated religious experience, it could challenge the future. This means that religion has the potential to challenge the future if it becomes more human.

Notes

1. In her morphogenetic scheme, Archer labels this phase T1.
2. In her morphogenetic scheme, Archer labels this phase T2→ T3.
3. This phase could be labelled T4.

References

Archer, M. S. (1995). *Realist Social Theory*. Cambridge: Cambridge University Press.

Archer, M. S. (2003). *Structure, Agency and the Internal Conversation*. Cambridge: Cambridge University Press. DOI: 10.1017/CBO9781139087315.

Archer, M. S. (2007). *Making Our Way Through the World. Human Reflexivity and Social Mobility*. Cambridge: Cambridge University Press. DOI: 10.1017/CBO9780511618932.

Archer, M. S. (2012). *The Reflexive Imperative in Late Modernity*. Cambridge: Cambridge University Press. DOI: 10.1017/CBO9781139108058.

Index

Note: Page numbers in *italics* indicate figures and **bold** indicates tables in the text.

agency 3, 6–14, 19, 25, 28–30, 35–37, 42, 43, 45, 47, 61, 63–64, 70–71, 85, 93–95, 107, 134, 151, 167, 170, 179–181, 183, 185–186
agrarian piety 26
Altermatt, Urs 26
American Catholic Church 98
American Catholicism 98
American culture 96–97
American Pew Research Center 12
American 'Polish colonies' 80
American religious culture 97
American society 87, 99, 164
Ammerman, Nancy 54
'analytical dualism' 58
anamnesis 4, 56, 185
Anglican Church 149
'anthropomorphic turn' 81
Archer, Margaret 2, 3–5, 6–10, 13, 37, 43, 45–47, 49–51, 56, 58–60, 62–63, 64n1, 64n3, 71, 87, 99–100, 107, 178, 180, 184–186; 'DDD scheme' 48
atheism 6, 21, 110
Aupers, Stef 55
Australia 145; and Polish Catholics 2; secularization in 1
'autonomous reflexivity' 184

Bailey, Edward 20
'Baptism of Poland' 2
Beck, Ulrich 27–28, 32, 62
Bell, Justyna 152
Bellah, Robert 28–29
Berger, Peter 5–6, 24–25, 29–30, 34, 46–47
Bhaskar, Roy 3, 15n1, 42, 64n1
Bible 96
Blachnicki, Franciszek 118
Blizinski, Waclaw 94

Boguszewski, R. 123
Bojarczuk, Sarah 159
Borowik, Irena 10
Botterill, Katherine 159–160
Boudon, Raymond 79
Bourdieu, Pierre 23–24, 38n2, 55
bourgeois religiosity 26
British Catholics 161
British Parliament 147
Bujak, Franciszek 10, 75, 91–92, 94–96
Bukraba-Rylska, Barbara 73, 77, 81
Buttiglione, Rocco 2
Bystron, Jan Stanislaw 10, 96

Cadge, Wendy 164
Caritas (Catholic social service organization) 94, 134n6
Casanova, Jose 115
Catholic Christianity 78
Catholic Church 2, 99, 101n2, 101n8, 108–112, 120, 134n3, 160; declaration of nullity of a marriage in 135n8; Good Friday in 135n11; Holy Rosary ('the Rosary') in 135n12; in Ireland 148
Catholic Dioceses 113
Catholic Ireland 148
Catholicism 12; American 98; folk 26; global 2; Irish 148, 150, 155, 162, 168; Irish-American 98; Roman 146; socio-cultural system of 4; traditional 9–10, 80, 90, 93, 134, 169, 184
Catholic societies 1, 119
Catholic University, Lublin 2
Catholic Youth Association 94
Celtic Tiger 148
Chalasinski, Jozef 10
changing: personal concerns 121–124; transcendental concerns 128–133

Christian Europe 147
Christianity 12, 36, 59, 70, 117, 147
'Christianity of choice' 118
Christianization of Poland 2
Christian Pentecostal Community 113
Christ Stopped at Eboli (Levi) 29
Churchill, Winston 108
'Church of choice' 117–118
Church of England 149
Church of Ireland 149
Cipriani, R. 22
Ciupak, Edward 10, 74–75, 79, 84, 90
Ciupak, Jozef 94
'codification of religious practices' 57
collective memory 27
collectivistic religions 36
commitment: emotional 4; human 47,
    50; personal 36, 50, 117, 171; religious
    52, 84, 95, 97, 124, 157; social 47;
    transcendental 50; unreflexive 36
common conscience 30
common religion 22
communicantes 126, *127*, 135n7
'communicative reflexivity' 184
Communism 2, 106–107, 108, 110, 153
Communist Poland 95
Comte, August 44
configuration 4, 8–11, 50, 56, 63, 76, 107,
    115, 144, 179, 181, 183, 186
conflation 37, 45–46
Constance Markievicz née Gore-Booth
    146
'conventional religions' 22
Conway, Martin 85
Copernicus, Nicolaus 2
Coppola, Francis Ford 70
Crimea Conference 108
'critical naturalism' 42
critical realism 42–43, 45; human
    person and experience 43–49;
    morphogenesis in 'late modernity'
    60–62; performing transcendence
    56–59; personal relationship to
    transcendence 49–52; religious
    identity from perspective of 42–64;
    shaping religious identity reflexively
    53–56
critical realist ontology 43, 178
cultural elaboration 60; of Polish
    Catholicism 107–115
'cultural religion' 115
culture: American 96–97; American
    religious 97; Irish 147, 153, 157, 163,

168–170, 182; Italian 29; modern 23,
    31, 54, 134, 151; Polish 7, 81–82, 84,
    87, 101, 107, 120, 152, 168, 172, 182,
    184
'customary religion' 22
Cywinski, Piotr 108
Czapinski, Janusz 124
Czarnowski, Stefan 10, 74, 76, 81, 87, 91

de Certeau, Michel 29
Demerath, Jay 115
detachment 12, 33, 50, 131, 160, 172
'Devotional Revolution' 148
'diffused religion' 22
Diocese of Katowice 126
Diocese of Koszalin-Kolobrzeg 126
Diocese of Szczecin-Kamien 115
Diocese of Tarnow 115, 126
Divine Mercy 2, 128
divine reflexivity 55
Dobbelaere, Karel 33
Domecka, Markieta 152
dominicantes 115, 124, 126, *127*, 135n7
Donati, Pierpaolo 11, 63, 64n4
dualism: analytical 58; epistemological
    21; ontological 20; in study of religion
    20–25
Duda-Dziewierz, Krystyna 163
Durkheim, Emile 20, 30, 81
dynamism: of Polish migration to
    Republic of Ireland 145–150; in
    religious life 30–36; of religious
    rituals 124–128
Dzwonkowski, Roman 86

Easter Rising 147
Ecklund, Elaine Howard 164
elaboration 7, 10, 49; cultural 9, 60,
    107–115, 133, 181, 183; reflexive 74–80,
    152, 186
emergence 12, 44–45, 48, 111, 183
Emigrants Protective Association,
    Warsaw 80
emotions 47–48; first-order 48; human
    4, 59; second-order 48
English Reformation 147
Enlightenment 21
Episcopal Church 149
'ethnic mobilization' 97
European Acts 3
European Christians 101
European Social Survey 149
European Union 144–146, 159

Evangelical Pentecostal Community
   113
Evans-Pritchard, Edward 20
events 55, 73, 92–93, 118–120
everyday life 5, 20, 23, 32, 46–47, 53–54,
   76, 78, 87, 90–91, 93, 109, 123, 129
experience 1, 4–8, 10–14, 19–25, 28–33,
   36–37, 42, 43–56, 73, 75–81, 85, 90,
   97–99, 101, 110, 118, 120, *128*, 157–160,
   167, 169–170, 185–186

faith 1, 3, 14, 26, 29, 32, 77–78, 80–82,
   85, 97, 110, 120, 129, 131, *132*, 147–148,
   154, 161, 167, 185
fake modernity 106
'false consciousness' 6
Ferdydurke (Gombrowicz) 70
Feuerbach, Ludwig 21
Finke, Roger 21, 98
Firlit, Elzbieta 112, 116
first-order emotions 48
First World War 2, 74, 81
'folk Catholicism' 26
'folk religion' 22, 25, 28
'folk religiosity' 10, 13, 77, 101, 180
France: 'religious vitality' in 5; rural
   Catholicism in 5
Frankowski, Edward 109
Frelak, J. 155

Garapich, Michal 158
Giddens, Anthony 27–28, 31, 35, 62
global Catholicism 2
global homogenization 1
Glock, Charles 5
Gmaj, Katarzyna 157
The Godfather (Puzo) 70
Gombrowicz, Witold 70
Gordon, Milton 87
Gorny, Agata 158
Grabowska, Izabela 151
Grabowska, Miroslawa 10, 118
Great Britain 14, 160; British Catholics
   in 161; Polish Catholics in 161; Polish
   migrants to 14, 145, 159–160; Polish
   minority in 145
Great Famine 148
Greek Catholic Church 112
Greek Catholics 101n2
Greeley, Andrew 86, 143
Grot, K. 155
Grygiel, Stanislaw 79, 91
Gutenberg 23

habitus 38n2, 55
Habsburg Monarchy 101n4
Hall, David D. 54
Hegel, Wilhelm 44
Henri VIII of England 147
Hervieu-Leger, Daniele 35
Hobbes, Thomas 21
Hodur, Franciszek 98
Holy Black Madonna (Virgin Mary)
   painting 101n7
Holy Roman Empire 2
Hornsby-Smith, Michael 22
'human biological nature' 5
human consciousness 6, 24, 45, 49, 76
human emotions 4, 59
humanistic naturalism 78
human being 4, 20–21, 27–28, 31, 35,
   44–46, 48, 56, 58–59, 61–62, 70,
   76, 101, 153, 170, 179–180, 182–183,
   185–186
human person 44; and experience
   43–49
human reason 4
human reflexivity 3, 49, 61, 63, 71, 100,
   144, 178–180
Hume, David 21

ideological sectarianism 78
Implemented Random Driven
   Sampling 172n2
individualization 11, 13, 15, 20, 32–35,
   131, 158, 170
Institute for Catholic Church Statistics
   (Poland) 12, 146
institution 28, 32, 55, 82, 88–89,
   109–111, 113, 116, 120, 131
institutionalization: of Catholicism 181;
   Polish Catholicism 112–115
integrating social and religious concerns 81–87
'intellectual rationalism' 26
'internalized natural law' 28
'invisible religion' 24
Ireland: attitude towards abortion
   in *149*; declared religious attitudes
   before and after migration to *155*;
   dynamism of Polish migration to
   145–150; Great Famine 148; Polish
   traditions by Polish migrants *165*;
   reasons for leaving Poland according
   to Polish migrants in *156*; reasons for
   remaining in Ireland according to
   Polish migrants *157*; religious beliefs

and religious concerns of Polish
migrants to *150*
Irish-American Catholicism 98
Irish Catholicism 148, 150, 155, 162, 168
Irish Catholic organizations 150
Irish Catholics 98, 148
Irish Christians 147
Irish Citizen Army 147
Irish culture 147, 153, 157, 163, 168–170,
182
Irish people 148, 153, 155
Irish Polish Society 146
Irish Sociological Association 143
Isambert, François-Andre 26
Israel and secularization 1
Italian culture 29

Jakelic, Slavica 36
Jankowski, Stanislaw 109
Jasna Gora Monastery 101n7
Jehovah Witnesses 112
Joas, Hans 11, 12, 35
John Paul II 2, 93, 109, 114, 129, 132,
146

Kaczynski, Lech 134n1
Kantian aesthetics 23
Kantian philosophy 23
Kapinos, Seweryn 160, 164
Kennedy, Ruby 86
Kieniewicz, Stefan 73
Knoblauch, Hubert 22–23
Komitet Obrony Robotnikow (Workers'
Defense Committee) 109
Konfederacja Polski Niepodleglej
(Confederation of Independent
Poland) 109
Kosela, Krzysztof 10, 85, 116
Krotofil, Joanna 160

'labour migration' 155
Lash, Scott 62
late modernity 9, 31, 182–183; culture
of 62; and human biographies 182;
morphogenesis in 60–62; Polish
Catholicism in 9, 183; religious
pluralization in 11; sociological characterization of 31
Latour, Bruno 55
"lay religion" 22
Le Bras, Gabriel 5, 143
Levi, Carlo 29
Light–Life Movement 118–119

'lived religion' 5, 54, 77, 181
'logic of opportunity' 62
love 21, 48, 50–52, 121
Lublin-Warsaw School of Sociology of
Religion 5
Luckmann, Thomas 12, 24, 33, 44
Luczewski, Michal 79
Luhmann, Niklas 23
Lynch, Gordon 23

Majka, Jozef 10, 77, 109–110
Marianski, Janusz 10, 79, 85, 93, 108,
129
Maritain, Jacques 11
Markievicz, Casimir 146
Marti, Gerardo 54, 58
Martin, David 32
Marx, Karl 44
Marxism 85
'material culture' 90
Mazowiecki, Tadeusz 110
McGuire, Meredith 54
'mechanical solidarity' 117
Mellor, Philip 55
Mensching, Gustav 26
'Meta-Reality' 15n1, 64n1
'meta-reflexivity' 184
'methodological nationalism' 151
Mieszko I, ruler of Polish state 2
migration: dynamism of Polish migration to Republic of Ireland 145–150;
emerging social engagement 167–170;
facing new cultural contexts 158–163;
performing religious rituals 163–167;
and reflexivity 150–155; search for
well-being 155–158; and shaping of
religious identity 143–172
Mikolejko, Zbigniew 132
Military Ordinariate 113, 134n4
Mill, John Stuart 44
mobility, emerging 93–99
mobilization 3, 34, 97, 106, 108–109,
111, 120, 181
modern culture 23, 31, 54, 134, 151
modernity: 'compulsive' 31; defined 35;
fake 106; late 9, 31, 60–62, 182–183;
and marriage 28
modernization 37, 62, 95, 97, 106, 116,
134
modern Polish society: changing
personal concerns 121–124; changing
transcendental concerns 128–133;
cultural elaboration of Polish

Catholicism 107–115; dynamism of religious rituals 124–128; between movements and events 118–120; and religious identity 106–134; social interactions 115–118
'modes of reflexivity' 184
modus vivendi 48–49, 62, 78, 96, 153, 171, 184
Molotov-Ribbentrop pact 107
moral/morality 24, 27–28, 33–34, 83, 86, 89, 93, 120
morphogenesis 179; in 'late modernity' 60–62
movements and events 118–120
Mühlau, Peter 159
Myers, Scott 163

'neo-Durkheimian' 81
Neuhaus, Richard 2
new cultural contexts and migration 158–163
New Evangelization Schools 119
Newman, John Henry 146
Niedzwiedz, Anna 77
Nipperday, Thomas 34
norms 22, 28, 32–33, 35, 47–48, 51, 58, 78, 86–87, 95, 109–110, 121–123, 131, 134, 151, 153, 158, 160, 172, 179, 182

objective/objectivity 6, 11, 20–21, 24, 25, 30, 118
O'Connell, Daniel 147
Odyssean refugees 158–159
'official religion' 22
Oplatek 135n9, 166
orders of reality 3–4, 46–47, 49–51, 53, 61, 64, 170, 178, 180, 185
'organic solidarity' 117
organization: agricultural 94; Catholic 12, 94, 117, 150, 158; parish 89, 118, 119, *119*; Polish 159; religious 1, 33, 36, 87, 111, 118, 119, 154; social 34, 80, 86–87, 156
Orsi, Robert 54
Orthodox Russia 148
Osipovic, Dorota 158
Otto, Rudolf 46

Palikot, Janusz 134n2
paradox 21, 61, 75, 154
parish 73, 75, 80–84, 86, 89–96, 111, 114, 116–119, 128, 162–166
Parsons, Talcott 44, 57

participation 46, 75, 79, 84, 91, 95, 107, 114, 117, 120, 123, 125–127, 164, 166, 170–171
Patton, Kimberley 55
Pawelczynska, Anna 75, 92
peasant piety 26
Pentecostal Church in Poland 112
performative order 4, 53
performing: religious rituals 163–167; transcendence 56–59
person: human 6, 11, 43–49, 59, 185; religious 8, 155
personal concerns, changing 121–124
personalism 2, 44
phenomenology (ical) 63
Piwowarski, Wladyslaw 10, 78, 83, 93, 110, 117, 118, 135n7
Poland: attitudes towards easter in *128*; attitude towards abortion in *149*; Catholics participating in parish-based organizations *119*; Center for Research on Public Opinion 92; changes in moral attitudes in Polish society *122*; Christianization of 2; 'crawling secularization' 129; declared belief in god, life after death, heaven and hell, in *133*; declared frequency of religious practice in *125*; declared frequency of religious practice of high school students *130*; declared importance of 'God in one's life' in *129*; declared relationship to the Church in *131*; declared religiosity of high school students *130*; faith in various beliefs *132*; 'folk religiosity' in 10; Institute for Catholic Church Statistics 12, 146; joining European Union 144; Military Ordinariate in 113, 134n4; number of Catholic parishes and priests *113*; partitions of 101n4; Polish traditions in Ireland by Polish migrants *165*; proportion of *communicantes* to *dominicantes* in Roman catholic dioceses in *127*
Polish Bishops' Conference 111
'Polish Catholic Church' organizations 158
Polish Catholicism 2, 150; cultural elaboration of 107–115; institutionalization 112–115; and John Paul II 109; in late modernity 9, 183; modern 14, 107, 112; modern religious forms within 10; morphogenesis of 144–145,

183; between movements and events 118–120; political influence of 116; recent history of 108; social morphogenesis of 8; traditional 8–9, 13, 38, 70–71, 75, 91, 94, 100, 183–184
Polish Catholics 2, 89, 123, 126, 146, 150, 161–162, 168, 184
Polish Central Statistical Office 12, 146
Polish cultural identity 99
Polish culture 7, 81–82, 84, 87, 101, 107, 120, 152, 168, 172, 182, 184
Polish diaspora 8, 86; Catholic parish in 80; internal conflicts within 99; in Ireland 11, 38; social organization in 86
Polish identity 14, 86, 160, 164
Polish-Lithuanian Commonwealth 2
Polish Lublin-Warsaw School of the Sociology of Religion 5
Polish nobility 73
Polish 'People's Church' 118
Polish Public Opinion Research Center 12
Polish religiosity 71; and Catholic Christianity 78; evaluation of 118; reductionist accounts of 11; traditional 69–102
Polish religious experience 19
Polish society 2; after Second World War 71; basis of moral attitudes in *122*; changes in moral attitudes in *122*; Communist dominated 118; dominant role of Catholicism in 7, 14; dynamics of religion in 85–86, 109–110; and 'mechanical solidarity' 117; modern 9, 106–134; modernization of 116; religious configuration of 10; religious identity in 7; religious statistics from 3; religious structure of 71; in Second Republic of Poland 71; traditional 8, 70–71, 73, 93, 99–100, 172, 180; transcendental order in 13–14
'Polonia' 172n4
Pope Benedict XVI 148
Popper, Karl 44
popular democracy 110
popular piety 26
popular religion 22, 23; defined 26; Isambert on 26
popular religiosity 79
The Possibility of Naturalism (Bhaskar) 42
'potential self' 156
'private life' 33

'prophetic religion' 26
Protestantism 35, 99
Protestant Prussia 148
Protestants 71, 86, 96
Public Religions in the Modern World (Casanova) 115
Puzo, Mario 70

Rahner, Karl 117–118
rational choice theory 54
rationality 33, 45, 62, 79, 169
rationalization 32, 59
A Realist Theory of Science (Bhaskar) 42
Reclaiming Reality (Bhaskar) 42
reconfiguration 3–4, 23, 64
'reflexive disposition' 55
reflexive elaboration of religious identity 74–80
The Reflexive Imperative in Late Modernity (Archer) 64n3
'reflexive modernization' 62
reflexivity 43, 48; Archer's definition of 48; autonomous 184; communicative 184–185; divine 55; human 3, 49, 61, 63, 71, 100, 144, 178–180; and migration 150–155; migration and 150–155; religious 54–55; theological 97
relationship 3–8, 10–12, 14, 20, 22–24, 27, 34–37, 43, 45, 47, 49–52, 59, 60, 63–64, 76, 81, 84, 88, 91, 97, 99–101, 107, 116, 120, 122, 124, 126, *131*, 133–134, 151–152, 158, 159, 161, 163, 167–170, 178–181, 186
religion: dualism in study of 20–25; dynamism in religious life 30–36; embodying 87–90; performing 90–93; sociology of 1, 5–7, 11–13, 19, 24–25, 37, 43–44, 51, 54, 64, 77, 128, 178, 180, 185–186; between subjectivity and structure 19–38; traditional religiosity 25–30
'religion of the masses' 25–26
religiosity: bourgeois 26; folk 10, 13, 77, 101, 180; traditional 25–30; traditional Polish 69–102
religious change 4, 8, 11, 13, 19, 30, 33–37, 42, 84, 107, 116, 118, 129, 144, 151, 156, 158, 171, 179, 181–182, 186
religious commitment 52, 84, 95, 97, 124
religious experience 1, 4–13, 19–25, 28–29, 32–33, 36–37, 43, 46–47, 50–56, 73, 75, 81, 85, 101, 118, 120, 126, 170, 185–186

'religious *habitus*' 55
'religious ideation' 30
religious identity 63; changing personal concerns 121–124; changing transcendental concerns 128–133; cultural elaboration of Polish Catholicism 107–115; dynamism of religious rituals 124–128; migration and shaping of 143–172; and modern Polish society 106–134; between movements and events 118–120; from perspective of critical realism 42–64; reflexive elaboration of 74–80; shaping reflexively 53–56; social interactions 115–118; traditional culture and 71–74
'religious individualization' 11, 32
religious institutions 1, 8–10, 23–25, 29, 32–33, 85, 88, 100, 108, 117–118, 156, 170–172, 178
religious knowledge 56
religious life 33; dynamism in 30–36
'religious nationalism' 85
religious people 53–54, 121, 123–124
'religious products of modernity' 35
'religious reflexivity' 54–55
religious rituals: dynamism of 124–128; migration 163–167; performing 163–167
'religious vitality' in France 5
Riesebrodt, Martin 34, 59
rituals 4, 14, 27, 29, 47, 49, 55–57, 59, 73–75, 79, 90–93, 100, 101, 118, 124–128, 157, 163–167, 170, 180, 182
Roman Catholic Church 101n5, 117
Roman Catholicism 146
Roman Catholics 71, 148
Roman Catholic tradition 7
Roosevelt, Franklin 108
Rosta, Gergley 116
Round Table Agreement 110
Rubicon refugees 158–159
Ruch Mlodej Polski (Young Poland Movement) 109
Ruch Obrony Praw Czlowieka i Obywatela (Movement for the Defence of Human and Civil Rights) 109
Ruch Palikota (Palikot's Movement) 111
Rules Governing the Formal Act of Defection From the Church 111
rural Catholicism in France 5
Russian Empire 101n4

Saint Faustina 2
Schaap, Julian 55
Schools of New Evangelization 119
Schutz, Alfred 46
Scruton, Roger 44
'second-order' emotions 48
Second Republic of Poland 2, 71
Second Vatican Council 118
Second World War 7–8, 70, 71, 74, 83, 84, 86, 107, 129, 148; Catholic religious education 114
Second World War Soviet 2
A Secular Age (Taylor) 12
'secular intelligentsia' 108
secularization 179; in Australia 1; in Israel 1; in Western Europe 1, 12
'sense of self' 45
Shilling, Chris 55
Siekierski, Stanislaw 94
'situational logic of opportunity' 9
Skype 160
Slany, Krystyna 152
Smith, Christian 44, 163
Smith, Timothy 88, 97
social engagement: emerging 167–170; migration 167–170
social interactions and religious identity 115–118
social mobility 62, 93, 95, 107, 123, 150, 152, 184
social order 3–5, 8, 26, 34, 46–48, 55–58, 64, 85, 109, 172, 179–180, 182, 185
social structure 3–4, 6–8, 10–13, 20–22, 24, 25, 27–29, 31, 33, 37, 43, 45–47, 49, 58, 61–64, 86, 89, 91, 100–101, 151, 167, 170, 181, 186
sociology of religion 1, 5–7, 11–13, 19, 24–25, 37, 43–44, 51, 54, 64, 77, 128, 178, 180, 185–186
Solga, Brigida 152
Solidarity Movement (Solidarnosc) 2, 109, 115
Sorokin, Pitirim 57
Soviet Union 2, 108
spirituality/spiritual 4, 23, 29, 54, 76–77, 78, 83, 88, 90–91, 100, 109, 119, 120, 132, 156, 178
Stalin, Joseph 108
Stalinism 83
Staples, Peter 22
Stark, Rodney 5, 21, 98
Stein, Joseph 69
Stomma, Ludwik 77

subjective/subjectivity 4, 7, 11–12,
19–38, 42–43, 46, 51, 53, 55, 59, 61–62,
63, 70–71, 76, 101, 122, 131, 152, 157,
178, 179, 180, 183, 185
'surrogate religion' 22
Swiatkiewicz, Wojciech 121, 123
Swiecicki, Andrzej 95
Swieconka 126, 135n10

Taras, Piotr 97
Taylor, Charles 12, 81, 116
Teheran Conference 108
Tevye the Milkman 69
'theodicy' 6
theological reflexivity 97
theology 75, 81, 185
Thomas, William 10, 79–80, 82, 88–89
'Three-Stage Model' 61
Tischner, Jozef 79, 91, 109
Tomicki, Ryszard 77
Tomka, Miklos 10, 28–29, 34
Toon, Richard 22
Towler, Robert 22
tradition 3–4, 6–7, 11, 27, 29–31, 35–36,
51–52, 56–59, 69–73, 85, 96–97, 100,
126–127, *128*, 132, 165–166, 171
traditional Catholicism 9–10, 80, 90, 93,
134, 169, 184
traditional culture and religious identity 71–74
'traditional elites' 27
traditional Polish religiosity 69–102;
embodying religion 87–90; emerging mobility 93–99; integrating
social and religious concerns 81–87;
performing religion 90–93; reflexive
elaboration of religious identity 74–80;
traditional culture and religious
identity 71–74
traditional religiosity 25–30
transcendence 6–7; performing 56–59;
personal relationship to 49–52
transcendental commitment 50
transcendental concerns 50–51, 171;
changing 128–133
'transcendental realism' 42
transcendental reality 50
'transhumanism' 186
'transnational migrants' 151
Troeltsch, Ernst 35–36
'Two-Stage Model' 61
Tyczynski, Antoni 94
Tylko nie mow nikomu 112

'ultimate concerns' 64n2
United States National Intelligence
Council 1
University College Dublin 146
Urbanska, Sylwia 154

values 1, 14, 21–22, 32–35, 47, 60, 73,
75, 79–82, 85, 87, 96, 107–108, 110,
120–121, 123, 133, 151–152, 168,
170–171, 179, 182, 184
Veblen, Thorstein 44
'verbal intermediaries' 56
Voivodeships 101n3; religious affiliation
in some Eastern Polish **72**
Volkreligiositaet 77
'*Volksreligion*' 26
Voltaire 21
Voyevodenship 71

Walesa, Lech 109
Warner, Stephen 158
Warsaw Confederation 3
Wat, Aleksander 83
Weber, Max 25, 27, 47, 53, 58–59, 185
Weigel, George 2
well-being: migration 155–158; search
for 155–158
Western Christianity 29
Western Europe: cultural aspects of 29;
Polish minority in 145; secularization
in 1, 12
White, Anna 151, 159
Whitehead, Alfred 44
Wierzbicki, Albert 74
Wierzbicki, Zbigniew 94–95
Wilson, Bryan 32, 85
Wisniewski, Ludwik 109
Witos, Wincenty 75, 91, 95
Wlodkowic, Pawel 2
Wojtyla, Karol 11
Wojtynska, Anna 165
Wolynskie Voyevodenship 71
World Youth Day (WYD) 12, 120
Wyszynski, Stefan 94

Yalta Conference 71, 108

Zdaniewicz, Witold 10, 135n7
Zieja, Jan 109
Znaniecki, F. 10, 79–80, 86, 88–89
Znaniecki, Stefan 82
Zubrzycki, Genevieve 85